"In this era of racial tension in the United Sta..., ... Charles and Soong-Chan Rah offer a corrective lens that brings into sharp focus the seed of Euro-American exceptionalism along with its enduring effects through history up to this present day. *Unsettling Truths* examines the racially charged yet unrecognized theology that unleashed the slave trade in West Africa and the dispossession of indigenous peoples' lands in North America: the Doctrine of Discovery. The United States' two original sins find their roots here, and the racial tensions that grow from them continue to overrun the American cultural landscape. These *Unsettling Truths* lead us to self-examination and offer hope for conciliation. This is the true American story."

Gene L. Green, professor emeritus of New Testament, Wheaton College and Graduate School

"If you're Native, you have been waiting for this book. It tells truths that we didn't learn in school about how the ideology of Christian discovery resulted in the dehumanization of the indigenous people of Turtle Island, and how those principles continue to oppress. If you are Native who follows Jesus, you have been hard pressed to explain the difference between your faith and the dysfunctional theology that birthed an exploitative Christian worldview that cultivated genocide and slavery. This book explains the concealed history and theology of truths that this country has not been able to own and shows how we might move toward a restoring narrative."

Lenore Three Stars (Oglala Lakota), cross-cultural facilitator in racial reconciliation

"Followers of Jesus say, Amen! to the emancipatory call of John 8:32. He is Truth, and the truth sets us free. Yet even as we go on to affirm, 'All truth is the Creator's truth,' we recognize we are not immediately emancipated by all truth. Sometimes truth is at first inconvenient, even outright offensive. That's why this narrative will trouble you—because while it is true, it chronicles the great lie that America, Canada, and other colonial nations arose *ex nihilo* from the land. Once embraced, however, this truth can reset your relationships in the land, creating a trajectory toward authentic freedom in Christ."

Terry LeBlanc, director of NAIITS: An Indigenous Learning Community, where he teaches theology and community development

"Charles and Rah offer critiques of American myths and white American Christianity that must be accounted for as Christians of all races reckon with and lament the brokenness of the past—to seek justice and unity in the present. Although the historical narrative lacks context, at times wrongly interpreting historical figures' actions and therefore caricaturing the past, the authors raise powerful questions. Charles and Rah have created theological space for wisdom to grow in the church if readers seriously engage their arguments."

Karen Johnson, associate professor of history, Wheaton College

"Oh that this book's thesis were merely 'unsettling' like a brisk wind or a cancelled flight might be. Instead, Charles's and Rah's argument feels more like an earthquake or a tsunami. To hear the Doctrine of Discovery this richly, poignantly, and painfully explicated will press readers to face 'truths' that are not merely unsettled but undone. Therein lies the book's hope."

Mark Labberton, president of Fuller Theological Seminary

"In Chicana/o Studies, many reject Christianity because of the unsettling truth that white racial nationalism has historically infected the American Church and perverted the biblical message of Jesus Christ. Drawing from a unique indigenous perspective, Charles and Rah persuasively trace the historical roots of such nationalism to the Doctrine of Discovery and settler colonialism, and call the church to lament and conciliation. *Unsettling Truths* tears down a stronghold that has held the American church in captivity for four centuries."

Robert Chao Romero, associate professor, UCLA César E. Chávez department of Chicana/o studies

"There is an inherent danger in attempting to decolonize and deconstruct one's faith without an understanding of how deeply Western Christianity wed itself to the false and dangerous Doctrine of Discovery. Mark Charles and Soong-Chan Rah skillfully give us an unflinching look at Western political and church history, weave in personal stories, and help connect the past to present policies, appealing to both our hearts and minds."

Kathy Khang, speaker and author of *Raise Your Voice*

"Reading *Unsettling Truths* hit me between the eyes. It's a worldview changer. Mark Charles and Soong-Chan Rah powerfully take us deep into the impacts of the Doctrine of Discovery on the 'new' world and on our faulty understandings of Christianity. I needed to read this book."

Michael O. Emerson, author of *Divided by Faith: Evangelical Religion and the Problem of Race in America*

"This volume offers a bold challenge to the simplistic and distorting ways in which the history of Christianity in North America is often told, refusing to accept any approach that denies the horrors of genocide. For any believer rigorously committed to the good news that the truth does set us free, this will not be an easy book. It will challenge many of us to relinquish our all-too-easy denials of past trauma and to taste the bitterness of tears of lament. It will also invite us to sense with astonishment the breadth and depth of what life with Jesus and with each other could look like, not only in the fullness of the coming kingdom but also in the near future of our life together in the land."

John D. Witvliet, Calvin Institute of Christian Worship, Calvin University and Calvin Theological Seminary

Unsettling Truths

THE ONGOING, DEHUMANIZING LEGACY OF THE DOCTRINE OF DISCOVERY

MARK CHARLES

AND

SOONG-CHAN RAH

An imprint of InterVarsity Press
Downers Grove, Illinois

InterVarsity Press
P.O. Box 1400, Downers Grove, IL 60515-1426
ivpress.com
email@ivpress.com

*InterVarsity Press® is the book-publishing division of InterVarsity Christian Fellowship/USA®, a
movement of students and faculty active on campus at hundreds of universities, colleges, and schools
of nursing in the United States of America, and a member movement of the International Fellowship
of Evangelical Students. For information about local and regional activities, visit intervarsity.org.*

Cover design: David Fassett
Interior design: Daniel van Loon
Images: vintage sailing ships: © DenPotisev / iStock / Getty Images Plus
  paper texture: © Zakharova_Natalia / iStock / Getty Images Plus
  *Navajo blanket: weaver, Katherine Marianito, courtesy of Steve and Gail Getzwiller, Nizhoni Ranch
  Gallery, Sonoita, AZ*

ISBN 978-0-8308-4525-5 (print)
ISBN 978-0-8308-8759-0 (digital)

Printed in the United States of America ⊗

*InterVarsity Press is committed to ecological stewardship and to the conservation of natural
resources in all our operations. This book was printed using sustainably sourced paper.*

Library of Congress Cataloging-in-Publication Data
Names: Charles, Mark, 1970- author. | Rah, Soong-Chan, author.
Title: Unsettling truths: the ongoing, dehumanizing legacy of the doctrine
 of discovery / Mark Charles and Soong-Chan Rah.
Description: Downers Grove, Illinois: IVP, an imprint of InterVarsity Press, [2019] | Includes bibliographical
 references and indexes.
Identifiers: LCCN 2019027951 (print) | LCCN 2019027952 (ebook) | ISBN
 9780830845255 (paperback) | ISBN 9780830887590 (ebook)
Subjects: LCSH: Indians of North America—Colonization—Religious aspects—Christianity. | Indians of
 North America—Cultural assimilation—United States—History. | Christianity and
 politics—United States—History. | Christianity and culture—United States—History. | White supremacy
 movements—Religious aspects. | United States—Race relations—Religious aspects—History.
Classification: LCC E93 .C428 2019 (print) | LCC E93 (ebook) | DDC
 261.7—dc23
LC record available at https://lccn.loc.gov/2019027951
LC ebook record available at https://lccn.loc.gov/2019027952
A catalog record for this book is available from the Library of Congress.

P 25 24 23 22 21 20 19 18 17 16 15 14 13 12 11 10

Y 37 36 35 34 33 32 31 30 29 28 27 26 25 24 23

Contents

INTRODUCTION: Who We Are and What We Bring   *1*

1: The Doctrine of Discovery and Why It Matters   *13*

2: The Power of Narratives and the Imagination   *24*

3: The Kingdom of God Is About Relationship Not Empire   *39*

4: The Rise and Defense of Christendom   *52*

5: A Dysfunctional Theology Brought to the "New" World   *69*

6: Exceptionalism and the Founding Documents of the United States   *82*

7: Dysfunctional Theology and the Spread of Settler Colonialism   *98*

8: Genocide, the Impact of a Dysfunctional Theology   *117*

9: Abraham Lincoln and the Narrative of White Messiahship   *132*

10: Abraham Lincoln and Native Genocide   *148*

11: The Complex Trauma of the American Story   *164*

12: The Christian Worldview and the Failure of Re-conciliation   *178*

CONCLUSION: Truth and Conciliation   *197*

ACKNOWLEDGMENTS   *207*

APPENDIX   *211*

NOTES   *221*

NAME AND SUBJECT INDEX   *235*

𝔚𝔥𝔬 𝔚𝔢 𝔄𝔯𝔢 𝔞𝔫𝔡 𝔚𝔥𝔞𝔱 𝔚𝔢 𝔅𝔯𝔦𝔫𝔤

Yá' át' ééh. Mark Charles *yinishyé. Tsin bikee dine'é nishłí. Dóó tó'aheedlíinii bá shíshchíín. Tsin bikee' dine'é dashicheii. Dóó tódích' ii' nii dashinálí.*

Hello. My name is Mark Charles. In the *Diné* culture, when you introduce yourself, you always give your four clans. We are a matrilineal people, and our identities come from our mother's mother. My maternal grandmother is American of Dutch heritage, and so I say *tsin bikee' dine,'* which translates as "the Wooden Shoe People." My paternal grandmother is from the Water Flows Together People. My maternal grandfather is also from the Wooden Shoe clan, and my paternal grandfather is of the Bitterwater clan, one of the original clans of our *Diné* people.

My mother, Evelyn Natelborg, and my father, Theodore Charles, were married less than two years after the historic Supreme Court ruling of *Loving v. Virginia.* This ruling, in 1967, invalidated all anti-miscegenation laws in the United States. Believe it or not, prior to 1967, interracial marriage was still illegal in many states throughout the United States. I encourage you to pause and ponder that for a moment. And it was not until 1967 that interracial marriage was legalized at the federal level throughout the entire United States.

In 2004, after pastoring a small church called the Christian Indian Center for two years, I moved with my family from Denver, Colorado, to the Navajo Reservation, located in the four corners area of the southwest United States. The Navajo Nation still resides on much of what we call *Dinétah*, our traditional lands located between our four sacred mountains. The eleven-year period we lived on our reservation was one of the hardest yet most rewarding experiences of my life. Never have I felt more lonely, isolated, and marginalized from both the church and our country yet more secure and grounded both in my humanity as well as in my identity as the son of a Navajo father and an American mother of Dutch heritage. And it is from that space that I would like to invite you into a conversation about race, culture, and faith.

This dialogue will not be easy. It will involve a history many would be happy to forget, and it will challenge a mythology that most would prefer to remain unchallenged. But it is a necessary conversation and one that has been put off for far too long. You may find significant portions of the book uncomfortable and disquieting. That's OK. I encourage you to stay engaged. This conversation will not be easy, but I am convinced that we can get to a better place.

My name is Soong-Chan Rah. I was born in Seoul, South Korea, and immigrated to the United States shortly after my sixth birthday. Raised in an immigrant family, an urban environment, and in the context of economic poverty, I have experienced a range of life settings in the American social fabric. I was raised in a single-parent family in the inner city of Baltimore and in the suburbs of Washington,

DC, native land of the Piscataway people. My father faced many challenges as an immigrant to the United States. His failure to adjust to life in America and his inability to carve a path forward as a Korean in a white man's world were both factors in the breakup of our family.

Despite these significant challenges, my mother's deep commitment to her children and her spiritual strength equipped her to keep our family together. She worked long hours at an inner-city carry-out complete with bulletproof plexiglass. She would follow this day job with a night shift at an inner-city nursing home, working as a nurse's aide. Despite working these long hours, money was always short, so our family was on food stamps and the school free-lunch program for several years. Years later, a United States president would label single moms who received help from the government as "welfare queens" with a strong implication of their laziness. I know of no single human being who worked harder than my mother to keep her family together. To this day, I am stunned by the power of the collective imagination to embrace a false narrative that became the norm for many Americans.

For our family, connection to our immigrant church community and commitment to education served as the way out of the hood. The Korean immigrant church of my youth provided for our family the spiritual resources of a faith community that embodied Christ. The immigrant church arose from a context of struggle, pain, and suffering. Even in the midst of these struggles, this church would thrive and grow as it sought to serve and lift up the oftentimes downtrodden of our society. Education was valued in our home and in the Korean immigrant church. As a consequence, I have spent an inordinate amount of time in school. I have pursued theological studies partially as a result of how education and faith have intersected in my life.

I have had the distinct pleasure of serving multiethnic and multicultural Christian communities, often in the urban context. After many years in pastoral ministry, God directed me toward fulfilling my call to ministry through the academic world, specifically at North Park Theological Seminary, where I have sought to integrate my passion for Christian ministry with academic thought.

⟨⟨⟨⟨⟨⟨⟨⟨⟨⟨⟨⟨⟨

The coauthors of this book have been friends for many years. We have traveled and ministered in many of the same circles and have found connection with those who are like-minded and like-"passioned." Our connection stems from our mutual love for Jesus and our mutual passion for justice, both of which have found expression in our mutual lament for the church. In our journey together, we have discovered the power of developing common experiences and a common memory, which move us toward a common purpose.

Much of this book describes history's impact on the Native peoples of North America. Whenever possible, we will refer to the specific tribal names when referring to Native communities. In other instances, the terms *Native, Native American,* and *indigenous people* may also be used as more general categories of identification. Occasionally we will use the term *American Indian(s),* which is often referenced in treaties and legislation by the United States federal government.

The book is primarily the story of Mark, his people, and their relationship to the church and to the nation. Mark's voice will be front and center in the narrative and will provide the melody, while Soong-Chan's role will be to provide the harmony to complement the main narrative. We hope that this book will serve as a unique chorus of both of our experiences and voices. May it be an expression of the truth we have learned and the power of common memory.

THE SPIRITUALITY OF THE SUNRISE

I (Mark) remember hearing a Navajo preacher exhort a congregation on our reservation by asking us, "How come, before the missionaries came, our people were able to wake up every morning to greet the sunrise with our prayers, and now we can hardly get to church by 10 a.m.?"

One of the most beautiful, beneficial, and sacred spiritual disciplines I have incorporated into my life is the discipline of watching the sunrise. It is one thing to watch the sunrise a couple times a year, perhaps on Easter for a sunrise service or when you have a 6 a.m. flight. Both times are beautiful and calming. If the clouds are just right, the sunrise can be breathtaking. But it is another thing altogether to intentionally rise five or six mornings a week and to be in a posture of prayer while watching the sun come up over the horizon.

When you do this, you notice something very different. Yes, it is beautiful, peaceful, and often breathtaking. But when you do it day after day, week after week, month after month, and eventually, year after year, something else happens. Subtle changes become glaring.

Every morning in the spring, the sun moves just a little further north; every morning in the fall, the sun inches a bit further south. The birds come and go, migrating in the general direction of the sun's path. It is quiet. In the spring the sun rises just a minute or two earlier as the days grow longer, and the earth warms as it begins to wake up. And in the fall, the sunrise happens just a minute or two later as the earth cools and prepares to go to sleep.

Even the days on the calendar begin to take on a different meaning. June 21 is the first day of summer, and most of the hemisphere is celebrating. The days are long, the weather is warm, and school is out. Pools are opened, barbeque grills are cleaned, and vacations are planned. But the twenty-first also marks an ending, and you can't help but feel just a slight mourning, a hint of lament, and a tinge of sadness. Because you don't just know—you actually see. The sun has completed its journey north, and tomorrow, June 22, it will rise just a moment or two later as it begins another long journey south.

The same is true on the twenty-first of December, the first day of
winter. Many people are feeling glum. Winter is starting. The days are
short, the weather chilly. Almost no one celebrates the first day of
winter, as it marks the start of a long, cold, and dark season. But on
that morning, you can't help but feel excited and find a new spring
in your step. The sun has completed its long journey south. The days
are through getting shorter, and a new journey is beginning. You are
hopeful because you know, you see, and you experience the very next
day will be nearly a minute longer as the sun once again begins its
slow and hopeful journey north.

Another benefit of watching the sunrise is the beauty of the sky.
After a while, you realize it's not so much a sky as it is a canvas. Creator
is not a far off and distant God. Creator is an amazing artist with a
personality, an eye for beauty, and even a sense of humor. Every
morning is a carefully orchestrated production, complete with a musical score. But the production is not a play or even a musical. The
production is the act of creation of a piece of art. The production is
the privilege of watching the artist painting the picture, shaping the
vase, and arranging the score.

So the beauty is not just the final product; the beauty is seen in
watching that piece of artwork come into being. All of creation is both
a grateful participant and a privileged observer—not on a single
morning but throughout the fullness of the seasons. Birds sing.
Flowers bloom. Winds blow. Leaves turn different colors. Clouds pass.
Animals stop. And donkeys bray.

Yes, it is true. Even the obnoxious bray of a donkey can add a
praiseworthy note to the production. While living on the reservation,
my daughter would frequently wake up early and join me as I walked
to the top of the hill near our house to watch the sunrise. As we walked
up the hill, we could hear in the background birds singing, dogs
barking, and the occasional car passing by. But the most distinct yet

infrequent noise we heard was that of a donkey braying. We didn't hear it every day, or even every week. It was sporadic and unpredictable yet surprisingly consistent. Every morning we would listen for it, and each time we heard it my daughter exclaimed, "Daddy! I hear my favorite donkey!"

If you've ever heard a donkey's bray you know that it can be an extremely loud sound that quickly becomes annoying. It usually goes on for several seconds and sounds about as pleasant as an untrained performer with laryngitis attempting to sing opera. Yet as my daughter and I watched the sunrise, we would pray, and whenever we heard it, her prayer included the phrase, "and Jesus, I thank you that I heard my favorite donkey."

My daughter knew this donkey. She listened for his bray and became filled with joy every time she heard it. Only a masterful artist with impeccable timing, a perfect knowledge of the breadth of the tools available, and a bit of a wacky sense of humor could ever pull off incorporating the annoying sound of a donkey's bray into something as breathtakingly beautiful as a sunrise and still elicit both joy and praise from the audience.[1]

But the biggest benefit from this discipline of watching the sunrise has come not from enjoying the beauty or even from experiencing the seasons but from an understanding much deeper in my soul. This understanding did not occur after one sunrise or even after thirty. It began happening after months and years of watching the seasons pass, of observing the birds migrate, of feeling the temperatures rise and then fall. It began happening after experiencing, over and over, the long journey of the sun, first to the north and then again back to the south. The longer I was privileged to see the masterful and artistic genius of Creator, and the longer I was blessed to stand in the midst of the grandeur of this masterpiece, the easier it became to acknowledge that neither I, nor all of humankind for that matter, was in control.

Ultimately, this production is not ours. We cannot make the sun rise faster. We are unable to change the order of the seasons. The birds sing, the flowers bloom, the grass grows, the seasons change—not because of us or even in spite of us, but because of Creator. This work of art, this amazing, ongoing, beautifully choreographed production, is our blessing to observe. It is our privilege to participate in and even our solemn responsibility to steward. But it is not ours to control.

For all of our science, our technology, our air-conditioned buildings, our chemically enhanced soils, our genetically modified foods, our dams, our weapons, our internet, and even our artificial intelligence cannot change that. Over the years I have learned that one of the best ways to remind myself of my limitations is to follow the example of my ancestors. To rise early in the morning, walk (or run) toward the east, and greet the sunrise with my prayers.

The Need for Lament

The assumption of the exceptional character of the American church leads to a belief in the inevitable triumph of the American church. Exceptional people will certainly triumph. The concepts of exceptionalism and triumphalism do not emerge from a proper understanding of the kingdom of God and its relationship over all the nations and kingdoms of the world. Instead, this exceptionalism and triumphalism is rooted specifically in a warped self-perception and theology.

Because of this self-perception that emerges from a dysfunctional theology, acts of aggression and dominance by exceptional people can be deemed as acceptable. At all costs, therefore, the exceptional American church must flourish. The excessive level of triumphalism results in the seeking of human power and human authority to assert the agenda of American Christianity. Ecclesiastical life that emerges from a triumphalist church results in the belief that God has ordained the American church agenda and therefore the actions of the American church—no matter how dysfunctional or destructive—to serve the purpose of God. Excessive celebration of exceptionalism and triumphalism results in the absence of lament for the American church. Human activity is elevated, and God's activity is diminished.

The spiritual practice of lament could counteract the human tendency towards self-elevation. Lament serves as a crucial expression of worship because it is truth telling before God. Lament recognizes that no matter what the circumstances, God is faithful, and God delivers. We can rely upon God to be faithful to his Word. Without lament, human effort and human success emerge as the driving force in the activity of the church. The message of a messiah who suffered and died for humanity is lost in the avalanche of triumphalism. The practice of lament is a necessary truth telling. This book, therefore, offers a lament over dysfunctional theology and a broken history.

THE PURPOSE AND DIRECTION OF THE TEXT

This text offers the hope that healing can occur when unsettling truths are confronted. For centuries we have kept hidden the stories of the oppressed people in our society. We have embraced the stories of success and exceptionalism rather than engaging the narrative of suffering and oppression. This obsession with the self-elevation of the American church and American society reflects an absence of truth telling. The American church has yielded the prophetic voice because it has not spoken a historical and theological truth.

The absence of truth has resulted in the presence of injustice. This injustice is particularly evident in the systemic racism that often defines American society. This text addresses the glaring need to expose the deceit and lies that mask how the United States operates as a systemically white supremacist nation. We will also challenge the

American church in its culpability through either its silence (at best) or affirmation of the elevation of the narrative of American exceptionalism. We will examine the historical and theological roots of systemic racism in the United States with particular attention to the Doctrine of Discovery and its impact on the United States. We will call our nation and the Christian churches of our nation to a truth telling that will begin to shed light and open the door to a future hope.

This book will challenge you to examine the imaginaries and the narratives you have embraced as American Christians or even simply as Americans. Our work of confronting the history of racial injustice requires an examination of the roots of sin that result through this injustice. In chapter one, we introduce the Doctrine of Discovery and how it was formed in the theological imagination of Western imperial culture. In chapter two, we examine how sinful social systems and structures are fueled by mediating narratives and shaped by the social and theological imagination. In chapter three, we examine the difference between the godly authority exercised by Jesus versus the supposed greatness of worldly power. Chapter four offers an overview of the rise of Christendom and its defense by the church. In chapter five, we will explore how the Doctrine of Discovery intersects with the myth of Anglo-Saxon superiority in forming a dysfunctional imagination that influenced American history.

Chapter six traces how the founding documents of the United States are shaped by the narrative of white American Christian exceptionalism. In chapter seven, we discuss how the US legal system codified the dysfunctional imagination of white supremacy in the discovery doctrine. Chapter eight continues the story of the brutal mistreatment and genocide of Native communities and the legal precedent that allowed this brutality. Chapters nine and ten examine how the absence of Christ within the heresy of Christendom led to the creation of a mythological white messiah by the name of Abraham

Lincoln. We will discuss how the dysfunctional narrative of white supremacy was not so easily shirked, even by the "Great Emancipator." In chapter eleven, we explore how this dysfunctional narrative that has held a centuries-long grip on the American imagination has resulted in the trauma of white America (both within and outside the church). Chapter twelve reveals how this trauma has hindered the work of racial conciliation.

Our book concludes with a call for conciliation with a new focus and emphasis that is necessary in order to deal with the deeply rooted dysfunction in our society. Because the more familiar term *racial reconciliation* implies a preexisting harmony and unity, we propose the use of the term *racial conciliation.*

Conciliation does not happen without truth telling. Conciliation without truth is trying to bring health without a comprehensive diagnosis. Truth telling requires the deeper examination of the existing narratives and the unearthing of the dysfunction surrounding those narratives. The broken system and the dysfunctional theological imagination that the broken system emerges from must be exposed. Once that broken system is uncovered, an authentic lament rooted in truth can commence. Lament, therefore, emerges from the confrontational nature of truth and our honest response to that truth. Truth telling will liberate the church to write a more biblical narrative that will integrate the lost practice of lament, the power of a shared journey, and the building of a common memory.

This book will examine both the history of the church and of the nation. It will ask uncomfortable questions and expose some horrifying narratives. But God's love for his creation is amazing. And his passion for the church is undeniable. We can get to a better place and in the end be grateful for the constant prodding of Christ to pursue truth, even if what is revealed serves as unsettling truth.

CHAPTER ONE

The Doctrine of Discovery and Why It Matters

"YOU CANNOT DISCOVER lands already inhabited."

I (Mark) said this almost under my breath, as I walked past a line of men dressed as Spanish sailors from the 1490s. I was in front of Union Station in Washington, DC, near the massive statue of Christopher Columbus overlooking the United States Capitol. Every Columbus Day, there is an official ceremony in this plaza honoring Columbus as the discoverer of America. I had stumbled upon this ceremony by accident the year prior. There were a few non-natives holding signs and protesting the ceremony but nothing very disruptive. I came back the following year primarily out of curiosity. I was not intending to protest, nor did I want to make a scene.

As I walked up behind the statue and approached the group of men dressed as Spanish sailors, the words just came out of my mouth: "You cannot discover lands already inhabited." As I walked farther down the line, I said it again, this time a little louder. "You cannot discover lands already inhabited." As I continued walking, I came to the front of the line, where a group of men dressed in suits were standing. I repeated myself, making sure they could hear me. "You cannot discover lands already inhabited." "Suck it up" was the reply I heard as I kept walking.

By this time, I had walked around the statue and reached the front, where a small stage had been erected and chairs set up for people to watch the ceremony. It hadn't started yet, but more than half the audience was seated, waiting for it to begin. So I stopped near the center, turned toward the gathering crowd, and in a calm but loud voice I said to the people: "You cannot discover lands already inhabited. That process is known as stealing, conquering, or colonizing. The fact that America calls what Columbus did 'discovery' reveals the implicit racial bias of the country—that Native Americans are not fully human."

Quickly one of the white men dressed in a suit walked over and interrupted me. "You are not welcome here," he said as he grabbed my arm and began walking me away. I attempted to explain the inappropriateness of both celebrating this holiday as well as hosting this ceremony. But instead of engaging in conversation, he threatened me with arrest and escorted me from the area. As I walked away from the gathering, I was amused at his words and at the irony of their context: a white man, participating in a public ceremony honoring Christopher Columbus as the discoverer of America, telling a Native man he was not welcome in that space.

WHAT IS THE DOCTRINE OF DISCOVERY?

How did a flawed assumption about the place of the indigenous population in US society become normative? How are assumptions so deeply ingrained in the American psyche and imagination that dysfunctional and oppressive actions emerge? How did a dysfunctional idea and worldview form that allows for the displacement of Native bodies? One of the explanations for the formation of this dysfunctional worldview is the Doctrine of Discovery.

The Doctrine of Discovery is a set of legal principles that governed the European colonizing powers, particularly regarding the administration of indigenous land. It is the "primary legal precedent that still controls native affairs and rights . . . an international law formulated in the fifteenth and sixteenth centuries."[1] From a theological perspective, the legal and political role of the Doctrine of Discovery is rooted in a dysfunctional theological imagination that shaped the European colonial settler worldview.

The doctrine emerged from a series of fifteenth-century papal bulls, which are official decrees by the pope that carry the full weight of his ecclesial office. On June 18, 1452, Pope Nicholas V issued the papal bull *Dum Diversas*, which initiated the first set of documents that would compose the Doctrine of Discovery. The official decree of the pope granted permission to King Alfonso V of Portugal "to invade, search out, capture, vanquish, and subdue all Saracens (Muslims) and pagans whatsoever, and other enemies of Christ wheresoever placed, and the kingdoms, dukedoms, principalities, dominions, possessions, and all movable and immovable goods whatsoever held and possessed by them and to *reduce their persons to perpetual slavery* (emphasis ours), and to apply and appropriate to himself and his successors the kingdoms, dukedoms, counties, principalities, dominions, possessions, and goods, and to convert them to his and their use and profit."[2]

Dum Diversas would identify Saracens (a common term for Muslims at the time) and pagans (essentially identifying any non-Christian or "others") as those who could be targeted for "perpetual slavery." The papal bull intentionally used language that identified those outside the European Christian world and enforced the Western theological imagination of non-Europeans as "other." The Portuguese took these ecclesial statements to heart and perpetrated the slave trade from the African continent to the European and the American continents. As a Christian ruler, the king of Portugal would have power endowed from the church to take possession of "the other" as slave labor from the continent of Africa. The pagan African body was just another commodity to be taken for the pleasure and profit of the European Christian body, the one made most fully in the image of God.

In January of 1454, Pope Nicholas V authored the bull *Romanus Pontifex*, also directed towards the kingdom of Portugal. Written as a logical sequel to *Dum Diversas*, *Romanus Pontifex* allowed the European Catholic nations to expand their dominion over "discovered" land. Possession of non-Christian lands would be justified along with the enslavement of native, non-Christian "pagans" in Africa and the "New" World. The church believed that Alfonso "justly and lawfully has acquired and possessed, and doth possess, these islands, lands, harbors, and seas, and they do of right belong and pertain to the said King Alfonso and his successors."[3] The abusive system of transcontinental slavery initiated by Portugal would be seen as just and lawful.

The church claimed that what benefited the European colonial powers would benefit the church. The warped Western social imagination that saw slavery as a just and legal institution would be rooted in the dysfunctional assertions of this papal bull. The Doctrine of Discovery deemed as just and lawful what benefited the European powers, affirming the privilege of the "pure" European Christian to determine what is right and just. Because the pure European body held an inherent spiritual worth, the actions of European Christians would be deemed just. King Alfonso as the true image bearer of God held the right to discover the land and to pass along the rights to the land to his children and to his people. Alfonso would operate as an agent of God, while the conquered and enslaved people would have no agency before God. The Doctrine of Discovery created the possibility of significant harm upon those outside the privileged position of the pure European body.

Romanus Pontifex revealed Pope Nicholas V's desire to seek "the salvation of all . . . [that] he may bring the sheep entrusted to him by God into the single divine fold, and may acquire for them the reward of eternal felicity, and obtain pardon for their souls."[4] The papal bull would cite spiritual and theological motivation for the acts of atrocity that followed the Doctrine of Discovery. The pope believed that "if we bestow suitable favors and special graces on those Catholic kings and princes, who . . . restrain the savage excesses of the Saracens and of other infidels, enemies of the Christian name, but also for the defense and increase of the faith vanquish them and their kingdoms and habitations."[5] There would be an unashamed elevation of the European rulers with a subsequent diminishing and demonizing of non-Europeans who would be rightly vanquished. The slave trade would become the fulfillment and material expression of the dysfunctional theology offered by the church.

The papal bull asserted the "noble personage" of Henry, uncle to King Alfonso of Portugal. Prince Henry would be one of the progenitors and propagators of the African slave trade. The pope would again assert the specious spiritual rationale that Henry would "bring into the bosom of his faith the perfidious enemies of him and of the life-giving Cross by which we have been redeemed, namely the Saracens and all other infidels." Henry's work of furthering the slave trade would therefore be seen in the most positive light, his pursuit of the slave trade being described as "growing daily more and more zealous in prosecuting this his so laudable and pious purpose."[6]

One of the immediate consequences of the Doctrine of Discovery, therefore, was the furtherance and establishment of the African slave trade by Prince Henry, the very person verified by the pope as an agent of God. The first captives from Africa were taken into slavery in 1441 by Portuguese explorers who brought twelve slaves back to Portugal. The timing of these papal bulls corresponded to the emboldening of the Portuguese to expand this initial action of subjugation. The year 1502 is often cited as the year that African slaves were brought to the American continent, and by 1525, the direct passage of slave ships began from Africa to the Americas. The papal bulls of the mid-fifteenth century, therefore, would provide the theological justification for the actions of the kingdom of Portugal and for other European powers to initiate and expand the slave trade from Africa.

Prince Henry would be affirmed and emboldened in his actions off the coast of Africa by the papal bulls. Not only would Henry relish in his status and position as an agent of God, his subjects and his ships' crews would likewise embrace Henry's role. Willie Jennings notes that the ritual that sealed the Portuguese prince's possession of African lives in chattel slavery was characterized as "deeply Christian": "Prince Henry following his deepest Christian instincts, ordered a tithe be given to God through the church. Two black boys were given."[7] So, the slave trade becomes an act of worship in the diseased imagination of the European explorers engaged in it.

Jennings also narrates the story of Zurara, who served as Prince Henry's historian at the onset of the transatlantic slave trade. Zurara is troubled by the inhumane treatment of African lives and "recognizes their humanity, their common ancestry with Adam."[8] Zurara's realization of the humanity of the African points towards the thought process of a well-intentioned bystander. Zurara's conscience and maybe even his upbringing in a Christian context aid his realization of the humanity of the African lives before him.

However, while disturbed by the scene before him, Zurara will accept these actions because Prince Henry has been affirmed by the pope as one who operates under the authority and sanction of the Christian church. Zurara describes Prince Henry as "mounted upon a powerful steed, and accompanied by his retinue, . . . he reflected with great pleasure upon the salvation of those souls that before were lost."[9] Zurara continues to give justification for the slave trade by asserting that "we, the Portuguese, will save them. They will become Christians."[10] The theological imagination of the Doctrine of Discovery would justify the actions of Prince Henry, in his own eyes and the eyes of those who would follow him.

THE DOCTRINE OF DISCOVERY AND THE "DISCOVERY" OF THE AMERICAS

On May 4, 1493, the year after Columbus sailed the ocean blue, Pope Alexander VI issued the papal bull *Inter Caetera*, addressed to "our very dear son in Christ, Ferdinand, king, and our very dear daughter in Christ, Isabella, queen of Castile, Leon, Aragon, Sicily, and Granada." Once again, the pope offered a spiritual validation for European conquest, "that in our times especially the Catholic faith and the Christian religion be exalted and be everywhere increased and spread, that the health of souls be cared for and that barbarous nations be overthrown and brought to the faith itself."[11] In particular, the bull served as an ecclesial affirmation of the state-sanctioned expedition and work of conquest by Christopher Columbus. In recognition of the hard work and zeal exhibited by these explorers, they were lauded for their evangelistic zeal in concert with their exploration, discovery, and conquest. The bull would affirm "the spread of the Christian rule to carry forward your holy and praiseworthy purpose so pleasing to immortal God. . . . who for a long time had intended to seek out and discover certain islands and mainlands remote and unknown and not hitherto discovered by others."[12]

In the papal bulls, Columbus would be singled out and honored for his efforts to expand the Christian empire:

> As was pleasing to the Lord, you [Isabella and Ferdinand], with the wish to fulfill your desire, chose our beloved son, Christopher Columbus, a man

assuredly worthy and of the highest recommendations and fitted for so great an undertaking, . . . the said Christopher has already caused to be put together and built a fortress fairly equipped, wherein he has stationed as garrison certain Christians, companions of his, who are to make search for other remote and unknown islands and mainlands . . . to bring under your sway the said mainlands and islands with their residents and inhabitants and to bring them to the Catholic faith . . . to lead the peoples dwelling in those islands and countries to embrace the Christian religion; nor at any time let dangers or hardships deter you therefrom.[13]

By this reasoning, Columbus could be considered the "discoverer" of the Americas, despite the continents already being filled with people and civilizations. As a European Christian fully endowed with God's presence, he would hold a superior position over and against the Native inhabitants of the land. A 2013 study by the Christian Reformed Church asserted that "framing Aboriginal peoples as enemies of God positioned Europeans as the harbingers of civilization and Christianity to the so-called pagans of the Americas. The doctrine of discovery became the justification for colonial actions."[14]

The authority to "discover" and to "conquer" drew from an assumed spiritual authority. The bull asserted that those who would oppose the authority and rule of the European powers would be opposing the will of God: "Let no one, therefore, infringe, or with rash boldness contravene, this our recommendation, exhortation, requisition, gift, grant, assignment, constitution, deputation, decree, mandate, prohibition, and will. Should anyone presume to attempt this, be it known to him that he will incur the wrath of Almighty God."[15] The assertion of European supremacy by these papal bulls had taken such a hold that anyone opposing this doctrine would be considered opposing the will of God.

In September of 1500, Columbus had been brought back from Santo Domingo in chains. The royal court was at Seville and he stayed for a number of months at the Carthusian monastery of Las

Cuevas across the Guadalquivir River from the city.[16] At the monastery Columbus compiled his notes, which he described as "a notebook of authorities, statements, opinions and prophecies on the subject of the recovery of God's Holy City and mountain of Zion, and on the discovery and evangelization of the islands of the Indies and of all other peoples and nations."[17] Christopher Columbus's self-perception reveals a connection to the heresies of both Christendom and the Doctrine of Discovery. Columbus's atrocities would find justification in the belief that all of these actions would result in evangelization. The spread of the European version of the Christian message would justify violence in all forms found in Western imperialism.

The Doctrine of Discovery, first directed towards Portugal then directed towards Spain, affirmed the imperial ambitions of these two European powers. It gave theological permission for the European body and mind to view themselves as superior to the non-European bodies and minds. The doctrine created an insider perception for the European while generating an outsider, other identity for non-Europeans; it created an identity for African bodies as inferior and only worthy of subjugation; it also relegated the identity of the original inhabitants of the land "discovered" to become outsiders, now unwelcome in their own land.

Those who stole the land now claimed power over those who originally held the land. In order to strengthen the claim to usurped land, the more pure, European-American Christian settler colonialists needed to elevate themselves over and against the indigenous inhabitants. The dominant powers created dysfunctional narratives derived from a diseased social and theological imagination that elevated the sense of worth of the dominant group. This lie of supremacy empowered the dominant group to define the other as inferior and claim authority over them.

THE IMPACT OF THE DOCTRINE OF DISCOVERY ON
THE INDIGENOUS NATIONS OF TURTLE ISLAND[18]

The collective expression of the papal bulls that would result in the Doctrine of Discovery fueled the conquest of non-European lands by Europeans. As Stephen Newcomb notes, "what is generally referred as the doctrine of discovery might be more accurately called the doctrine of Christian European arrival, or, better still, the doctrine of Christian European invasion."[19] The Doctrine of Discovery served a dual function: a theological "doctrine" that served as an affirmation from the church for European atrocity and a political, even military doctrine (akin to the Monroe Doctrine or even the Bush Doctrine) that provided political boundaries and mediation between colonial settler powers.

The doctrine as expressed to Portugal furthered the African slave trade and as expressed to Spain affirmed the "discovery" of the Americas. This military and political doctrine that defined the parameters of European imperial greatness arose from an ecclesial treatise rooted in a dysfunctional theology. At the foundation of this doctrine was a narrative of European Christian purity and supremacy that negated the value and worth of the other and permitted European Christians to assume their own supremacy and privilege on specious theological grounds.

An individual questioning the appropriate presence of a Native American at a Columbus Day celebration reveals a dysfunctional narrative embedded within Western society. The concept of the other stands in direct opposition to the teachings of the New Testament. Theology that arises from Scripture and from the teachings of Jesus does not allow for the identification and exclusion of the other. A Christian Reformed Church task force concluded that "the doctrine encoded racial ideas that created a hierarchy within humanities that invariably placed European Christian nations in the position of power."[20] The assumption of white supremacy took root in the imagination of the Western mind. This imagination and narrative have become embedded realities in the American Christian worldview.

CHAPTER TWO

The Power of Narratives
and the Imagination

HOW DID THE NARRATIVE OF WHITE SUPREMACY and the
social imagination of "otherness" develop in Western society? How
do dysfunctional narratives emerge from a social reality and in turn
shape that reality? As social reality gets constructed, the social imagination plays a significant role in the formation and sustaining of that
social reality. In a society with significant religious influences, the
theological imagination can impact the social imagination. The Doctrine of Discovery presents an example of the impact of a dysfunctional Christian theological imagination on social reality.

Peter Berger and Thomas Luckmann present a theory on the construction of social reality.[1] They argue that social systems are formed
through the interaction of multiple factors including externalization,
institutionalization, and internalization. Individuals entering a social
system contribute to that system through the externalization of that
individual's identity and values. The individual's values and perspectives are externalized into the system, helping to shape the system.

The full construct of a social system, however, is not simply attributable to the influence of individuals. Berger and Luckmann assert that institutions can take on a life of their own through the process of institutionalization. The social system becomes an external object that is institutionalized and now begins to exhibit a value system that has moved beyond the specific values of the individuals who may have initially shaped the system.[2] The institution has the capacity to outlast the individuals that originally established the system.

In turn, the institution begins to influence individuals within the system through the process of internalization. This institutionalization of the social system helps create an external objective reality, and individuals within the system now begin to take on and internalize the values of that reality. The process of internalization completes the cycle. The institution has fully moved beyond the influence of the individuals that initially created the system. And the institutionalized system now has the power and capacity to perpetuate itself with continued influence upon anyone entering the system.[3]

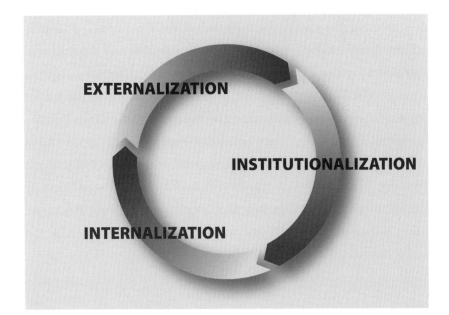

The social construction of reality reveals the power of internalization. Dysfunctional messages generated by the dysfunctional
system impact those within the system. Even individuals who may
have a strong sense of self-worth and who seek to retain their cultural
identity may eventually succumb to the power of internalization,
which can diminish both their self-worth and their cultural identity.

One Sunday I (Mark) was teaching in one of the churches on our
reservation and I concluded with a call to bring the gospel to the
ends of the earth. I specifically challenged the church to consider
participating in missions outside of our reservation. After the service,
I was approached by one of the grandmothers of the church. She
appreciated my message but wanted to remind me that while such a
call to missions might be possible for someone who had earned a
college degree, she and many other members of the church never
went to college. They didn't have degrees and therefore could not
become missionaries.

In the Western mission model, which is rooted in the Doctrine of
Discovery, the primary role for the "heathens" is to simply receive the
message and the charity of their benevolent, generous, and well-
educated missionaries. If they show real potential and demonstrate
extraordinary ambition, they might be able to work their way up to a
support role, but they will never become full partners in the gospel.
The message that was externalized by the early missionaries became
institutionalized in the churches throughout the reservation and is
still being internalized by the congregants. In a similar fashion, the
Doctrine of Discovery emerged from an externalized worldview by
the European Christian powers that became institutionalized in the
European colonial powers and would become internalized by the
world conquered by the European powers.

THE POWER OF THE IMAGINATION

The human imagination serves as a powerful tool in the construction of social systems. Imagination shapes the worldview and the subsequent actions of an individual and can be internalized in the individual within social reality. In the same way, the social imagination has the capacity to profoundly influence and shape society. The construction and preservation of social reality depends on the power of the imagination.

The formation of the imagination emerges from the way individuals and communities process social reality and how they are shaped by social reality. The social imagination helps us to make sense of the world around us and allows us to consider possibilities in the systems and structures where we dwell. Sociologist C. Wright Mills notes that "the sociological imagination enables us to grasp history and biography and the relations between the two within society. . . . It is by means of the sociological imagination that men now hope to grasp what is going on in the world, and to understand what is happening in themselves as minute points of the intersection of biography and history within society."[4] William Cavanaugh adds that "the imagination of a society is the sense of what is real and what is not; it includes a memory of how the society got where it is, a sense of who it is, and hopes and projects for the future. . . . [it] is the condition of possibility for the organization and signification of bodies in a society."[5] Therefore the social imagination possesses the power to shape and influence society.

Differentiated from the social imagination, the theological imagination has the power to generate a view of the world that expands beyond the limitations of one's own immediate reality. The possibility of transcendence, an experience beyond normal physical human capacity, is offered by the social imagination and may be buttressed or furthered by the theological imagination.

Willie Jennings asserts that theology is the "imaginative capacity to redefine the social."[6] Walter Brueggemann calls the church to a theology that engages the prophetic imagination. Brueggemann believes that "the task of prophetic ministry is to nurture, nourish, and evoke a consciousness and perception alternative to the consciousness and perception of the dominant culture around us."[7] The power of theology is the power to expand our imagination, so theology offers the possibility of a prophetic imagination that can transform the individual and society.

Christian theology can contribute significantly to the development of a transcendent imagination, which can provide a positive function in broadening the imaginative capacity of the individual. However, this capacity for transcendent vision can also lead to a sense of arrogance and privilege by limited human beings. The belief that the theological imagination allows the Christian to connect with the divine can lead the Christian to assume that they speak from a position of privilege, chosen and preferred by God, and that the Christian has the capacity to know what is best for the rest of the world.

The reality of a broken world and broken systems within the world, therefore, means that Christians often engage in a dysfunctional theological imagination. As Jennings asserts, "Christianity in the Western world lives and moves within a diseased social imagination."[8] The diseased social imagination of the United States has been shaped by the dysfunctional theological imagination of the Western world known as the Doctrine of Discovery, which has resulted in the formation of the dysfunctional social systems of the United States. These dysfunctional systems find fuel from the dysfunctional narratives of our society, which are shaped by the social and theological imagination.

On June 4, 2017, a terror attack occurred in London, claiming seven lives and injuring nearly fifty people. A few hours later evangelical leader Franklin Graham posted the following to his public Facebook account:

> The threat of Islam is real. The threat of Islam is serious. The threat of Islam is dangerous. . . . We need to pray that God would give our President, our Congress, and our Senate wisdom—and the guts to do what is right for our nation.[9]

Franklin Graham identified Muslims and the entire religion of Islam as the enemy. Graham urged prayer to God not for the victims or even for the church but for his own nation-state, for his President and political leaders to have the "guts to do what is right for *our* nation" (emphasis ours). Graham is identifying his own country as Christian and the war as religious. He aligns the United States on the side of God and of the good, while relegating Muslims and all of Islam on the side of evil. His rhetoric of moral superiority and the mindset of religious supremacy is similar to the imagination of the leaders of previous iterations of Christendom.[10] Franklin Graham reveals a disturbingly dysfunctional social imagination of European/American superiority buttressed by his dysfunctional theological imagination of European-American Christian supremacy.

THE POWER OF METAPHORS

Another layer of analysis for the power of the imagination is offered by communication scholar George Lakoff. Lakoff asserts that certain forms of communication, particularly metaphors, impact the formation of social reality and the functioning of institutions within society. Lakoff argues that the traditional view of reason is that it is abstract and disembodied. It "sees reason as literal, as primarily about propositions that can be objectively either true or false." But the new view sees reason as having a bodily, even imaginative, basis. In the new view, "metaphor, metonymy, and mental imagery" are central to reason rather than peripheral.[11] The imagination that can shape the social system is more deeply impacted by metaphors than by logical reason. Despite the assertion of the Enlightenment, human beings are more than simply chemical responses to a stimulus. We not only respond with reason in our minds, but we also respond with the body and with feelings emanating from the mind and body.

Jesus understood the power of metaphors in his use of parables. Jesus did not simply list the aspects of God's character but appealed to people's imagination by telling parables about how God is like a father—not just any father, but a rich, generous, and forgiving father. He did not talk about heaven and the kingdom of God in stale, abstract terms. He compared finding the kingdom of God to the experience of finding a lost coin or a treasure buried in a field. Jesus also talked bluntly not only about his own impending crucifixion, but about how his followers must also pick up their cross and follow him. Therefore, he frequently used metaphorical communication and appealed to people's imagination regarding the character of God and the rewards of heaven because he understood that pure logic and reason alone would not be enough to get his followers through persecution.

While Jesus used metaphor to spark a kingdom imagination to endure persecution, Satan also stirred a fearful imagination. In Luke 4:13, after Jesus resisted the temptations of Satan, we are told that the devil "left him until an opportune time." In Luke 22, just before his arrest, Jesus told his disciples, "Pray that you will not fall into temptation" (v. 40). He then went a stone's throw beyond them and "being in anguish" over the prospect of his coming persecution, he prayed so earnestly that "his sweat was like drops of blood falling to the ground" (v. 44).

In the Garden of Gethsemane, Jesus realized the temptation to have the cup pass from him and not suffer and die on the cross. In this, Satan found an opportune time to tempt Jesus. Temptation may have been easier to resist when Jesus was standing on a high mountaintop discussing a persecution years away, but a more opportune time was the night before the persecution, when the soldiers were walking into the garden to make an arrest. But even then, Jesus prayed to his *Abba* and resisted the temptation to flee persecution and settle for an earthly kingdom. Jesus worshiped God alone by surrendering his will and saying to his Father, "Not my will, but yours be done" (Luke 22:42).

Throughout the twenty-first century, many white Christian leaders in the US have frequently expressed the anxiety that the United States of America has lost its Christian values, even fearing that Christians in our country are facing persecution. This embedded fear and anxiety often drives many Christians in the US to seek out comfort through partisan politics and to embrace the heresy of Christendom. Successful Christian leaders will often embrace partisan political leaders that tap into the metaphors which serve the retention of Christian empire.

In 2016, Donald Trump won the presidential election with overwhelming support from white Evangelicals and white Catholics. Many questions were raised as to how Trump won the support of the conservative Christian right. This was a candidate who stormed onto the political scene by asserting the unfounded accusations of the birther movement. This was a candidate who at his first campaign event said about immigrants from Mexico: "They're bringing drugs, they're bringing crime, they're rapists."[12] This was a candidate who, on the stage of a conservative Christian college in Iowa, bragged that he could stand in the middle of Fifth Avenue in New York and shoot somebody and not lose a single voter. This was a candidate who was caught on a live mic bragging that his celebrity and fame gave him the right to sexually assault women. This was a candidate who was unrepentant of his multiple affairs. This was a candidate who on national radio bragged about his sexual exploits and even allowed the host, Howard Stern, to refer to his daughter as "a piece of ass."[13] This was a candidate who claims to be a Christian but, when asked at the Family Leadership Summit in July 2015 if he had ever asked God for forgiveness, responded, "I am not sure I have, I just go and try to do a better job from there. I don't think so. I think, if I do something wrong, I think I just try to make it right. I don't bring God into that picture. I don't."[14] Very little about Donald Trump reflects either a desire for the high moral standards associated with Christian life and practice or the humility of a hurting person grateful for the forgiveness and healing mercies of Christ.

Trump himself revealed his playbook to garner the vote of white Evangelicals in an interview with the Christian Broadcast Network on October 27, 2016, where he stated:

> We're doing very well with evangelicals. And if they vote we're going to win the election. And we're going to have a great Supreme Court. And we're going to have religious liberty. Because religious liberty, let's face it. I saw a high school football coach the other day and they were praying before the game. You know they're going into combat, they're in the locker room praying, and, I think they're going to fire him. And. You know they suspended him. I think they want to fire him. Whoever heard of a thing like this. And I always say to you, we're going to all be saying Merry Christmas again. But the truth is religious liberty is under tremendous stress.[15]

While Trump raised the specter that "religious liberty is under tremendous stress," he had no qualms enacting a ban on Muslims entering the United States and approving the Dakota Access pipeline that ran through lands considered sacred to the Dakota people.

When Trump and the religious right use the term "religious liberty," what is actually meant is "Christian liberty." Donald Trump promised religious liberty by claiming that his election would allow Americans to "all be saying Merry Christmas again." Trump used metaphor and mental imagery to appeal to the dysfunctional imagination of the voters. He exacerbated the church's fears of persecution in order to tempt the faithful away from the difficult teachings of Christ and towards the ease and temporal safety found in the heresy of Christian empire.

Lakoff claims "evidence that the mind is more than a mere mirror of nature or a processor of symbols, that it is not incidental to the mind that we have bodies, and that the capacity for understanding and meaningful thought goes beyond what any machine can do."[16] The individual imagination, the social imagination, and the theological imagination can profoundly shape and influence social systems. These imaginaries, however, are not simply formed by linear and reasonable proposition. Instead, Lakoff points towards the possibility of the imaginary and narratives that govern social systems being formed by feeling, emotions, and bodily experience.

For the church, the social imagination can be influenced by the theological imagination, which can generate an even deeper embodied experience or feeling. The theological imagination can have a logical component, but it can also shape and be shaped by emotional experiences. This interconnection is found in the power of the collective imagination. Contrary to our assumptions, both of these imaginations (social and theological) may not be rooted in the rational order. It is the arrogance of Western theology to assume that all of our theological musings are rooted in rationality and logic and therefore must not be susceptible to dysfunction. However, a diseased theological imagination can put forth a dysfunctional expression that ultimately forms a dysfunctional social imagination. The diseased theological imagination (such as Christendom, the Doctrine of Discovery, and the myth of Anglo-Saxon purity) contributed to a dysfunctional social imagination (white supremacy) that has perpetuated unjust leaders, systems, and structures.

THE POWER OF NARRATIVES

Lakoff's explanation of the use of metaphor and its impact on the social imagination takes on another layer of meaning with the analysis offered by Walter Wink. The human imagination has the great power to generate, foster, and perpetuate existing systems and structures through the individuals within the system. The social and theological imagination can arise from individuals and from the system itself. The social theological imagination can have a direct effect on the system of the institution and subsequently impact the individuals within the institution. Wink uses the language of "the powers that be" to explain how systems and structures can take on a life of their own and influence both the system and individuals through the power of mediating narratives.

To Wink, the powers that be "are more than just the people who run things. They are the systems themselves, the institutions and structures that weave society into an intricate fabric of power and relationships. These Powers surround us on every side. They are necessary. They are useful. . . . But the Powers are also the source of unmitigated evils."[17] The captivity to individualism in the West leads many to reject the possibility of institutions and systems inflicting social harm that requires a social response.[18]

Scripture testifies to the reality of systems and structures beyond the personal, individual, and the material. When John 3:16 speaks of how God loves the world, it speaks of the *cosmos*, the systems and structures of our social reality which impact our lives. Ephesians 6:12 is even more explicit in revealing a power beyond the individual and material by stating that "our struggle is not against flesh and blood, but against the rulers, against the authorities, against the powers of this dark world and against the spiritual forces of evil in the heavenly realms." Powers, according to the Bible, can operate in evil ways in the larger context of the *cosmos*.

Wink claims that "greater forces are at work—unseen Powers—that shape the present and dictate the future."[19] These powers reflect a spiritual reality. "The spirituality that we encounter in institutions is not always benign. It is just as likely to be pathological. . . . Corporations and governments are 'creatures' whose sole purpose is to serve the general welfare. And when they refuse to do so, their spirituality becomes diseased. They become 'demonic.'"[20] These systems with a diseased spirituality are shaped and influenced by narratives that are also profoundly diseased. Narratives, therefore, have significant influence on systems and structures as well as on the social imagination. Narratives are also not neutral and have the capacity to express evil intention and influence on social reality.

Walter Wink postulates that social structures need mediating narratives in order to sustain dysfunctional systems. For example, the dysfunctional system of Western society needs the myth of redemptive violence to sustain its authority and legitimacy over its residents: "Unjust systems perpetuate themselves by means of institutionalized violence."[21] Violence can now be justified and redeemed. Something that inherently brings harm is now considered to bring about healing. The entirety of the system has become so corrupt that it perpetuates dysfunction.

The dysfunctional narrative of redemptive violence has taken firm root in the social imagination of America. America assumes it has the capacity to use violence in redemptive ways while the rest of the world does not have that capacity. Walter Brueggemann points out that there is "a militant notion of US exceptionalism, that the US is peculiarly the land of freedom and bravery that must be defended at all costs. It calls forth raw exhibits of power, sometimes in the service of colonial expansionism, but short of that, simply the strutting claim of strength, control, and superiority."[22] The myth of redemptive violence allows Americans to see themselves as having superior intellect and value and therefore the ability to handle weapons capable of incredible violence in an appropriate manner. The dysfunctional social imagination of American exceptionalism informs the mediating narrative of the myth of redemptive violence.

Currently, there is appropriate concern regarding weapons of mass destruction in the hands of the wrong people. Specifically, there is concern that Kim Jung Un of North Korea possesses nuclear capabilities. It is self-evident and logical to deny a WMD to the North Korean dictator. Kim Jung Un should not have nuclear weapons. However, there is no conversation on who else should be allowed to have nuclear weapons. For example, if you were to walk into a room where five people possessed AR-15 rifles, you should be legitimately concerned about the guy in the corner who just got the weapon and is muttering to himself trying to figure out how that weapon works. You don't want that guy to have a weapon of violence.

But the person you should be most worried about in the room is the one guy who has the weapon and has used the weapon to kill people (even civilians) in the past. That guy not only knows how to use the weapon, he has actually used it. While Kim Jung Un's possession of a weapon of mass destruction is a scary prospect, we never consider how the rest of the world might view the one nation on the entire planet that has used a weapon of mass destruction not just once, but twice, on a civilian population. The social imagination of white American Christian exceptionalism feeds the narrative of the myth of redemptive violence, which continues to perpetuate fallen and broken systems.

The challenge to a fallen system requires confrontation on the structural level and of the mediating social narratives that drive those dysfunctional systems. "The task of redemption is not restricted to changing individuals, then," Wink explains, "but also to changing their fallen institutions. . . . Redemption means actually being liberated from the oppression of the Powers, being forgiven both from one's own sin and for complicity with the Powers."[23] The corrupt system that emerges from a diseased social imagination now results in a broken system that perpetuates a dysfunctional narrative. The problem of the Doctrine of Discovery is that it affirms the perspective of a diseased social and theological imagination. It established the false notion of a more ethnically pure, European Christian supremacy, and today it furthers the mythology of American exceptionalism, which is rooted in the blatant lie of a white racial supremacy.

The mediating narratives rooted in a dysfunctional imagination that fuel the social systems provide a locus of evil that must be confronted, and evil must be confronted in its proper geography.[24] Because mediating narratives provide the fuel for dysfunctional systems, they can hold a power that we can oftentimes overlook. For instance, if there is an overriding narrative of white supremacy that fuels a dysfunctional system, the demise of that system does not necessarily mean the end of the narrative.

In the United States, the narrative of white supremacy is a central theme that fuels our dysfunctional systems. The horrid institution of slavery fulfilled the narrative of white supremacy. Yet even after the institution of slavery was abolished, the dysfunctional narrative of white supremacy continued; therefore a new dysfunctional system of Jim Crow laws took the place of slavery. When the dysfunctional system of Jim Crow was overturned through the Civil Rights movement, the mediating narrative of white supremacy remained, and Jim Crow was replaced with the New Jim Crow, a system of mass incarceration and disenfranchisement that allowed the narrative of white supremacy to continue.

The power of the mediating narrative is the ability to create new systems to take the place of old systems that still function to further the diseased imagination and corresponding mediating narrative. (See figure 2.2.) The power of narratives should not be underestimated as they form and shape public opinion and response in ways that logic and reasoning may not.

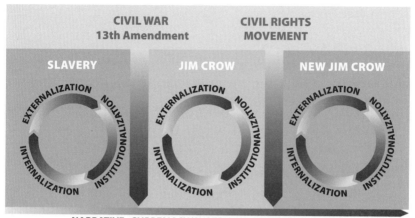

NARRATIVE : SUPREMACY/SUPERIORITY/EXCEPTIONALISM

Systems and structures will seek to maintain and preserve themselves. Systems and structures, therefore, will form metaphors, narratives, and imaginaries that help to sustain the values that have become embedded within the system. The Doctrine of Discovery serves the social system of the Western world. The dysfunctional imagination that shapes and perpetuates the Doctrine of Discovery helps maintain the social construct of Western reality, even when the system operates in a dysfunctional fashion. The dysfunctional imagination forms dysfunctional narratives that help to sustain the dysfunctional system.

In the work of healing brokenness in the world, the failure to recognize the power of narratives could derail any progress. Attempts to simply change the individual and to rid individual prejudices prove to be insufficient in this endeavor. Even attempts to change systems and structures may not be sufficient as new systems and structures take the place of old ones. Narratives, formed by the social and theological imagination, are the powers and principalities that must be addressed so that all levels of social reality are confronted. The Doctrine of Discovery, rooted in fifteenth-century theological dysfunction, is one of the most influential yet hidden narratives in American society that continues to impact social reality in American society well into the twenty-first century.

CHAPTER THREE

The Kingdom of God Is About Relationship Not Empire

STOLEN LANDS, BROKEN TREATIES, MASSACRES, boarding schools, forced assimilation, and Indian reservations populate a partial list of not only sins but unspeakable crimes that have been perpetrated against Native peoples in the name of Christ. These realities cause even the most devout Christian to question their loyalties: How can Natives call themselves Christian and consider themselves members of the church? The testimony of Scripture, however, stands in contrast to the dysfunctional narratives that have shaped the oppression of Native peoples.

Narratives have the power to shape both positive change and negative change. Unfortunately, dysfunctional narratives adversely shaped the story of the United States as well as the Christian church. The history of European conquest of the American continent arose from not only a grab for land, wealth, and power—but a grab for worldly greatness. Dysfunctional narratives would fuel these imperial ambitions and systems of dominance.

This quest for dominance resulted in the enslavement of Africans and the genocide of Native Americans. In order to justify this unholy grab for land, wealth, and power, the so-called Christian nations of Europe needed a theological justification for their unjustifiable actions. Devastating outcomes emerged from these dysfunctional theological narratives. An examination of Scripture, however, reveals that God's intention for creation was not the wielding of destructive power by one group over another. Instead, God had intended for the church to be an expression of his ongoing desire for a relationship with his creation.

THE CREATOR SEEKS A RELATIONSHIP WITH CREATION

In Genesis 3:8-9, Creator was walking in the Garden of Eden, seeking out Adam and Eve and calling out to them "Where are you?" God had created the heavens and the earth. The stars were set in their place. The plants and animals were spoken into existence. The seas teemed with fish, and the air was filled with birds. At the pinnacle of his work, God created humans: "In the image of God he created them; male and female he created them" (Genesis 1:27). Sadly, the perfection of created order was disrupted by human rebellion. So we read that God moves through the garden, calling out to his creation, seeking a restoration of a relationship broken by sin.

God is not an uninvolved force who set the world in motion and oversees it from a distance. God is a relational being who spoke the heavens and the earth into existence and stepped into it for the sake of building relationship with his creation. But sin broke that relationship when Adam and Eve disobeyed God's commandments and were expelled from the garden. In Genesis 12, Creator tried to reestablish a relationship with creation by speaking to an ancient Near Eastern nomad who would come to be known as Abraham.

Abraham was by no means perfect, but he believed the words of Creator, and God credited his faith as righteousness. God established a covenant with Abraham that included a promise of land for his descendants. So close was the relationship between Creator and Abraham that Abraham would be considered as a formative influence on multiple religions.

In the book of Exodus, God reaffirmed his covenantal relationship with the descendants of Abraham, Isaac, and Jacob by calling Moses to lead the Hebrew people out of Egypt and bring them to their Promised Land. Creator intended to be their king and God's presence dwelt among them through the Ark of the Covenant. In Deuteronomy 29 and 30, God clarified the terms of his land covenant with them, setting up their relationship to the land as a reflection of their relationship with him. When they were obedient, they would be blessed and prosper in their land. And when they were disobedient, they would be punished and exiled from their land. The people of Israel's relationship to their land was to be a barometer of their relationship with God. Upon entering their Promised Land YHWH continued leading them through relational proxies: Joshua, the judges, the prophets, and through Samuel. Towards the end of Samuel's life, the people of Israel rejected God and demanded a physical, human king. They wanted an earthly empire.

At God's direction, Samuel anointed Saul, who later rejected God. Then came David, a man after God's own heart. King David crushed the enemies of Israel and expanded the earthly kingdom. God was with David and throughout his reign the people of Israel prospered in their Promised Land. But his hands were so bloody that he was not allowed to build the temple of the Lord. His son Solomon sought wisdom from God, and it was granted, along with tremendous wealth, which he used to build God's temple. Unfortunately, he was led astray from the worship of YHWH. Soon after his death the kingdom of

Israel split, which began a long cycle of the kings and the people of God forgetting the Lord, being conquered by their enemies, returning to the Lord (and subsequently to flourishing in the land), and then forgetting him again. Throughout these cycles, God continued to speak through the prophets and never ceased trying to establish a relationship with his people.

THE MESSIAH RESTORING BROKEN RELATIONSHIPS

Woven throughout the Old Testament is the promise of a messiah who would bring final redemption and ultimate rescue from Israel's enemies. In Genesis 3:15, God states, "I will put enmity between you and the woman, and between your offspring and hers; he will crush your head, and you will strike his heel." In John 1, we are told that Jesus was in the beginning with Creator. At the formation of the heavens and the earth, Jesus was there. In the Garden of Eden, seeking out Adam and Eve after the fall, Jesus was there. Throughout the entire biblical narrative, Jesus was there. Since the beginning, Jesus was there. "Through him all things were made; without him nothing was made that has been made" (John 1:3).

Jesus is the promised Messiah. He is the embodiment of the good news. Not only because he was born to a virgin (Isaiah 7:14), healed the sick, and gave sight to the blind (Isaiah 35:5), and offered his life as a blood sacrifice (Isaiah 53:4-12), but because on the cross, he crushed the serpent's head and reconciled a sinful and rebellious creation back into relationship with Creator (Genesis 3:15).

From the beginning, Jesus understood the rebellious desires of humanity. He knew that there had been a constant struggle between the human desire to create an earthly empire and God's desire for relationship with creation. When Jesus physically entered into human history, he recognized the expectation to establish an earthly political kingdom rather than a restored relationship with Creator. The oppressed people of Israel expected a return to the greatness of the kingdom of David, but God remembered the communion of community in the Garden of Eden.

Jesus sought to challenge and change Israel's expectations. He was conceived by the Holy Spirit but out of wedlock. He was born in Bethlehem but in the humblest of environments. His arrival was announced by angels but to a bunch of shepherds. He lived in Egypt as a refugee. He grew up in an insignificant backwater town called Nazareth. Jesus did everything he could to enter into the world in a way that communicated that while he was indeed the Messiah, he did not come in power to militarily or politically overthrow their Roman oppressors and establish another earthly kingdom. But changing those expectations was one of the biggest difficulties that Jesus faced throughout his earthly ministry.

Even before he began his public ministry, Jesus rejected outright the lure of earthly kingdoms. In Matthew 4, Satan tries to tempt Jesus with the tantalizing reward of earthly kingdoms, if only Jesus would bow and worship him. Instead, Jesus rebukes Satan, refuses to bow, and rejects the temptation of earthly kingdoms.

In Luke 6 and 7, after hearing reports of Jesus' anti-imperial and even politically damaging efforts that included raising the son of a widow from the dead and healing the servant of a Roman centurion, John the Baptist sent messengers to Jesus asking, "Are you the one who is to come, or should we expect someone else?" (Luke 7:19). Jesus did his best to change John's expectations.

> At that very time Jesus cured many who had diseases, sicknesses and evil spirits, and gave sight to many who were blind. So he replied to the messengers, "Go back and report to John what you have seen and heard: The blind receive sight, the lame walk, those who have leprosy are cleansed, the deaf

hear, the dead are raised, and the good news is proclaimed to the poor. Blessed
is anyone who does not stumble on account of me." (Luke 7:21-23)

Jesus demonstrated to John that the true power of the kingdom of
God was not political but relational.

In John 6, after feeding the five thousand, Jesus knew the people
"intended to come and make him king by force" (v. 15). But an earthly
kingdom was not the plan, so he withdrew and went away by himself.
In Luke 9:46-48, the disciples were arguing among themselves about
who was the greatest, but Jesus knew their thoughts and, like any good
teacher, decided to turn their discussion into a teaching moment.
Jesus did not rebuke or attempt to squelch their desire for greatness,
but he was intentional to seize the opportunity to change the context
for their definition of the word: "Jesus, knowing their thoughts, took
a little child and had him stand beside him. Then he said to them,
'Whoever welcomes this little child in my name welcomes me; and
whoever welcomes me welcomes the one who sent me. For it is the
one who is least among you all who is the greatest'" (Luke 9:47-48).

The word *great* is a comparison and its definition is contextual.
A lottery winner may choose a lump sum payment of a million dollars
and feel that is a "great" amount of money. But that same amount
would feel like chump change to Jeff Bezos, Warren Buffett, and Bill
Gates, each of whom alone are worth upwards of $90 billion. We
allow our definition of greatness to be dictated by our environment,
our history, and the world around us. When the topic of greatness
came up among the disciples, Jesus brought a child into their midst.
This child was to be their comparison, not the might of their Roman
oppressors, nor the stories of King David, nor the wealth of Solomon,
nor the exploits of the prophets. The basis of greatness was how they
accepted and treated a weak and vulnerable child. Earthly empires
seek power and wealth to demonstrate their greatness, but greatness

in the kingdom of God is not to be measured by such standards. But the disciples didn't get it.

In Luke 9, Jesus set out for Jerusalem and sent messengers ahead to a Samaritan village. But the Samaritans rejected the messengers, which prompted James and John to ask if Jesus wanted them to call down fire on this village to destroy it. Based on examples from throughout the Old Testament, this request is actually not that outlandish. There are many stories of God sending his prophets with a call for repentance. When that call was heeded, God was merciful. But when the call was rejected, God brought judgment (Noah and the flood, Pharaoh and his soldiers in the Red Sea, and the wall of Jericho). The Old Testament is filled with examples of God using Israel to judge the nations and also using the nations of the world to judge Israel. There is even direct precedent for judgment to take the form of fire coming down from heaven (Sodom and Gomorrah, Elijah and the prophets of Baal, and Elijah and the soldiers of King Ahaziah).

The disciples, like the rest of Israel, viewed the Samaritans as other, a rebellious and sinful people. The Samaritans had intermarried with Gentiles and worshipped God on a mountain instead of in Jerusalem. The disciples most likely felt ambivalent going to a Samaritan village in the first place. The Samaritans, however, rejected the messengers and thereby rejected Jesus. They had their chance. They missed their opportunity. The disciples did not directly ask Jesus if the village should be destroyed. James and John assumed it would be and boldly asked if they could be the ones to destroy it by calling down fire on the Samaritans. But Jesus turned and rebuked them. The disciples still did not get it.

In Mark 9, John, on behalf of the rest of the disciples, comes to Jesus, saying, "Teacher, we saw someone driving out demons in your name and we told him to stop, because he was not one of us" (v. 38). Jesus is incensed at how his disciples have elevated themselves above others and immediately tells them, "Do not stop him . . . anyone who gives you a cup of water in my name because you belong to the Messiah will certainly not lose their reward" (vv. 39-41). But Jesus doesn't stop there: "If anyone causes one of these little ones—those who believe in me—to stumble, it would be better for them if a large millstone were hung around their neck and they were thrown into the sea" (v. 42). He goes on to warn that if their hand or their foot causes them to believe they are better than others, they should "cut it off" (v. 45). He also warns them that if their eye causes them to believe they are better than others they should "pluck it out. It is better for you to enter the kingdom of God with one eye than to have two eyes and be thrown into hell" (v. 47).

These verses are some of the strongest warnings that Jesus gives. They are not directed at the Samaritans who rejected Jesus nor are they directed at sinners like tax collectors or women working as prostitutes. They are also not directed at the Roman oppressors or even the pious religious leaders. The strongest warnings Jesus gives are directed at his disciples when they begin believing that because they are with Jesus they are somehow privileged and better than others.

In Luke 21, Jesus is in Jerusalem with his disciples, who are astonished with the structures of a physical kingdom and the magnificence of the temple. But Jesus responds by reminding them that what they are so taken by is only temporary and will not last. A worldly kingdom is not the goal. "As for what you see here, the time will come when not one stone will be left on another; every one of them will be thrown down" (v. 6).

A New Barometer—Persecution and Suffering

A new paradigm on power and a rejection of earthly kingdom are not the only challenging aspects of Jesus' message. Persecution also serves as a crucial aspect of his teaching. In Matthew 16:15-16, Jesus asked his disciples "Who do you say that I am?" Peter replied, "You are the

Messiah." After the disciples understood Jesus' identity, Jesus began to teach them that "the Son of Man must suffer many things and be rejected by the elders, the chief priests and the teachers of the law, and that he must be killed and after three days rise again" (Luke 9:21).

This plan contrasted so sharply with Peter's image of the Christ that he arrogantly took his teacher aside "and began to rebuke him" (Matthew 16:22). But Jesus responded with a rebuke of his own, telling Peter, "Get behind me, Satan! . . . You do not have in mind the concerns of God, but merely human concerns" (v. 23). He then continued teaching and told his followers that "whoever wants to be my disciple must deny themselves and take up their cross and follow me. For whoever wants to save their life will lose it, but whoever loses their life for me will find it" (vv. 24-25). Peter's human ambitions, earthly imagination, and even his own desire for self-preservation all conflicted with the truth of Jesus' message.

Jesus outlines in greater detail the persecutions the disciples would suffer on his account.

> "They will seize you and persecute you. They will hand you over to synagogues and put you in prison, and you will be brought before kings and governors, and all on account of my name. And so you will bear testimony to me. But make up your mind not to worry beforehand how you will defend yourselves. For I will give you words and wisdom that none of your adversaries will be able to resist or contradict. You will be betrayed even by parents, brothers and sisters, relatives and friends, and they will put some of you to death. Everyone will hate you because of me." (Luke 21:12-17)

In the Beatitudes, given in the Sermon on the Mount, Jesus takes this teaching on suffering and persecution even further when he says: "Blessed are you when people insult you, persecute you and falsely say all kinds of evil against you because of me. Rejoice and be glad, because great is your reward in heaven, for in the same way they persecuted the prophets who were before you" (Matthew 5:11-12).

Jesus gives his disciples a new barometer. Throughout the Old Testament prosperity and flourishing in their Promised Land was a gauge by which the Israelites' relationship with YHWH was measured. But now Jesus is telling his disciples that persecution, suffering, and even death will not only be his fate but will also be the fate of anyone who seeks to follow him. Their discipleship is not to be gauged by their wealth, their power, or their prosperity here on earth. They will know they are following Jesus correctly when they are rejected, insulted, and even persecuted—just like Jesus and the prophets who were before them. But his disciples did not want to accept this new barometer.

Even at the end of his life, Jesus struggled to manage the expectations his followers had for an earthly kingdom and for the old barometer of worldly prosperity. In the Garden of Gethsemane, Jesus prayed, "My Father, if it is possible, may this cup be taken from me" (Matthew 26:39). Yet Jesus knew he had to suffer, so he continued praying, "My Father, if it is not possible for this cup to be taken away unless I drink it, may your will be done" (Matthew 26:42).

Jesus knew that the message about the kingdom of God was so offensive to the power of worldly empire that persecution and even death was inevitable—not just for him, but also for his followers— which explains why he became so angry with his disciples for sleeping in the garden while he was praying: "Then he returned to his disciples and found them sleeping. 'Simon,' he said to Peter, 'are you asleep? Couldn't you keep watch for one hour? Watch and pray so that you will not fall into temptation. The spirit is willing, but the flesh is weak'" (Mark 14:37-38). Jesus knew the temptation to flee the persecution that was coming. He had already warned Peter about it and was modeling for them how to prepare for it. But his disciples missed this teaching because they were asleep.

When Jesus was arrested in the Garden of Gethsemane, Peter refused to give up his vision for a physical, earthly kingdom and therefore, having a sword, "[he] drew it and struck the high priest's servant, cutting off his right ear" (John 18:10). But Jesus again rebuked Peter and told him to put away his weapon. Jesus allowed himself to be arrested and "everyone deserted him and fled" (Mark 14:50). Later, standing alone before Pilate, Jesus said, "My kingdom is not of this world. If it were, my servants would fight to prevent my arrest by the Jewish leaders. But now my kingdom is from another place" (John 18:36).

Jesus had no intention of creating an earthly "Christian" empire, and he was adamant that both he and his followers would endure persecution. But it wasn't until he allowed himself to be killed, rose from the dead, appeared to his disciples, and was taken into heaven that his followers finally began to understand. When God poured out his Holy Spirit at Pentecost, the people who joined the believers (the church) knew that they were doing so in opposition to the religious establishment and the Roman Empire. The first members of the Way were convicted by the words of Peter that they had sinned by siding with evil men—the religious and political leaders of the worldly empires—to kill Jesus (Acts 2).

After healing the lame beggar in Acts 3, Peter and John were brought before the religious leaders and warned with threats to stop speaking in the name of Jesus. But they refused and replied, "Judge for yourselves whether it is right in God's sight to obey you rather than God. For we cannot help speaking about what we have seen and heard" (Acts 4:19-20 NIV 1984).

Saul was a Pharisee who persecuted followers of "the way," and he was on the road to Damascus when Jesus appeared to him and blinded him. Christ did not charge Saul to now use his power to "conquer" the enemies of the church. Instead he blinded Saul and asked, "Why are you persecuting me?" He then sent Saul stumbling into Damascus and three days later sent Ananias to heal Saul's blindness and to commission him for the ministry of suffering. Ananias brought the message that "I (Jesus) will show him how much he must suffer for my name" (Acts 9:16). God was not punishing Saul; rather this message revealed to Saul that to follow Jesus was to suffer.

The call of Christ is intimately tied to the expectation of impending persecution. Jesus told his followers to pick up their cross, an element of extreme and excruciating torture, and follow him. Following Jesus is not to aspire towards an elevated existence in the clouds but to follow Jesus as he crawls along the ground carrying the cross, headed towards an agonizing death. After seeing the vision of Christ, Paul understands the pending and unavoidable persecution and writes, "We also glory in our sufferings, because we know that suffering produces perseverance; perseverance, character; and character, hope" (Romans 5:3-4).

The church was meant to be prophetic. The church is strongest when it is subversive. Jesus, the bridegroom of the church, was crucified on a cross for upsetting the religious establishment and posing a threat to the Roman Empire. Central to the call to be prophetic is the call to suffer and to endure persecution. Our restored relationship to Creator is through the suffering of Jesus. The gift of that relationship is not meant to be hoarded or used as a source of misappropriated and misapplied power.

Biblical reconciliation arises from the restoration of creation back to Creator—every nation, every tribe, all people, everywhere. That could not happen through another earthly empire. The God of the Bible is not only the God of Abraham, the God of the Bible is Jesus. He was there at the beginning with Creator. He is the God of creation and his kingdom is not of this world. If it were, his servants (the angels) and not his followers (whom he called friends) would have fought to prevent his arrest. They didn't because Jesus wouldn't let them. He knew he had to be killed because his kingdom is from another place.

The call of the Messiah was for followers to pick up an instrument of torture and carry it to their deaths. Once the disciples understood this truth, they willingly followed in Jesus' footsteps. Stephen was the first to be martyred, and his stoning is recorded in Acts 7. Paul, Peter, Andrew, "Doubting" Thomas, Philip, Matthew, Bartholomew, James, Simon the Zealot, and even Matthias, the disciple who replaced Judas, are all believed to have died for their faith. This legacy of martyrdom continued for hundreds of years as the church continued to grow while it stood in opposition to the empire. This biblical narrative of prophetic opposition to empire, however, unfortunately faded in subsequent centuries.

CHAPTER FOUR

The Rise and Defense of Christendom

About the time of the midday sun, when day was just turning,
he said he saw with his own eyes, up in the sky and resting
over the sun, a cross shaped trophy formed from light, and
a text attached to it which said, "By this conquer."

IN AD 312 THE ROMAN EMPEROR Constantine attempted to consolidate his power in a civil war with another Roman emperor, Maxentius. On October 28 the conflict between the two emperors culminated in the Battle of Milvian Bridge. At the end of the day, Constantine's armies prevailed, and Maxentius was dead. Constantine's vision of the cross is often identified as the point of his conversion to Christianity. In AD 313, Constantine signed the Edict of Milan, which proclaimed religious tolerance throughout the Roman Empire. In AD 325, Constantine called the Council of Nicaea, which produced the Nicene Creed. In AD 330, after defeating Emperor Licinius and consolidating the entire Roman Empire under his rule, Constantine moved the capital city to Byzantium and renamed it Constantinople.

This series of events established and solidified Christianity as the official religion of the Roman Empire. Christendom had been born. Rome was now a Christian empire, and formerly persecuted Christians throughout the land felt a profound sense of relief. This relief is best expressed by Eusebius, the Bishop of Caesarea, who wrote: "To him, therefore, the supreme God, granted from heaven above, the fruits of his piety, the trophies of victory over the wicked, and that nefarious tyrant with all his counsellors and adherents, he cast prostrate at the feet of Constantine."[1] But Jesus was absolutely clear, an earthly Christian empire was not God's plan. Christ's bride, the church, did not have a land covenant with the God of Abraham. Promised lands and earthly prosperity were not the barometer for the followers of Jesus. So where did this heresy of Christian empire originate?

JUSTIFYING CHRISTIAN EMPIRE

In AD 325, Eusebius, the Bishop of Caesarea, published a volume of eleven books titled *Ecclesiastical History*. A common theme throughout this work is the persecution of Christians. In books 1-8, Eusebius not only describes in vivid and even gory detail the suffering of Christian martyrs, but he also articulates the joy with which they embraced their persecution.

In book 8 Eusebius introduces Constantius, who is the father of the Roman emperor Constantine. He records that Constantius "was the kindest and mildest of the emperors," who "had no share in the hostility raised against us, but even preserved and protected those pious persons under him free from harm and calumny."[2] Eusebius writes that after Constantius's death his son Constantine was "proclaimed supreme emperor and Augustus by the soldiers." Eusebius seemed to ordain Constantine's rule by declaring that even before this,

Constantine was proclaimed supreme emperor and Augustus "by the universal sovereign God."[3]

This declaration of divine ordination of Constantine by Eusebius at first appears confounding. In a volume of ecclesiastical history that highlights the faith and piety of martyrs, words expressing God's ordination of an emperor from the pagan and oppressive empire of Rome seem out of place. However, Eusebius's motivation can be detected in the very next book.

Between books 8 and 9, Eusebius included a "Book of Martyrs," which contains thirteen chapters detailing persecutions that took place in Palestine and Caesarea (Eusebius's hometown), many of which were witnessed by Eusebius himself. This period, known as the "Great Persecution," occurred in AD 303 under the reign of the Roman emperor Diocletian. It was this persecution that Constantine's father, Constantius, had no share in, and it was after this persecution that Constantine ruled. However, another Roman emperor (at this point there were three), Maxentius, not only participated in the Great Persecution in AD 303 with tremendous zeal, but continued the persecution of Christians throughout his reign.

In AD 312 Constantine attempted to consolidate his power through a civil war with Emperor Maxentius. The results of this war would have huge implications not only for Christians throughout the Roman Empire but also for Eusebius personally. Eusebius's interest in establishing, validating, supporting, and ordaining a rising yet sympathetic political and military ruler such as Constantine is evident in how he records Constantine's victory at the Battle of Milvian Bridge.

> As, therefore, anciently in the days of Moses, and the religious people of the Hebrews, the chariots of Pharaoh, and his forces were cast into the Red Sea, and his chosen triple combatants were overwhelmed in it; thus, also, Maxentius, and his combatants and guards about him, sunk into the depths like a stone, when he fled before the power of God that was with Constantine,

and passed through the river in his way, over which he had formed a bridge by joining boats, and thus prepared the means of his own destruction.[4]

Eusebius not only includes a temporal secular victory in his historical account of the church, he offers a glowing spiritual account of the battle and compares the victory by Constantine to Moses parting the Red Sea and destroying Pharaoh and his army, one of the greatest military victories in the entire history of Israel.

The beginning of this chapter included a vision reportedly given to Constantine the night before his battle with Maxentius, which instructed him to "Conquer" (his enemies) through the power of the cross. Eusebius writes that Constantine was "wondering to himself what the manifestation might mean, then, while he meditated, and thought long and hard, night overtook him. Thereupon, as he slept, the Christ of God appeared to him with the sign that had appeared in the sky, and urged him to make a copy of the sign which had appeared in the sky, and to use this as protection against the attacks of the enemy."[5]

Constantine's vision occurred in AD 312, but it is not mentioned in Eusebius's *Ecclesiastical History,* published in AD 325. Constantine died in AD 337, but it was not until AD 339, in *The Life of Constantine,* which Eusebius was writing at the time of his own death, that a narrative of the vision was published. Eusebius was probably aware of the credibility issues surrounding this vision, so he wrote that "the victorious Emperor himself told the story to the present writer a long while after, when I was privileged with his acquaintance and company." Eusebius also reported that Constantine confirmed his story with oaths, so "who could hesitate to believe the account?"[6]

Further complicating the matter of credibility, Eusebius did not personally meet the emperor until Constantine convened the Council of Nicaea in AD 325. By that point, many competing narratives of the Battle of Milvian had already been circulated: "All of the early accounts of the battle, whether a panegyric, an apologetic pamphlet, a historical narrative, or a decorated monument, had been typically written, orated, or sculpted independently of the emperor's opinions."[7] Each narrative had a competing political and social agenda: "These accounts had been aimed at Constantine, as recommendations of how he ought to behave as ruler, and were not derived from him. . . . By the time the emperor told his stories, he had been thinking for years not just about the battle but also about the subsequent accounts of the battle."[8]

In the decade following the Battle of Milvian Bridge, a Constantinian imagination and narrative were constructed. So when Constantine finally relayed the account of his vision of Christ, the "stories were hence reactions, not catalysts." Constantine was adding to the "myth of himself,"[9] a myth that Eusebius had an active hand in constructing. Yet when the persecution of Christians reached his own hometown and touched Eusebius personally, his attitude towards persecution changed. In seeking to end it, Eusebius ordained the most likely emperor from the powerful and oppressive Roman Empire as "God's chosen ruler." Constantine's dubious account of Jesus taking sides in a violent conflict was not condemned as heretical and as inconsistent with the biblical account of Jesus.

Jesus repeatedly stressed the reality of suffering rather than the triumph and victory of an earthly Messiahship. When Jesus stood trial (John 19), Pilate was looking for an excuse to free Jesus and asked him, "Do you refuse to speak to me? . . . Don't you realize I have power either to free you or to crucify you?" (v. 10). Jesus could have acknowledged Pilate's power, flattered him, and ordained him as God's chosen ruler for such a time as this. As Eusebius did for Constantine, or white Evangelicals did for Donald J. Trump, or as progressive Christians did for President Obama, Jesus could have played to Pilate's ego and coaxed Pilate to set him free. Instead Jesus spoke prophetically to Pilate and was handed over to be crucified.

Eusebius, however, after being personally touched by the Great Persecution, exhibits an affinity towards the earthly ruler who represented the best possible chance of ending the persecution of the church. In a rejection of Christ's barometer of suffering, Eusebius aligned himself with Constantine, a young ruler attempting to consolidate power and looking for political allies. Eusebius helped construct the mythology of Constantine by sprinkling his writings with references to divine ordination and promises of honor and a legacy of supremacy. Eusebius affirmed Constantine's exceptionalism and the inevitability of his triumph, being "only too ready to claim Constantine as a Christian, long before he heard about the Emperor's conversion resulting from his vision of a cross."[10]

Before his death, Constantine issued an edict that allowed the right to religious freedom, halted the persecution of Christians, and even put a Christian stamp on the empire. But he reinforced his own mythology as a God-ordained military leader with his story of a vision for military conquest in the name of and under the cross of Jesus Christ. This heretical vision fit Eusebius's hopes to end the persecution of the church; therefore, he recorded and promoted the vision not only as historical fact, but also as a sound theological conclusion.

The idea of Christendom, an earthly Christian empire, is an extrabiblical concept that is not aligned with the teachings of Jesus. Participation in the early church was based on repentance (Matthew 3:2; Mark 1:15), baptism (Acts 2:38), confession (2 Timothy 2:19), discipleship (Matthew 28:19), and community (Acts 2:46-47). The church of Jesus Christ was solidified, refined, and strengthened through the shared and promised experience of persecution (Luke 21:12-17). A convert to Christianity would join a community of believers as an act of submission to the kingdom of God knowing full well that their conversion would result in carrying a cross.

With the advent of Christendom under Constantine, admission into the kingdom of God became entangled with participation in and protection from an earthly empire. In seeking to end the persecution of Christians, Eusebius allowed Constantine to fundamentally alter what membership in the church looked like. Instead of joining the church intentionally, sacrificially, and in opposition to empire, membership in the church now depended upon citizenship in, and allegiance to, one of the most powerful and historically oppressive empires in the world.

The conflation of the kingdom of God with an earthly empire was not what Christ intended for the church. The teachings of Jesus, his disciples, and the apostle Paul do not gesture towards Christendom. Central to Christianity is sacrificial love and the laying down of one's life. Empires are concerned with self-preservation, conquest, and expansion. The means of an empire are military power and financial resources. Jesus' disciples left everything—their livelihoods and their security—to follow him. Jesus sent them out with nothing, "like sheep among wolves" (Matthew 10:16). In Mark 10, a rich young ruler couldn't bring himself to be counted among the ranks of Jesus' disciples because he decided to walk away when Jesus challenged him to "sell everything you have and give to the poor" (Mark 10:21).

The creation of a Christian empire forced a paradigm on the church that was never imagined at its beginning. Military expansion, wealth, conquest, and colonization were how the Roman Empire was created and how it sustained, protected, and preserved itself. Converting from a pluralistic religion that included worship of the emperor to Christendom did not change the reality of an empire rooted in the myth of redemptive violence. Despite what could be considered teachings contrary to the empire offered by the New

Testament, the Roman Empire continued to operate under the narrative of violence, war, and colonial expansion. Christianity would be more adversely affected by the empire than the empire was positively impacted by Christianity.

AUGUSTINE AND THE AFFIRMATION OF CHRISTENDOM

With the onset of Christendom and a worldly empowerment of a previously disenfranchised Christianity, Christians began to reconsider their role in society. Christian leaders and thinkers who had focused on survival in the context of an oppressive empire now sought to justify the power of the empire that could potentially serve them rather than oppress them. The Christian imagination shifted from a mindset of suffering to a mindset of exceptionalism and triumphalism. The emergence of just war theory reflected this shifting mindset that emerged with Constantine and found its way throughout church history to the modern era.

Augustine of Hippo asserted just war theory as a means of understanding the relationship between the City of God (the heavenly kingdom) and the City of Man (the earthly kingdom). Augustine's early justification of war would be further developed by the church in subsequent centuries. These principles included, among other aspects: seeing war as a punitive act; a sense of confronting moral injustice and evil; and seeking a proper authorization for war from an authorized power such as a state.[11] Implicit within just war theory was the belief that those who claimed this position stood on the side of God and acted as the just actors in the scenario.

Augustine proposed the foundational aspects of just war theory believing that the church stood on the side of justice and reflected the values of the kingdom of God. Augustine sought to better understand how the heavenly kingdom could operate within the earthly empire.

At the same time, Augustine was concerned about the preservation of
Christian doctrine and theology in the context of the earthly kingdom.
The intersection of these two perspectives resulted in the burgeoning
just war theory.

In response to the fourth- and fifth-century schismatic movement
of the Donatists, who advocated for the purity of the clergy and some
of whom had engaged in violence, Augustine offered guidelines of a
just war. The violence of war could be justified under certain conditions. "The purpose of the war must be just. . . . A just war must be
waged by properly instituted authority . . . [and] even in the midst of
the violence that was a necessary part of war, the motive of love must
be central."[12] The earthly kingdom, if under the proper authority such
as the church, could engage in violent action in order to maintain just
order in the City of Man, so that the City of God could continue
uninterrupted. Augustine would give justification for the state to act
violently. Just war theory justifies violence, particularly violence
against those who would seek to contradict the teachings of the church.

In responding to the Donatist heresy, Augustine leaves room for
violent action by the state on behalf of the church. In chapter five of
his work *On the Correction of the Donatists*, Augustine investigates
the role of a Christian king.

> How then are kings to serve the Lord with fear, except by preventing and
> chastising with religious severity all those acts which are done in opposition
> to the commandments of the Lord? For a man serves God in one way in that
> he is man, in another way in that he is also king. In that he is man, he serves
> Him by living faithfully; but in that he is also king, he serves Him by enforcing
> with suitable rigor such laws as ordain what is righteous, and punish what is
> the reverse.[13]

A Christian king is one who enforces the commandments of the Lord.
He must also prevent and chastise with religious severity those who
oppose the commandments of God—in this case, the Donatists. The

commands of God, which by extension would include the doctrines of the church, must be enforced by the Christian king. As theologian Richard Hartigan notes: "In the majority of his works he set out to refute blatant heresies, false charges against the Christian religion, and erroneous teachings which had sprung up within his Christian church. It is in this last respect that his statements on war and killing primarily fall."[14]

We see evidence of this perspective in chapter 6, where Augustine asserts:

> It is indeed better (as no one ever could deny) that men should be led to worship God by teaching, than that they should be driven to it by fear of punishment or pain; but it does not follow that because the former course produces the better men, therefore those who do not yield to it should be neglected. For many have found advantage (as we have proved, and are daily proving by actual experiment), in being first compelled by fear or pain, so that they might afterwards be influenced by teaching, or might follow out in act what they had already learned in word.[15]

Augustine makes the argument that there are more peaceful ways to confront heresy, such as through teaching. However, if that approach does not work, it is permissible to compel them through "fear of punishment and pain."

As Catholic theologian John Langan notes, "Augustine's primary concern is with a conversion of mind and heart, and his preference is for achieving this by the example of patience. But . . . there is also reliance on punitive methods. . . . [Augustine's position] includes both the affirmation of the priority of spiritual goods and a strong paternalistic tendency, in which one is willing to take action overriding others' conception of what constitutes their good."[16] Augustine offers the possibility of using violence against those who would teach in opposition to the doctrines of the church, for their own good. A Christian king would be responsible, even obligated, to enforce these doctrines providing a justification for violence.

These quotations offer two examples of where Augustine of Hippo directly contradicts the model and teaching of Jesus. He concludes that the role of the Christian king is to use the resources of the state to enforce (through fear, punishment, and pain) the commandments of God and the doctrines of the church. This perspective was not taught by Jesus nor was it what Jesus modeled. When given the option to use force and heavenly power, Jesus instead chose the way of the cross. Instead of calling fire down from heaven, Jesus rebuked the disciples who sought this form of resolution. When Jesus was arrested, Jesus went willingly towards his execution. On the cross, Jesus did not call down angels from heaven to rescue him, but instead commended his spirit to the Father. Augustine's establishment of just war theory reveals a political expediency with a furtherance of empire and worldly power rather than the seeking of God's kingdom.

Ongoing Expressions of a Dysfunctional Imagination

Just war theory develops more fully in church doctrine following Augustine. Augustine's theological acceptance of Christian empire, his collusion through just war theory, and his justification of imperial power to enforce church doctrine set the stage for the Crusades in the eleventh century. In subsequent years, just war theory provided justification for various atrocities of the state. Even as Augustine attempted to provide a clearer articulation of this theory, the central theme remained the justification of the right of Christendom to use violent means, particularly if it meant defending the foundational beliefs of the Christian faith.

In the thirteenth century, Thomas Aquinas would further Augustine's perspective on the justification for violent action. "Aquinas lived in an era characterized by the blurring of the lines between Church and State," theologian Nico Vorster notes, adding that "Aquinas considered just war as a legitimate means to address injustice, wrong-doing and heresy. In doing so, God's eternal law that binds all people is enforced."[17] In *Summa Theologica*, in the chapter titled "Whether heretics ought to be tolerated?" Thomas Aquinas concludes:

> They deserve not only to be separated from the Church by excommunication, but also to be severed from the world by death. . . . Wherefore if forgers of money and other evil-doers are forthwith condemned to death by the secular authority, much more reason is there for heretics, as soon as they are convicted of heresy, to be not only excommunicated but even put to death.[18]

Aquinas elevates heresy to an action punishable by death by a secular authority, furthering the narrative of Christendom and the power of the church within the state.

Similar to the perspective of Augustine, Aquinas believes that just war must be conducted by "[1] the due authorities (princes) who received the power of the sword from God . . . [2] the cause must be just . . . [3] that wars must be waged with the right intent, namely to 'promote good and avoid evil.'"[19] Like Augustine, Aquinas assumes that the church (in this case the Christian church in Europe) stands on the side of justice and that those within the boundaries of Christendom will act justly to stamp out the heretics of those outside Christendom.

In the thirteenth century, the writings of the church begin referring to a subhuman class known as the infidel. The theological problem of the other would undergird the dysfunctional theological narrative needed for the European powers to justify violent conquest of the entire world. Because those living outside the boundaries of European Christendom could be deemed as infidels, justification could now be established for the enslavement and genocide of those who were others. Once the category of others was established as the "infidels"—that is, those who are outside of the Christian faith—violence towards the infidel other could now be justified.[20]

The formation of the Doctrine of Discovery in the fifteenth century was the culmination of the development of a diseased theological imagination that resulted in the severely dysfunctional expression of the church. This imagination operated beneath the surface of the European mind, particularly towards those deemed as outsiders or infidels. This identification of non-Europeans as infidels would amplify the church teaching that those who are outside of right doctrine could be subject to violent action by the state. The empire would serve the church by engaging in violence towards those deemed as others by the church; the earthly kingdom would be served by the church, as the church would deem the enemies of the state as those outside the faith. Thus, instead of seeking to restore relationships with the other, the church would aid the state in seeking to expand the empire, even at the cost of human lives.

THE BEGINNING OF THE END?

Eusebius sought to end the persecution of the church by ordaining the emperor of the most powerful empire in the world. Constantine fulfilled that expectation but in turn inaugurated Christendom. Augustine does not rebuke Christendom but colludes with it by offering a theological foundation for Christendom and affirming violence as a justifiable action for a Christian king. Aquinas further colludes with the Christian empire and the furthering of dysfunctional earthly power when he claims for the church the authority to "not only excommunicate [heretics] but even put [them] to death." An insider versus outsider reality has been formed that puts European Christianity on the inside, while others fall on the outside.

The theological efforts of Eusebius, Augustine, and Aquinas proved to be self-serving, as they would affirm the earthly empires with an elevated self-perception of their own worth. Exceptional Christian rulers governing the City of Man could operate in violence and war as long as they had the support of the church. A church caught in the throes of Christendom would have no choice but to rubber stamp the violent tendencies of an earthly empire. Affirming the just cause of war would give higher standing for the church in that society. By affirming just war for the sake of secular power, the church would yield its independent and prophetic role vis-à-vis the secular state. Instead of embodying the values of the kingdom of God and the self-sacrificial example of Christ, the church would grab power by affirming earthly power and the right of that earthly power to engage in violence.

Jesus' goal is not an earthly empire rooted in human power. In his teachings, there is no room for Christian empire. In Mark 2, Jesus tells a parable comparing himself to a bridegroom. In Ephesians 5, Paul writes about Christ's love for the church using the analogy of marriage: "Husbands, love your wives, as Christ loved the church and gave himself up for her, that he might sanctify her, having cleansed her by the washing of water with the word, so that he might present the church to himself in splendor, without spot or wrinkle or any such thing, that she might be holy and without blemish" (vv. 25-27 ESV).

Jesus loves the church. He laid his life down for her and he does not want his bride to prostitute herself out to a worldly empire. When Jesus was presented with the expectation or temptation to collude with empire or to create an earthly kingdom, Jesus reacted negatively. He did not come to establish an earthly empire. He came to make disciples, inaugurate the kingdom through the establishment of his church, and offer himself as a living sacrifice. He was here to lay down his life, not to save it or to promote it. Jesus warned his disciples that they should expect and do the same. Had Jesus been physically present on earth to hear Eusebius's affirmation of a secular emperor, Augustine's conclusions about the justification of violence, and Aquinas's affirmation of murder, Jesus would have responded in the same way he responded to Peter: "Get behind me, Satan! . . . You are not on the side of God, but of men" (Matthew 16:23 RSV).

When Eusebius made the decision to align the church with the emperor of Rome and Constantine Christianized the Roman Empire and created Christendom, they were both doing so in contrast to the teaching and example of Jesus. The church needed to reject Christian empire, but instead the church leaders, thinkers, and theologians sought for a way to make Christendom work. Augustine's just war theory provided a theological justification for the empire's violence and provided the church with standing within the empire. Aquinas furthered the self-perception of exceptionalism of the church and cemented the power of the church within the structures of Christendom. The church gained imperial power. The heresy of Eusebius, the actions of Constantine, and the collusion of Augustine and Aquinas were "Get behind me, Satan!" moments. But instead, the church was largely silent.

How did the church move from the ministry of compassion and care as commanded by Jesus and advocated by Paul to a Doctrine of Discovery that affirms violence and injustice in extreme forms? How did it get from following a Savior who was persecuted and executed for his faith to a church that enacted persecution and executed its enemies in the name of Christ? How did we get from the Holy Spirit enabling the followers of Jesus to speak the languages of the nations in Acts 2 to Christian missionaries washing out native children's mouths with soap for having the gall to speak in their own tongue?

Christendom is the prostitution of the church to the empire that created a church culture of seeking power rather than relationships. Jesus laid down his life, but the empire must save its life. Jesus emptied himself, but the empire must protect and expand itself. There is a fundamental conflict between the goal of the earthly empire and the direction of the kingdom of God. Greatness in the world and greatness in the kingdom of God stand in opposition.

In chapter 2 of Book 1 of *Ecclesiastical History*, Eusebius states his goal to provide a "summary view of the pre-existence and Divinity of our Lord and Saviour Jesus Christ."[21] He further seeks to "record the successions of the holy apostles, together with the times since our Saviour, down to the present." Church history, however, does not end with Eusebius's account. According to Scripture, the history of the church will not conclude until Christ returns. In Acts 1, two angels address the disciples and state, "'Men of Galilee,' they said, 'why do you stand here looking into the sky? This same Jesus, who has been taken from you into heaven, will come back in the same way you have seen him go into heaven'" (v. 11). Jesus consummates the kingdom, not an earthly ruler.

However, in concluding *Ecclesiastical History*, Eusebius does not emphasize the soon and returning king, but focuses on the Emperor Constantine. After control of the Roman Empire is consolidated under Constantine, after the persecution of the church has ended and Christendom has been created, Eusebius records that the Roman Empire has been restored "to its ancient state of one united body; extending their peaceful sway around the world." He records that:

> All things were filled with light, and all who before were sunk in sorrow, beheld each other with smiling and cheerful faces. With choirs and hymns in the cities and villages, at the same time they celebrated and extolled first of all God the Universal King, because they thus were taught, then they also celebrated the praises of the pious Emperor, and with him all his divinely-favoured children. There was a perfect oblivion of past evils, and past wickedness was buried in forgetfulness. There was nothing but enjoyment of the present blessings, and expectation of those yet to come.[22]

The language of the final chapter reflects the language of the end of human history. The text bears a remarkable similarity to the language of Revelation, where every tear will be wiped away and the old order of things has passed away (Revelation 21:4). Rather than the history of the church continuing to be written, Eusebius hints at a consummation of the church.

The final chapter, "The Victory of Constantine, and the blessings under him accrued to the whole Roman world," contains a single (passing) reference to Christ. The chapter is devoted to Constantine and his "divinely favoured" children, especially his "most pious son," Crispus Caesar. According to Eusebius, it was Constantine and not Jesus who was the "protector of the good, combining his hatred of wickedness with the love of goodness, went forth with his son Crispus, the most benevolent Cesar, to extend a saving arm to those who were perishing."[23] With Christendom, Christ had been replaced. According to Eusebius, *Ecclesiastical History* concluded not when Jesus returned, but when "the Supreme God, granted from heaven above, the fruits of his piety, the trophies of victory over the wicked, and that nefarious tyrant with all his counsellors and adherrents, he cast prostrate at the feet of Constantine."[24]

CHAPTER FIVE

A Dysfunctional Theology
Brought to the "New" World

ON MARCH 3, 2015, at the invitation of US House Speaker John Boehner, Israeli Prime Minister Benjamin Netanyahu addressed a joint session of the United States Congress. The speech was controversial on many levels, and some even considered it to be unconstitutional. Article II, Section 2, Clause 2 of the United States Constitution states that the President "shall have Power, by and with the Advice and Consent of the Senate, to make Treaties."[1] The Obama administration was working hard to finalize the terms for a nuclear treaty with Iran. The Republican Speaker of the House went behind the back of the Democratic president and invited the Israeli prime minister to address (technically, to lobby) a joint session of Congress. A political slight of this magnitude was without precedent.

Furthermore, because the speaker was white and the president was black, many interpreted it as a racist move. Not only was Netanyahu vehemently opposed to the proposed nuclear treaty with Iran, he was actively campaigning for re-election. Speaking to a joint session of

Congress could be interpreted as a political endorsement by the United States for the prime minister and his party. As a result, about thirty members of Congress boycotted the speech.

Netanyahu faced a daunting task. He was addressing an extremely partisan and divided Congress. His speech was being broadcast to a racially divided and politically unsettled US public. He had to find a way to thread the needle and get as many people as possible on the same page and in agreement with him. So early in his speech he hit on one of the most unifying and bipartisan themes in US politics, American exceptionalism. He said, "Because America and Israel, we share a common destiny, the destiny of promised lands."[2]

THE DOCTRINE OF DISCOVERY AND THE PROMISED LAND

The narrative of American exceptionalism finds an early expression in the colonial history of North America. In 1630, on a ship bound for the Massachusetts Bay Colony, John Winthrop, a Puritan pastor who would come to serve as the governor of Massachusetts, preached a sermon titled "A Modell of Christian Charity." He invoked the Old Testament passage in Micah "to do justly, to love mercy, to walk humbly with our God." He exhorted the colonists to "uphold a familiar commerce . . . delight in each other, make other's conditions our own. . . . The Lord will be our God and delight to dwell among us, *as his own people* (emphasis ours) and will command a blessing upon us in all our ways, so that we shall see much more of his wisdom power goodness and truth then formerly we have been acquainted with."[3] Winthrop envisioned the new colony as a community expressing care and love towards each other. These qualities exhibited by the commonwealth of Massachusetts would demonstrate that they were uniquely God's people and deserving of special favor from God. He envisioned the Puritans as God's people among whom God dwells with great delight.

In the second half of his sermon, Winthrop sought to motivate the colonists towards a divine destiny: "He (God) shall make us a praise and glory, that men shall say of succeeding plantations: the Lord make it like that of New England: for we must consider that we shall be as a City upon a Hill, the eyes of all people are upon us."[4] The "City upon a Hill" reference is taken from the teachings of Jesus in his Sermon on the Mount: "You are the light of the world. A town built on a hill cannot be hidden. Neither do people light a lamp and put it under a bowl. Instead they put it on its stand, and it gives light to everyone in the house. In the same way, let your light shine before others, that they may see your good deeds and glorify your Father in heaven" (Matthew 5:14-16). Winthrop, therefore, proclaimed the colonists to be those who had been endowed with a special, spiritual favor by God, whose life and example would be a shining light into all the world. Through their very embodiment, they would perform evangelism in a broken and sinful world.

Puritans in the New World believed themselves to be especially favored by God, the vessel through which the light of the gospel would shine forth into this dark world. Winthrop concluded his sermon by quoting from Deuteronomy 30. The Old Testament passage reveals God reiterating for Moses and the people of Israel the threats and promises of his land covenant with them. God instructs them that if they obey him, he will bless them, and they will flourish in their land, but if they disobey him, he will curse them and exile them from the land. Winthrop goes on to quote: "But if our hearts shall turn away, so that we will not obey, but shall be seduced, and worship and serve other Gods. . . . It is propounded unto us this day, we shall surely perish out of the good land whither we pass over this vast sea to possess it." However, Deuteronomy 30:17-18 concludes with the statement "whether we pass over the Jordan to possess it." John Winthrop changes "the Jordan" (a river) to "vast sea." The change in language reflects the fact that their ship didn't cross a river, it crossed an ocean—specifically, the Atlantic Ocean.

Drawing from Jesus' exhortation to be a city on a hill and referring to the land covenant that the God of Abraham established with the people of Israel, Winthrop asserted that the colonists were on the shores of their own promised lands, about to take possession of them. While not directly referencing the papal bulls of the Catholic Church and the Doctrine of Discovery, the understanding of chosen-ness and the legacy of promised lands align closely with the worldview and theological imagination found within the Doctrine of Discovery. The colonists claimed their identity as the chosen people. The narrative of European supremacy, now fully realized in the European body and mind, compelled them to seek out the mantle of being God's chosen people, which had been previously reserved only for the Jewish people. This dysfunctional theological imagination now affirmed the European body as superior to the Native body that already inhabited the Americas.

The conflation of Old Testament Israel with US history becomes even more troubling with the trajectory of Deuteronomy and the historical narrative in the book of Joshua: "However, in the cities of the nations the LORD your God is giving you as an inheritance, do not leave alive anything that breathes. Completely destroy them—the Hittites, Amorites, Canaanites, Perizzites, Hivites and Jebusites—as the LORD your God has commanded you" (Deuteronomy 20:16-17). According to this passage, promised land for one people is God-ordained genocide for another. Winthrop's assertion of a special status for the Puritans in the New World justified the resulting genocide of the existing population in the American continent. A dysfunctional social and theological imagination influenced by the assertions of the

Doctrine of Discovery allowed Native genocide to be understood as a holy act of claiming the promised land for European settlers, akin to the claiming of the Promised Land and the subsequent destruction of the people of the land by the chosen people of Israel.

So when Netanyahu publicly ordained both the United States of America and the modern nation state of Israel as having "promised lands," he revealed the very dysfunctional and codependent relationship that exists between the two countries. The US needs Israel's Old Testament legacy of promised lands to justify the history of enslavement of African people and ethnic cleansing and genocide of Native people. The modern nation-state of Israel needs the continued flourishing of the United States as a shining city upon a hill to justify their current unjust actions against the Palestinian and Bedouin people.

Christopher Columbus, anointed as the "discoverer" of America, operated under the claims of the Doctrine of Discovery. The church acknowledged Columbus as doing evangelistic work for the church and specially favored by God. The elevated narrative of Christopher Columbus would fuel the dysfunctional theological imagination that exceptional people discovered the New World and replaced less valued bodies on the American continent. The Doctrine of Discovery influenced the perspective that the "discovery" of the Americas was a God-ordained act that demonstrated the superiority of the exceptional European Christian. This doctrine sustained a strong influence over Western society beyond the conflict between the Catholic nations of Spain and Portugal. It would seep its way into the social imagination of the European powers that would find no challenge to the assumption that they were the chosen people, endowed by the Creator with certain inalienable rights, and able to bring civilization and Christianity to a savage "New World," which would serve as their promised land.

ANGLO-SAXON EXCEPTIONALISM

The Doctrine of Discovery not only shaped the imagination of the European powers and spurred their imperial and colonial ambitions—it also helped to shape the social and political foundations of the United States. The social imagination of the founding of the United States derived from the application of the long-standing Doctrine of Discovery intersecting with a Puritan worldview that elevated the value and worth of Anglo-Saxon peoples. The myth of Anglo-Saxon superiority contributed to this ongoing dysfunction established by the Doctrine of Discovery.

Kelly Brown Douglas in her work *Stand Your Ground* traces the origins of the Anglo-Saxon identity back to a first-century text titled *Germania,* written by the Roman historian Publius Cornelius Tacitus.

> In *Germania* Tacitus provides a meticulous portrait . . . of the Germanic tribes . . . "a distinct unmixed race . . . with fierce blue eyes, red hair, huge frames." Tacitus commended these Germans for their bravery and strong moral character. . . . Tacitus portrayed these ancient Germans as possessing a peculiar respect for individual rights and an almost "instinctive love for freedom." This was evident, he said, by the way in which they governed themselves . . . and most final "decision[s] rest with the people." . . . According to many later interpreters, Tacitus was describing the perfect form of government.[5]

Douglas notes that "even though the precise ethnic makeup of these Germanic tribes was not certain, they are considered the progenitors of the Anglo-Saxon race. Tacitus's ethnological description spawned the construction of the Anglo-Saxon myth."[6] The description of these Germanic tribes provides the beginnings of the claim to exceptionalism for European people. They held certain characteristics such as lighter skin and lighter hair, which were linked to a superior capacity for self-governance and, therefore, they could claim status as an exceptional people.

This narrative of European superiority and the correlation to the physical features of Europeans coupled with the proclamations of the Doctrine of Discovery would result in the self-perception of exceptionalism for the European body and mind. This perspective would find its way to the British Isles and find a narrative home in the myths of the British people. Historian Hugh A. MacDougal explains the four main components of the Anglo-Saxon mythology:

> (1) Germanic peoples, on account of their unmixed origins and universal civilizing mission, are inherently superior to all others, both in individual character and in their institutions. (2) The English are, in the main, of Germanic origin. . . . (3) The qualities which render English political and religious institutions the freest in the world are an inheritance from Germanic forefathers. (4) The English, better than any Germanic people, represent the traditional genius of their ancestors and thereby carry a special burden of leadership in the world community.[7]

This mythology would take hold among a group of religious reformers who would see themselves in the narrative of purity. In England, "the Pilgrims and the Puritans thought the Church of England did not go far enough in the eradication of Catholic and Norman abuses." They would see themselves as a pure faith and people that would uphold the purity of the Anglo-Saxon lineage as well as religion. These reformers (the Pilgrims and the Puritans) would "transport the Anglo-Saxon myth to America" and eventually have "the greatest impact on America's religious and political culture."[8]

Seeing themselves in the line of a special people that combined the best of exceptional European peoples, the colonial settlers of the American continent would indeed be especially endowed by their Creator to be a chosen people with a promised land to claim.

> The Pilgrims and Puritans fled from the Church of England to build a religious institution more befitting Anglo-Saxon virtue and freedom. They considered themselves the Anglo-Saxon tenant that was continuing a divine mission. . . . They saw themselves "as the Israelites in God's master

plan." . . . These reformers' exodus from England was first and foremost a
religious mission. . . . A part of their mission, therefore, was not simply to
build a nation that was in keeping with their Anglo-Saxon political heritage,
but also to build a religious nation.[9]

The worldview of the Pilgrims and the Puritans was profoundly
shaped by the dominant European perspective. They were formed by
the worldview established by the Doctrine of Discovery and reinforced by the myth of the exceptional nature of the pure Anglo-Saxon
people. As the Puritans found their way to New England, these sen-
sibilities and narratives would dominate the formation of the nascent
United States. "According to Tocqueville, (1) Americans found their
origins in Puritan theology, (2) the civilization they build displaced
a wilderness, and (3) their pursuits were directed more toward
making the most of life here on earth. . . . The portion of Englishmen
who settled in America were going to be focused on taming the
wilderness and building civilization in North America."[10] The imagination of a civilized people conquering the wilderness aligned with
the biblical narrative of God's chosen people. Israel wandered
through the wilderness and emerged from a nomadic, primitive
experience to conquer a pagan people. The wilderness represented
an uninhabited and wild land that required discovering and taming
by exceptional people.

The motif of an exceptional, chosen people ordained by God to
tame the savage world of the Natives of North America became the
driving narrative for the colonial settlers. Steven Newcomb points out
that the mental models of the early colonists would shape the
formation of American jurisprudence and governance:

> The Chosen People—Promised Land cognitive model serves as a significant
> part of the conceptual and religious backdrop. . . . This model is the source of
> the perspective that the American people of the United States are a new
> "chosen people" analogous to the chosen people of the Old Testament.
> According to this view, and in keeping with the Conqueror model, "God" is

considered to have granted the United States the divine right to conquer and subdue the "heathen" or "pagan" lands of North America.[11]

This mindset of the exceptional white European/American conqueror taming a savage new world is used by politicians even in the twenty-first century. On Friday May 25, 2018, President Trump gave the commencement address at the Naval Academy in Annapolis, Maryland. About one-third of the way through his speech he attempted to affirm and motivate the graduates by reminding them of America's past military conquests when he said, "There is nothing Americans can't do. Absolutely nothing. In recent years and even decades, too many people have forgotten that truth. They have forgotten that our ancestors trounced an empire, *tamed a continent* (emphasis ours), and triumphed over the worst evils in history."[12]

From the unchallenged assertion of the Doctrine of Discovery put forth by the widely accepted heresy of Christendom, there arose a narrative of European supremacy. The Doctrine of Discovery provided a theological foundation for the assertion of white superiority. This religious and theological perversion would intersect with a self-perceived exceptionalism that would elevate the mythical Anglo-Saxon people who were fair in skin, fair in hair, and excelled in self-governance. These exceptional Anglo-Saxon people crossed the vast Atlantic Ocean (akin to the Israelites crossing the Jordan River) to take possession of a newly discovered land (i.e., discovered by true image bearers of God and not by the savages that dwelled there) in order to establish a shining city on a hill. These pure and exceptional people would establish a nation that far surpassed the existing systems and peoples and would be a shining light and beacon to the world.

The dysfunctional impact of a worldview that affirms white American exceptionalism not only has a historical precedent but a current expression. Contemporary American politics are rife with examples of an American exceptionalism that continues to dominate American self-perception. The language of exceptionalism masks an unequal economic system, a failing educational system, and a crumbling society. The assumptions of an exceptional nation that stands as a city set on a hill with a desire to stretch from sea to shining sea undermine any necessary course correction.

Wilsey notes that "it may be safe to suggest that *exceptionalism* has largely replaced *patriotism* as a word expressing American conceptions of national devotion. That is not surprising, since exceptionalism became the rallying cry of both Newt Gingrich and Mitt Romney in their presidential campaigns during 2011 and 2012."[13] In the 2008 election, the vice-presidential candidate Sarah Palin accused the presidential candidate Barack Obama of not believing in American exceptionalism.[14] Throughout his first term in office, President Obama would seek to redefine that term, but towards the latter half of his second term, as every US politician does, he ultimately ended up embracing it.[15]

By the time the 2016 elections rolled around, the language of American exceptionalism had become deeply embedded in the American political ethos. The eventual winner of the 2016 presidential race, Donald Trump captured the imagination of a large segment of the American populace with the slogan, "Make America Great Again." Implicit in this statement was the exceptional nature of American society and history. What the Trump campaign was able to establish was the mediating narrative and metaphor that to make America great *again* would harken back to a time when the United States was defined by a white Protestant identity. American exceptionalism would not be connected to diversity or pluralism, but instead American exceptionalism would be connected to the reclamation of the American narrative by white Americans.

This is not solely a Republican problem. The myth of American exceptionalism is a bipartisan and unifying theme for most every American. One of the major challenges for a nation that believes in its own exceptionalism but also has a simplistic two-party political system is that when any flaw is uncovered that might blemish the exceptional nature of the whole, that flaw is blamed on the opposing political party (or any other available scapegoat). That way the mythology of American exceptionalism can remain intact. The problem is isolated and contained within a substandard subset, while the whole remains exceptional.

After her win in the South Carolina primary, Hillary Clinton responded to the Trump Campaign slogan "Make America Great Again" by telling the cheering Democratic audience that "America never stopped being great." On July 27, the day before taking the stage at the Democratic National Convention to accept her party's nomination, Hillary tweeted to her approximately sixteen million Twitter followers: "America is great already." And on July 28, 2016, in her acceptance speech of the nomination for president by the Democratic party, Hillary Clinton once again reminded her supporters (and the world) that "America is great." But she didn't stop there. She told the audience that "America is great because America is good."[16]

The 2016 presidential candidates from both the Republican and Democratic parties agreed on America's history of exceptionalism. They both agreed that our past, our foundations, and our history were great. Where they disagreed was if America was great in 2016. Donald said no, while Hillary was adamant that we were. On October 9, 2016, in the third presidential debate, Hillary repeated her position when she said, "And I think it is very important for us to make clear to our children that our country really is great because we are good." And Donald Trump concurred: "Well, I'll actually agree with that. I agree with everything she said."[17] In the 2016 presidential campaign the candidate from the Grand Old Party was a white land-owning male who was campaigning to make America explicitly white supremacist, racist, and sexist again. The Democratic candidate was a white woman who was pleading for the opportunity to help keep our nation's white supremacy and racism implicit.

At the 2016 Democratic National Convention, President Obama jumped into the fray and told the cheering audience that "America is great already." And Cory Booker, an African American senator from New Jersey, in his endorsement of Hillary Clinton, acknowledged that in our foundations Natives are referred to as savages, women are never mentioned, and black Americans only counted as 3/5th of a person. Most national politicians do not have the courage to mention even a single flaw in our country's foundations. That Booker mentioned all three was unprecedented. But he kept his political ambitions intact when he concluded that section of his speech by telling the audience, "But those facts and other ugly parts of our history don't detract from our nation's greatness."[18]

When movements, institutions, or nations that believe in their own exceptionalism cry out for equality and justice, the voices of the marginalized are neutered. When the roots of the mythology of exceptionalism are threatened, and in order to maintain the greater national narrative, those marginalized voices who have found some stake in the broader system will even neuter themselves. The dysfunctional imagination that was expressed through the Doctrine of Discovery not only found roots in the founding of the United States, it continues to perpetuate into all aspects of American life.

Exceptionalism finds expression not only in the political structures of US society but is amplified in the context of the US church as well. The white American church continues to envision itself as the main missionary thrust of the church even in the twenty-first century. While the growth of the church continues in the non-Western world in unexpected regions like China, India, Central America, and sub-Sahara Africa, the white American church will reject immigrants and refugees from these regions as not reflecting the Christian values of the West. It is noble for the exceptional white American church to go help those "over there," but not for them to come over here to a nation reserved for exceptional white Americans. This assumption of exceptionalism hinders the work of reconciliation as a dysfunctional imagination of white supremacy and exceptionalism continues unabated in the US church and in US society.

CHAPTER SIX

Exceptionalism and the Founding Documents of the United States

THE SEED OF EXCEPTIONALISM planted in the early stages of the American colonies percolated and overflowed into subsequent centuries. The narrative of exceptionalism not only found expression in the self-perception of the colonizers, but also became embedded in the founding documents of a nascent nation. In the middle of the 1700s, the European colonists moved farther west into and beyond the Appalachian Mountains. This movement of discovery of uncharted and "undiscovered" territory shaped the quest for independence and influenced the foundations of the United States government. The desire for independence from England emerged due to the desire to expand their God-ordained government and the influence of an exceptional people into the vast, "undiscovered" regions of the New World.

A Declaration Motivated by Discovery

Through a proclamation in 1763, King George drew a line down the Appalachian Mountains and declared that the colonies no longer had the right of discovery of the Indian lands west of the mountains. Only the Crown could thereafter negotiate treaties and buy or sell those lands. This proclamation upset the colonists who wanted the right of discovery and to lay claim to the "empty" Indian lands themselves. Several years later, the irate colonists wrote a letter of protest where they accused the king of "raising the conditions of new appropriations of land."

The letter would go on to claim that King George "has endeavoured to bring on the inhabitants of our frontiers, the *merciless Indian Savages* (emphasis ours), whose known rule of warfare, is an undistinguished destruction of all ages, sexes and conditions."[1] The stark language reveals an assumption of superiority of one people group over another people group, as well as the self-perception of exceptionalism that would spur the American colonies' desire to expand and extend their influence and presence among the savages, as was ordained and to some extent required by the Doctrine of Discovery. The colonists signed their letter on July 4, 1776.[2]

While the Declaration of Independence may initially assert that "All men are created equal," thirty lines below that assertion, indigenous people are referred to as "merciless Indian savages." The Founding Fathers could use the seemingly inclusive term "all men" because they had a worldview informed by the Doctrine of Discovery that gave them a very narrow definition of who was actually human.

The Declaration of Independence reflects the theological imagination of its time. The Doctrine of Discovery and the myth of Anglo-Saxon superiority girds the imagination that elevates the white body, mind, language, and culture. The Declaration of Independence gives foundation for a framework of white supremacy as it is rooted in the assumption of the exceptional rational capacity of the ethnically pure, white European—now American.

Both American Christian theology and American society at-large during the time of the writing of the Declaration of Independence relied upon Scottish Common Sense philosophy for their foundation. Scottish Common Sense philosophy operates under specific presuppositions, endemic to these assumptions being a level of perspicuity and rationality. "Common sense" assumes that rational people will come to a common sense or common understanding. When rational and intelligent people are presented with evidence, they will come to the self-evident conclusions. The Declaration of Independence, therefore, assumes the common sense of the white American colonists by claiming "we hold these truths to be self-evident." The assumption of the right conclusions drawn from evidence is found in the assertions of the Declaration of Independence and the prominent theological framework of the time.

A society and a theology that relies upon Common Sense philosophy gestures towards a bias towards one's own point of view. Common Sense philosophy has the potential to attribute nonnegotiable status to certain assumptions deemed to emerge from a rational mind. If Americans believe that there exists a divinely sanctioned "common sense" and that they are an exceptional people with exceptional minds, then an assumption emerges that their own point of view is intuitively and correctly derived. The perspective that arises from the rational mind with common sense assumptions, therefore, would emerge as the most accurate perspective. With common sense as the measure of truth, the rational assumptions of white Americans reign supreme. So the theological and social imagination dominant during the establishment of the United States elevated the "rational" white mind as superior over all others.

Common sense assumptions become problematic when confronted with a theological understanding of human anthropology. Western Christian theology claims a high anthropology and places humanity as "the highest creature God has made an image-bearer of God, who is only a little lower than God, and under whose feet all of creation has been placed."[3] Every human being is believed to be made in the image of God. The sin of the Doctrine of Discovery is the determination that the full expression of the image of God is found only in certain races. If the full expression of God's image is found in the rational common sense mind of the European, then the white European American is elevated above other bodies and minds. Racism in the United States is rooted in the theological distortion that elevates white bodies and minds to a privileged position over others. This sinful expression racializes the image of God and links God's image to whiteness. Whiteness becomes the embodiment of all that is good, true, and honorable, including the positive godly attribute of self-governance and the desire to spread this form of godliness to savages.

Human hubris leads to the assumption that our own judgments of the world are equal or even superior to God's judgments. The assumption of rational capacity allows the white American to embrace the racial superiority of whites as a common sense assumption. The diseased theological imagination assumes that a superior expression of God's image exists in the body and mind of the white American, allowing the diminution of those who differ from the image of the white American, particularly those of African or Native American descent. This belief reflects a fundamental violation of the Christian doctrine that asserts that the image of God is found in all people.

The image of the white person becomes the norm by which other races are judged and measured, whiteness becoming elevated to the level of godliness. The person of color becomes the opposite of what is closest to God. The determination of white superiority and the relegation of blacks and Natives to the opposite end of the spectrum is a theological perversion. The creation account is at the whim and mercy of white supremacy, rather than arising out of an understanding of the Christian Scriptures. White American Christian exceptionalism depends on the fundamental assumptions of white supremacy. A dysfunctional American theology provides the dysfunctional imagination that American exceptionalism builds upon.

The underlying assumption of the centrality of whiteness in theology is evident in the worship life of most American congregations. Native American theologian Richard Twiss, who wrote about the need for contextualization in the worship life of the American church, notes "the guidance of Creator's Spirit behind the widening critique and correction to the hegemonic assumptions of modernity and colonization/decolonization."[4] Twiss observes that there is an increasing awareness of the need to contextualize worship as an act of defiance over the assumptions of Western, white centrality in the worship life of the American church. All worship is contextual, but there may be an underlying assumption of European American primacy in worship and the failure to recognize the captivity of the church to European American norms.

I (Mark) was asked to lecture on the topic of contextual worship at a Christian college class comprised of a majority of white students with some representation of international students of color. I asked if any of them have ever participated in a contextualized worship. A couple of the students from the continent of Africa raised their hands as did one white student who was the son of missionary parents. But the bulk of the class did not raise their hands. I looked at the class and asked how many of them went to church. Every person raised a hand. "So," I surmised, "I assume that the rest of you attend Jewish synagogues and worship in Hebrew on Saturday." They quickly assured me that they all attended Sunday church services complete with three-point sermons, hymns, and regular prayers.

All of them were attending highly contextualized Christian worship services. The Western Christian church worships on Sunday, elevates the standing position of the pastor physically above the congregation, and offers a lecture-like sermon, with the duration of the entire service usually lasting no longer than an hour—all highly contextualized forms of worship. That is not how Jesus, the disciples, Paul, or even the early church worshiped. European Christians have taken incredible liberties to contextualize their worship of Christ for their culture. The broad acceptance of the commercialization of Christmas and the imagery of bunnies at Easter are both highly contextual practices adapted from not only secular but even pagan European practices. These forms of contextualized worship are not only seen as benign, but they have been accepted as normal.

The gospel was meant to be contextual, which is why Jesus told parables. He was attempting to contextualize the story of God and an understanding of the kingdom of heaven for the Jewish culture and people. For centuries, the church throughout Europe also contextualized their worship of Christ for their culture. However, a Lakota Christian worshiping in a sweat lodge with a drum or a Navajo Christian praying for a sick family member in a ceremony in their hogan is scrutinized by the Western church and frequently condemned as syncretism.

The rise of the concept of American exceptionalism, therefore, is a theological problem. Belief in exceptionalism is fundamentally related to how people view themselves in relationship to God. The sin of setting up one's own image as the ultimate ideal results in an exaggerated self-perception. This assumption of superiority allows the white American Christian to take a position of final authority over who has greater access to the benefits of American society.

Rather than confronting sinful racist perspectives theology becomes the tool of ongoing oppression. A warped understanding of
the doctrine of the image of God becomes the justification for white
supremacy. As Willie Jennings explains:

> Whiteness was being held up as an aspect of creation with embedded facili-
> tating powers. Whiteness from the moment of discovery and consumption
> was a social and theological way of imagining, an imaginary that evolved into
> a method of understanding the world. . . . It was a theological imaginary
> because whiteness suggested that one may enter a true moment of creation
> gestalt. . . . Whiteness was a global vision of Europeans and Africans but,
> more than that, a way of organizing bodies by proximity to and approxi-
> mation of white bodies.[5]

The Western theological imagination was rooted in the assumption of
white superiority and the elevation of white flesh. White American
Christians have made their own bodies the standard of reference in
the determination of values and norms, and so whiteness has become
universalized and held up as the embodiment of all that is good, true,
and honorable.

The Doctrine of Discovery preyed upon the human tendency towards hubris and self-elevation, contributing to the diseased theological imagination that could not envision a world with any other
expression of the fullness of humanity other than white flesh. As the
European colonial Christian mind began to encounter inhabitants of
the African continent, the doctrine affirmed that they were encoun-
tering a people who were inferior. This sense of superiority paired
with the motif of dominance and power assumed by the European
Christians resulted in a severely dysfunctional theological imagination. The assumption of superiority and the concomitant sense of
dominance and power would also form the European colonial
Christian perception of Native Americans.[6] The encounter with the
other resulted in the elevation of white bodies and minds over and
above African and American Indian bodies and minds.

Steve Kabetu, who is from Kenya and serves as the Canadian director of Resonate Global Mission, tells this story about his grandfather. When the first European Christian missionaries arrived in the lands today known as Kenya, they brought a message to the Kikuyu about a holy man named Jesus, a man who performed miracles and brought people back from the dead. A man who loved his enemies and forgave sins. A man who died an excruciating death on a Roman cross and then three days later came back to life. A man who claimed to be the Son of God.

To the tribe this message was new but rooted. It was rooted in their stories and legacy of Ngai. Ngai was a divine being that the people had known for generations. Stories were told about Ngai and how he brought all things into being. He was mighty, great, benevolent, and mysterious. The village was open to this new message, and some of them even believed. They learned from the teachings of the missionaries and grew in their faith. The people requested that the stories of this Jesus and his Father be translated into their own language. So the work began, translating the Bible into the language of Kikuyu.

The missionary had become fluent in the language of the Kikuyu and was working with Steve's grandfather on the translation but was adamant about one thing. The people referred to Creator as Ngai but he demanded that the translated Bible only use the English word for God.[7] He did not want the Holy Scriptures to be blemished by the tribe's pagan word for Creator. This request bewildered the Kikuyu. They already had a relationship with Creator, which the missionary was now dismissing. The missionary seemed to view the people, the language, the culture, and the faith of the tribe as inferior.

So the elders went to the missionary and simply told him, "We have known Creator for generations. Ngai is not new to us. We simply did not know he had a son. If you force us to use the English word for God in this translation, this book will only be about the white man's

God. But if we use our word Ngai, this book will be an extension of the revelations we have already received and the relationship we have already been building."

The ideas of white supremacy originated out of the European imagination, much of it rooted in the Christian imagination. The heretical positions that buttress the categorization and the subsequent gradation of the races as possessing differing levels of humanity and spiritual capacity stem from a catastrophic theological failure. Rather than confronting sinful racist perspectives, theology became the tool of ongoing oppression. The worldview generated by this diseased theological imagination resulted in a social imagination that assumed the superiority of the white body, mind, language, and culture.

THEOLOGICAL DYSFUNCTION AND THE CONSTITUTION OF THE UNITED STATES

In 1787 this dehumanizing worldview was again evident when the Founding Fathers wrote another document that began with inclusive sounding language. The preamble to the Constitution of the United States begins with "We the People" and is quoted frequently by both citizens and politicians as proof that the United States is a nation of equality and just laws. However, very seldom do people read Article I, Section 2, a mere four sentences into the body of the document. This section defines who is represented within this Union and who the Constitution was written to protect:

> Representatives and direct Taxes shall be apportioned among the several States which may be included within this Union, according to their respective Numbers, which shall be determined by adding to the whole Number of free Persons, including those bound to Service for a Term of Years, and excluding Indians not taxed, three fifths of all other Persons.[8]

Upon declaring themselves free from the shackles of England, the superior body, mind, and soul of the Anglo-Saxon colonists could now cement the myth of their own supremacy into the founding documents of their new union. A union that would indulge and protect their sense of exceptionalism by excluding anyone who was not like them. This assumption of the superiority of the white European Christian male against other races, sexes, and religions is evident, therefore, throughout the entire US Constitution.

Beginning in Article I, Section 2, women are never mentioned as having representation in the federal government or as beneficiaries of that government. In the Constitution, from the Preamble through the Twenty-Seventh Amendment, there are fifty-one gender-specific male pronouns. When referring to who can run for office, who can hold office, and even who is protected by this Constitution, not a single female pronoun is used. Next, indigenous people are explicitly excluded. And finally, all other persons (i.e., black slaves) are counted as three-fifths human. This article reduces those included in "We the People" primarily to white landowning men, and so the Constitution of the United States was originally written to protect the interests of white landowning men.

We should not be surprised, therefore, that in 2017, women earned eighty cents on the dollar compared to men,[9] and when measured by total earning over the most recent fifteen year period women earned only 49 cents to the man's dollar.[10] Our prisons are filled with people of color. In 2010, the United States Supreme Court sided with Citizens United and ruled that corporations now have the same rights to political free speech as individuals—allowing the creation of super PACS and unlimited support of political candidates. None of these realities should surprise us as US citizens. The original intent of the Constitution is accomplishing exactly what it was set up to accomplish, protecting the interests of white landowning men.

About ninety years after its establishment, there was an attempt to address the problematic aspects of the Constitution through the

Thirteenth Amendment. The popular perception is that the Thirteenth Amendment abolished slavery. But reading the entire amendment reveals that is not the case. The Thirteenth Amendment states, "Neither slavery nor involuntary servitude, *except as a punishment for crime whereof the party shall have been duly convicted* (emphasis ours), shall exist within the United States, or any place subject to their jurisdiction." This clause in the Thirteenth Amendment means that slavery was never abolished but merely redefined and codified under a criminal justice system. It could be argued that a form of slavery now continues through the legal venue of incarceration.

The current state of incarceration, therefore, proves troubling given the full scope of the Thirteenth Amendment. According to the Prison Policy Initiative, the United States incarcerates people at a rate of 693 per 100,000. That is by far the highest incarceration rate of any country in the world, with second place falling to Turkmenistan (583 per 100,000). The US rate of incarceration is more than five times higher than most other countries. And the numbers get even worse when broken down by race/ethnicity.

Blacks. . . . . 2,306 per 100,000
Hispanics. 831 per 100,000
American Indians. . . . . 895 per 100,000[11]

At 450 per 100,000, white people in the United States are incarcerated at rates much lower than the national average. To this day, slavery is alive, well, and legal in the prison system of the United States of America, under the jurisdiction of the judicial branch of our government.[12]

A few years later, in 1866, the US Congress also passed the Fourteenth Amendment. This amendment was written specifically to address the shortcomings of Article I, Section 2 of the Constitution.

All persons born or naturalized in the United States, and subject to the jurisdiction thereof, are citizens of the United States and of the state wherein they reside. No state shall make or enforce any law which shall abridge the privileges or immunities of citizens of the United States; nor shall any state deprive any person of life, liberty, or property, without due process of law; nor deny to any person within its jurisdiction the equal protection of the laws.

The Amendment starts with the inclusive language "all persons" and extends the rights of citizenship to anyone born or naturalized in the United States under the jurisdiction of the government. However, Section 2 of this amendment is not nearly as inclusive.

Representatives shall be apportioned among the several states according to their respective numbers, counting the whole number of persons in each state, excluding Indians not taxed. But when the right to vote at any election . . . is denied to any of the male inhabitants of such state, being twenty-one years of age, and citizens of the United States, or in any way abridged, except for participation in rebellion, or other crime, the basis of representation therein shall be reduced in the proportion which the number of such male citizens shall bear to the whole number of male citizens twenty-one years of age in such state.

Indigenous peoples were still explicitly excluded. Women were again left out. And, for a second time, criminal courts are given the role of gatekeeper to the full rights of citizenship. When paired with the Thirteenth Amendment, the Fourteenth Amendment had very little impact on the long-term prospects of freedom and equality for anyone not white, landowning, and male. It granted conditional rights of citizenship to former male slaves but still left huge segments of the population marginalized and disenfranchised.

Women didn't get the right to vote until 1920, an outcome of the women's suffrage movement. The entirety of the Native community didn't become citizens until 1924, and in some states like Arizona and New Mexico, didn't get the right to vote until 1948. Jim Crow laws were still written after the Fourteenth Amendment; Indian boarding schools were established after the Fourteenth Amendment. Lynching, Indian removal, internment camps, segregation, and mass incarceration of people of color—all these and more—took place after the Fourteenth Amendment. And in 1970 the Fourteenth Amendment was used in *Roe v. Wade*, which concluded unborn babies are not human enough to be considered a person by the Constitution and therefore could be aborted.[13]

At the heart of our Constitution and in the worldview of the original framers, there is not a comprehensive value for life or a true belief in equality. Instead, there is the persistent practice of marginalization and dehumanization. The prevailing value tends towards exploitation of the marginalized and profit for the dominant. Since its origins, the Constitution of the United States has proved to be a white supremacist and sexist document that assumes that the white landowning male has the authority to determine who is and who is not human.

The US Constitution may have been a revolutionary collection of ideas for the white landowning men who wrote it, but to nearly everyone else it served (and still serves) as an extremely oppressive document. Some white American males claim that the only unprotected group in America today is the white male. This perspective reflects a profound ignorance of both the Constitution and US history. Various groups such as women, African Americans, and indigenous tribes need protection because the original documents specifically excluded them. For the white landowning men who have enjoyed centuries of favor, benefit, privilege, and wealth from our founding documents, the prospect of "We the People" actually meaning "All the People" not only feels daunting, but even oppressive.

THE CHRISTIAN IMAGINATION AND THE JUSTIFICATION OF SLAVERY

The founding documents of the United States reveal a deeply embedded narrative of white supremacy. The United States drew from the wells of a dysfunctional European theological imagination to formulate flawed documents that centered the rights of the white male landowner. This theological dysfunction that shaped the United States found expression in the Doctrine of Discovery. In 1452 Pope Nicholas V asserted the right of Europeans to take non-Europeans into slavery with one of many pronouncements that would become the Doctrine of Discovery. Nicholas's pronouncements reveal the racist assumptions of the European mind steeped in the narrative of white supremacy. With this theological justification of the European right to slave ownership, the American version of slavery would extend the self-perceived notion of the theological right of the superior white Christian body to own the inferior black pagan body.

Despite claims that America has a Christian foundation and that the founding documents of the United States reflect a revolutionary form of democracy and equality, the reality of the history of the United States points towards an acquiescence to the dominant narratives of white supremacy. Christian theology provided the justification for the onset of the transatlantic slave trade, and it would continue to provide the mediating narrative for slavery in its specific and brutal iteration in the United States.

While some white Christians opposed slavery, the institution of slavery was often left unchallenged by Christian leaders as they willingly participated in slave ownership or passively participated in allowing its existence and flourishing in American society. Prominent ministers including Cotton Mather and American Christian revivalist and theological icon Jonathan Edwards owned slaves.[14] Ibram X. Kendi points out:

> During America's first century, racist theological ideas were absolutely critical to sanctioning the growth of American slavery and making it acceptable to the Christian churches. These ideas were featured in the sermons of early America's greatest preacher and intellectual, Boston divine Cotton

Mather. . . . Cotton Mather preached racial inequality in body while insisting that the dark souls of enslaved Africans would become White when they became Christians.[15]

Neither church membership nor Christian faith, therefore, constrained slave ownership. Historian Albert Barnes notes that "in the aggregate the number of members of the church, in all the religious denominations, who hold their fellow men in bondage, is not small."[16]

The Doctrine of Discovery served as theological justification for European Christian atrocities. One of the central explanations for the rightness of European conquest was the correlation of Christian evangelism and conversion with the expansion of European power as outlined in the Doctrine of Discovery. Enslavement could be justified because heathens would come to Christian faith. Some evangelistic efforts, therefore, were made on the plantation, but conversion would not provide a primary motivation for slaveholders. Evangelistic efforts on the plantation were stifled because of the incongruence of slavery with the message of the gospel.

Whether through silence, through passive support, or through actual complicity, many Christian ministers ended up affirming the institution of slavery. In the South, historian Charles Irons notes that "white Christians penned compelling defenses of slavery for the secular and denominational presses, guarded against insurrection by policing worship meetings in the quarters, gave regional apologists grounds for boasting by converting thousands of slaves to their faith, and enabled those skeptical of slavery's justice to subvert their concerns through mission work among the enslaved."[17] Many Christians participated in abolitionist efforts, but many others offered support for slavery and opposed abolitionist efforts.

In 1835 in Charleston, South Carolina, at a public meeting to exclude anti-slavery publications from circulation and ferret out persons suspected of favoring abolition, the Charleston Courier reported that "the Clergy of all denominations attended in a body, lending their sanction to the proceedings, and adding by their presence to the impressive character of the scene."[18]

Majority culture Christians are often unaware of the deep complicity of white American Christians in the atrocity of slavery as well as of the pervasiveness of white supremacy within American culture and throughout the church. Throughout American history, the theme of white supremacy and the concomitant oppression of nonwhite others remained central.

The complicity of the church in the horrid institution of slavery reflects the catastrophic failure of the theological imagination to challenge or change the social imagination of the times. Instead, the institution of the church was more likely to support or even expand the reach of slavery. The extant social imagination of the time, left unchecked by a prophetic theological imagination, resulted in the entrenchment of the basic idea that whites were inherently superior to other people groups. This narrative becomes further entrenched in the systems and structures that are fueled by this narrative. And thus the assumption of white supremacy as established by the Doctrine of Discovery and the myth of Anglo-Saxon purity is evident in the founding documents of the United States.

Dysfunctional Theology and the Spread of Settler Colonialism

"IF SLAVERY WERE LEGAL, I'd probably have two myself. That would not have made me a racist."

I (Mark) get my fair share of ignorant comments on my social media. But this one took the cake. A few minutes later another person commented, challenging the above statement as dehumanizing and calling for this person to "have a heart." But the individual quickly shot back: "On the contrary my dear, I have a big heart but the law is the law. I would have slaves but I wouldn't treat them harshly because after all, we are all humans. Last time I checked, slavery was acceptable back in the Bible days. So, if slavery was cool with God, it's cool with me."

Human beings will often attempt to justify their blatantly sinful biases. This individual does not want to view himself or be known as an evil person. But he also does not have a moral or ethical problem with owning another person and forcing them to work for him without choice or compensation. He clearly stated that the only thing preventing him from participating in the dehumanizing institution of slavery was the question of its legality. If it were legal, he would happily participate.

As a general rule, I do not respond to comments on social media. However, this individual nearly caused me to break my rule. But I restrained myself. If I had responded, I would have wanted to ask this individual: "If slavery were legal today, what makes you so confident that you would be a slave owner and not one of the enslaved?"

The Kirwan Institute for the Study of Race and Ethnicity at Ohio State University defines implicit bias as "the attitudes or stereotypes that affect our understanding, actions, and decisions in an unconscious manner." They also identify some characteristics of implicit bias:

> Implicit biases are pervasive.
>
> Implicit and explicit biases are related but distinct mental constructs.
>
> The implicit associations we hold do not necessarily align with our declared beliefs or even reflect stances we would explicitly endorse.
>
> We generally tend to hold implicit biases that favor our own ingroup.[1]

Implicit biases reveal how our brains create associations between ourselves and those around us. In the United States, the human construct of race is vitally important to how we relate to one another—so important that we include questions for it on surveys, the US census, and nearly every important application. Racial biases exist in the atmosphere of American society, and most every American, regardless of race, has an implicit racial bias.

The implicit racial bias of the person commenting on social media was that he was somehow superior to others. This implicit bias is what allowed him to condone the institution of slavery, which was based on race. He revealed his biased assumptions when he said that if slavery were legal, he would gladly participate in it. He would certainly have a different opinion of the institution of slavery if he and his race were the ones being enslaved.

THE PERSISTENT EXPRESSION OF A
DISEASED IMAGINATION

With the passing of the Thirteenth Amendment, the explicit racist institution of chattel slavery for African people abated in the latter half of the nineteenth century, but it quickly gave rise to the abhorrent lynchings and the segregation of Jim Crow. Meanwhile, the ethnic cleansing and genocide of Native people increased in frequency in the second half of the nineteenth century. Going into the twentieth century, chattel slavery had ended, but the destructive narrative of white supremacy was in full bloom and finding new systems and structures through which to express itself. The country was not growing a conscience nor was the dysfunctional social imagination being rehabilitated. Instead, modern American Christian society was finding increasingly creative ways to justify the blatantly evil lie and actions of white supremacy. Implicit expressions were replacing more explicit ones. A diseased mediating narrative had formed and became deeply embedded in the American social imagination and in American society. In the latter part of the nineteenth century, the implicit assumption of white supremacy found particular expression in the rhetoric around the Indian problem.

The United States claimed rights derived from the Doctrine of Discovery and from the mythology of the exceptional nature of their God-endowed spirituality and humanity in its founding documents. As was their supposed God-given right, the American colonies could fulfill their destiny with further westward expansion. The American colonies and later the nation of the United States would see their presence in North America as a God-blessed, even a God-ordained event. Over the next several centuries, this thinking matured into an understanding that not only was this new nation to be a city on a hill, but it also had a divine mandate to conquer, occupy, and rule this land from "sea to shining sea."

The Second Great Awakening of the late eighteenth century witnessed both spiritual renewal and numerical growth in churches. As religious fervor swept throughout the land, the colonists continued to move westward. White settlement surged past the Appalachian Mountains and past the Mississippi River. Western expansion would also often be seen in religious terms. For example, in the early nineteenth century, the term "Manifest Destiny" was introduced, reflecting the belief that this young nation has the God-given right to rule the entirety of the North American continent.

John L. O'Sullivan, editor of the *United States Magazine and Democratic Review* coined the phrase "Manifest Destiny" in 1845. O'Sullivan used the term "to explain God's unique mission for America. That mission was to civilize and democratize the North American continent through the acquisition of territory westward to the Pacific Ocean."[2] If the thirteen colonies had been founded by an exceptional people with superior, physical, intellectual, and spiritual characteristics, that exceptionalism would have no choice but to seek expansion. The Doctrine of Discovery had encouraged the conquest of a lesser people by a greater people. Therefore, the exceptional Anglo-Saxon people of the thirteen colonies would need to expand their influence and power: "America saw itself as a bulwark of Western civilization centered on belief in God. . . . And in the twenty-first century, most Americans continue to believe that their nation is indispensable and exceptional. . . . The concept of exceptionalism remains the guiding paradigm in self-identification for most Americans."[3] While Manifest Destiny does not directly reference the papal bulls of the fifteenth-century Catholic church, the understanding of chosen-ness and the legacy of promised lands align closely with the imagination and narrative of the Doctrine of Discovery.

The theological imagination of the young nation would both contribute towards and be shaped by the social imagination of American exceptionalism and the impetus to spread this exceptionalism to the Pacific coast. The familiar patriotic anthem "America the Beautiful" contains the phrase from "sea to shining sea." This patriotic song was originally written as a hymn in the late nineteenth century by Katharine Lee Bates, an English professor at Wellesley College. The lyrics would be published in the denominational journal of the Congregational Church, *The Congregationalist,* in 1895.[4]

In "America the Beautiful" we see the blatant conflation of American greatness with Christian faith. A hymn sung in the church would be steeped in the dysfunctional social imagination of American greatness and the inevitability of American triumph. The lyrics speak of a majestic land of "amber waves of grain . . . purple mountain majesties . . . [and] fruited plain" that has been conquered by "heroes proved in liberating strife, who more than self their country loved." Both the social and theological imagination are emboldened with the prayer, "God shed His grace on thee, and crown thy good with brotherhood from sea to shining sea."[5] A Christian hymn explicitly justifies the white American Christian quest for Manifest Destiny. Even a modern interpretation of the hymn states that "each time we join together in singing the vividly descriptive lines of 'America the Beautiful,' we are moved emotionally as we contemplate the wonders of our great nation. The scenic beauties, the courage of the early settlers, and the sacrifices of heroes in battle all stir us to avid appreciation of our country's heritage."[6] The enmeshment of the social and theological imagination resulted in a deepening of the dysfunctional mediating narrative of American society.

As the nation began to grow and expand, the social imagination of the Founding Fathers became entrenched in society as well as in various social structures and systems, including the legal system. For example, the *Dred Scott* decision of 1856 affirmed the dysfunctional social imagination of the Founding Fathers. The decision asserted that African Americans "are not included, and were not intended to be included, under the word 'citizens' in the Constitution, and can therefore claim none of the rights and privileges which that instrument provides for and secures to the citizens of the United States. On the contrary, they were at that time considered as a subordinate and inferior class of beings, who had been subjugated by the dominant race."[7] A Supreme Court case filed by an individual seeking freedom through legal channels affirmed that the United States Constitution was not written for nonwhites. The great project of democracy was launched with only white men in mind as beneficiaries.

The *Dred Scott* decision also touched upon the US government's relationship to the Native community. Native tribes would be seen as foreign entities. The Supreme Court had already ruled in 1831 (*Cherokee Nation v. Georgia*) that Native tribes were "'domestic dependent nations' existing 'in a state of pupilage. Their relation to the United States resembles that of a ward to his guardian.'"[8] The case left open the possibility that the US government could provide instruction and correction for the Native tribes. An inherently racist bias is also evident: "The people who compose these Indian political communities have always been treated as foreigners not living under our Government. It is true that the course of events has brought the Indian tribes within the limits of the United States under subjection to the white race."[9]

The *Dred Scott* decision, therefore, affirmed what was already embedded in the social imagination of the American people. Africans and Natives were considered less than human. They would be candidates for correction and tutelage by a superior people group. The entrenchment of this social imagination from the very beginnings of the United States would find a wide variety of expressions throughout the country's history.

JOHNSON V. M'INTOSH AND
NATIVE LAND RIGHTS

In the process of westward expansion, the Doctrine of Discovery would be directly invoked to justify the stealing of land from people who already occupied it. The landmark Supreme Court decision of 1823, *Johnson v. M'Intosh* (21 US 8 Wheat. 543),[10] provided that legal justification: "The Supreme Court said that, under Discovery, when European, Christian nations discovered new lands, the discovering country automatically gained sovereign and property rights over the lands of non-Christian, non-European peoples, even though, obviously, the native peoples already owned, occupied, and used these lands."[11] The Native occupants of the land would be deemed inferior to the superior claims of the image-bearing Christian presence of European settlers. This sense of sovereignty and superiority of the European-American people would be a common-sense assumption explicitly and implicitly expressed throughout US history.

In 1823, litigation over a piece of land in Illinois escalated to the Supreme Court, which would issue the *Johnson and Graham's Lessee v. M'Intosh* verdict. As legal scholar Eric Kades describes,

> *M'Intosh* involved conflicting claims to large tracts of land in southern Illinois and Indiana. The plaintiffs made their claim under deeds obtained directly from the Indians. . . . The defendant countered with supposedly conflicting claims to some of the same land under a United States patent. . . . The *M'Intosh* verdict held that a discovering sovereign has the exclusive right to extinguish Indians' interest in their lands, either by purchase or just war.[12]

While seemingly a simplistic legal statement, the unique aspect of the verdict was how the Supreme Court would invoke the Doctrine of Discovery, which was rooted in the warped theological imagination of the European mind, as legal precedent for federal Indian law. At the heart of the case was the question of whether the United States government would recognize the human agency and authority of Native tribes to have primacy over their land.

Stuart Banner in *How the Indians Lost Their Land* explores the question of whether the English colonists viewed the Native Americans as the actual owners of North America. If the land rights of Native Americans were recognized, the colonists would have to purchase the land. Banner argues that there was a general understanding among the colonists that Native Americans owned the land. Even beginning with the baseline assumption that recognized "the Indians as owners of the whole continent," the land was believed to be "disproportionately large to the Indians' small numbers."[13] Native claims to land, therefore, were recognized in the colonial era. Any additional claim would need to be superseded by another legal assertion to deny the common assumptions that Natives owned the land.

In line with this belief, the story of the *M'Intosh* case begins with a land purchase from the Illinois tribes. The Illinois Land Company under the direction of William Murray purchased land in southern and central Illinois in a deal "with the remnants of the once great Illinois tribes, [whose] population had dropped from around 12,000 in 1680 to 1,720 in 1756, to 300 in 1800, as they fell victim to European disease and Indian enemies on all sides." The Illinois tribes closed the land deal on July 5, 1773, in exchange for a wide variety of goods.[14]

A few years later, the same William Murray who negotiated the first deal "recruited a prominent local Frenchman, Louis Viviat, as a partner and agent." Viviat would negotiate with the Miami Indians on behalf of the Wabash Company. "Like the Illinois tribes, the Miami as a group suffered precipitous population declines after contact with Europeans; their numbers fell from 7,500 in 1682 to just over 2,000 in 1736." The deal closed on October 18, 1775, with similar conditions negotiated between the Illinois Land Company and the Illinois tribes, which would have been a very low price given the very large swath of land.[15]

On March 13, 1779, the two companies would merge, and Wilson would become the chairman of the now single company.[16] The land in question in the *M'Intosh* verdict, therefore, would trace their land ownership to purchases from both the Miami and Illinois tribes that would cover all of the land in question. Furthermore, the circumstances of the land sale would indicate that tribes shrinking from the adverse effects of European colonial settlers needed to sell the land for survival. In other words, the Illinois and Wabash companies purchased land from Native tribes who were under duress from the very incursion that these companies would represent.

The United Illinois and Wabash Companies attempted to lobby for legislation to affirm their rightful ownership of the land. However, in 1792, a United States Senate committee ruled that "deeds obtained by private persons from the Indians, without any antecedent authority of subsequent confirmation from the government, could not vest in the grantees . . . a title to the lands."[17] The United States government sought to leave open the question of rightful land ownership and reserve the right to claim the land for its own use. According to Miller, et.al., President Thomas Jefferson told a gathering of tribal leaders in Washington, DC, "that they owned their lands and possessed the legal rights of use and occupancy, and that the United States was the only possible buyer of their lands whenever they were willing to sell."[18]

In the following administration, the Americans would claim against the British Empire, the "right of preemption because Indian nations did not have 'the right to sell their lands to whom they pleased' or 'to dispose of their lands to any private persons, nor to any Power other than the United States.'"[19] Using the Doctrine of Discovery to declare themselves the only eligible purchaser of tribal lands, the United States government manipulated the land market by creating a monopoly through which it was able to suppress land prices, thus effectively cheating Native tribes out of their lands. These actions reveal the diseased social imagination of the United States government, as it brazenly claimed its "promised land" from a defeated, and supposedly inferior, people. As Kades points out: "The meager surviving bands ceded their lands in large part for the protection of the United States."[20]

Both claims in the *M'Intosh* case, therefore, held specious claims on the land. The land purchased from the Native tribes would have been purchased under duress and for an unreasonably low sum. The United States government claimed jurisdiction over the land based upon power and authority over the Native groups that had diminished in number in the land. Furthermore, there is evidence that indicates that the case itself was a sham that was brought to establish land rights over Natives rather than adjudicate an actual land dispute. Ultimately, the Supreme Court case would claim to consider two different claims of ownership of the land: one obtained the land from Native tribes, while the other obtained the same land through the US government. The Supreme Court ruled in favor of the defendant (Johnson) who had purchased the land from the United States government.

The Supreme Court, led by Chief Justice John Marshall, in a unanimous opinion referenced the Doctrine of Discovery as a legal precedent for the ruling:

> As they [European colonizing nations] were all in pursuit of nearly the same object, it was necessary, in order to avoid conflicting settlements, and consequent war with each other, to establish a principle, which all should

acknowledge as the law by which the right of acquisition, which they all asserted, should be regulated as between themselves. This principle was, that
discovery gave title [emphasis ours] to the government by whose subjects, or
by whose authority, it was made, against all other European governments,
which title might be consummated by possession.

So in the end, the discovery doctrine of the fifteenth century was established as a legal instrument that governed land acquisition and
land ownership in nineteenth-century North America.

The court acknowledged that a group of European colonizers
created a governing doctrine that determined land title rights among
the European nations. Native rights would not be taken into account
because those rights would be superseded by the authority of the
Christian European governments over against all other claims. The
Doctrine of Discovery, steeped in the diseased social and theological
imagination of Anglo-Saxon ethnic purity and European Christian
supremacy, would become the rationale for the *M'Intosh* decision.

Stephen Newcomb summarizes the unanimous decision written by
Chief Justice John Marshall. In that decision, Marshall argues "that
'Christian people' had 'discovered' the lands of North America and
that this event had given Christian Europeans 'dominion' over and
'absolute title' to the lands of 'heathens.'"[21] Lindsay Robertson con-
tributes that "Marshall identified an additional ground for decision:
that upon discovery by European nations, the Indians lost to the discovering sovereign title to the lands they occupied. . . . In the Court's
words: 'their [Native tribes] power to dispose of the soil of their own
will, to whomsoever they pleased, was denied by the original fundamental principle, that discovery gave exclusive title to those who
made it.' It was this ground—the discovery doctrine—that proved
Johnson's most important legacy."[22] The indigenous tribes of North
America only had the right of occupancy to the land, while Europeans
had the right of discovery to the land, and therefore the true title to it.

The *M'Intosh* ruling confirmed the historical treatment of Natives and also set a legal precedent for the future mistreatment of Natives. As Stephen Newcomb surmises, "A key point expressed in the *Johnson* ruling is that the US government formally adopted the argument that 'Christian people' had 'discovered' this 'heathen' continent and that the 'civilized inhabitants' of the United States therefore collectively 'hold this country' on the bases of a 'right of discovery.'"[23] The case "strangely linked to fifteenth-century Vatican papal documents of subjugation, a case that continues today as the cornerstone of federal Indian law."[24]

The *M'Intosh* case helped form a cluster of cases in the Marshall Court era that created legal precedent for land titles as it related to Native Americans and the United States government. Robertson notes that "in two very important Indian law cases in 1831 and 1832, the Supreme Court touched on issues of Discovery and demonstrated its continued adherence to the Doctrine."[25] Not only did the 1823 Supreme Court led by Chief Justice John Marshall, and subsequent Supreme Court judicial interpretations, perpetuate the dehumanizing worldview of the Doctrine of Discovery, but they transformed the discovery doctrine into a modern-day legal instrument that has become the bedrock of the legal principle for land titles in the United States.

LEGAL JUSTIFICATION FOR INDIAN REMOVAL AND GENOCIDE

An immediate impact of the 1823 *M'Intosh* decision was felt in the state of Georgia. Robertson notes that "the state of Georgia seized on *Johnson's* formulation of the discovery doctrine to support the state's legal claim to the right to coerce the removal of the Cherokee Indians from their lands within Georgia's charter limits."[26] Understandably, the Cherokees resisted the attempts by the state of Georgia to take over their lands. In 1828, emboldened by the 1823 *M'Intosh* ruling, the state of Georgia sought to "enforce its claim to jurisdiction based on its ownership of the Cherokee Nation's land. . . . [Furthermore], the election of pro-removal General Andrew Jackson to the White House in 1828 gave Georgians the resolve to attempt it."[27] Georgia would not only add Cherokee land to their state jurisdiction, they would extend Georgia law to those lands occupied by Cherokee Indians. The state of Georgia felt significant confidence in the direction of the country against the independent agency and worth of Native tribes.

As Georgia sought to usurp Cherokee land, the United States government under Andrew Jackson expanded its legal authority against the Cherokee people. Because the Cherokee now occupied land in the United States, they were accused of attempting to establish a new and separate government. Robertson notes that "the United States could not countenance the creation of new states within the bounds of existing states, and these governments could not stand. The Indians must submit to the states or leave."[28] The groundwork was being laid for Indian removal. The cascading effect of these actions was made possible by the *M'Intosh* decision, which gave preemptive authority to the European American gaze over actual Native possession of the land. Furthermore, the assumption of Anglo-Saxon superiority in self-governance exacerbated the belief that Natives were inferior, lacking the agency to own their land and the capacity to self-govern. The assumption of superior governing capacities by Anglo-Americans would result in the desire to take over land owned by Natives, bring them under the jurisdiction of a superior form of government run by superior beings, or to remove them from proximity.

On May 28, 1830, Andrew Jackson signed into law the Indian Removal Act. The legislation stated that the president possessed the right to distribute land west of the Mississippi River for Native tribes. Seemingly a benevolent statement, the legislation would go on to state that these western lands would be in exchange for the lands where Indians currently resided, and that they could be removed from those districts of residence. The law stated:

> That it shall and may be lawful for the President of the United States to cause so much of any territory belonging to the United States, west of the river Mississippi, not included in any state or organized territory, and to which the Indian title has been extinguished, as he may judge necessary, to be divided into a suitable number of districts, for the reception of such tribes or nations of Indians as may choose to exchange the lands where they now reside, and remove there.[29]

The Christian Reformed Church of North America, in its teaching on the Native American experience, explains that

> the Indian Removal Act gave power to the government to make treaties with Native nations that forced them to give up their lands in exchange for land west of the Mississippi. These treaties on the surface, spoke to a voluntary exchange and removal of nations, though in reality, most of these treaties were made forcefully, by withholding food, through the decimation of food sources, such as the buffalo, and through violent acts including warfare.[30]

The Indian Removal Act empowered the United States government to physically displace Natives from east of the Mississippi to lands west of the Mississippi. In a specific expression of this act, the "Cherokee, Creek, Choctaw, Chickasaw, and Seminole were all marched out of their ancestral lands to Indian Territory, or present Oklahoma. . . . The Trail of Tears differed for each of the nations, but all Indians suffered. . . . An exceptionally harsh winter plagued the Choctaw, the first nation to face the forced migration."[31] The harsh treatment of the Cherokee tribe has also been well documented: "During the fall and winter of 1838 and 1839, the Cherokee were forcibly moved west by the United States government. Approximately 4,000 Cherokees died on this forced march."[32] The Trail of Tears remains one of the darkest moments in US history.

Cherokee leader William Shorey Coodey describes when the first group of Cherokee were moved west:

> At this very moment a low sound of distant thunder fell on my ear. In almost an exact western direction a dark spiral cloud was rising above the horizon and sent forth a murmur I almost fancied a voice of divine indignation for the wrongs of my poor and unhappy countrymen, driven by *brutal* power from all they loved and cherished in the land of their fathers, to gratify the cravings of avarice.[33]

The journey proved brutal to the Cherokee as many fell to illness and death along the trail. Reverend Daniel Butrick, an American missionary who accompanied the Cherokee on the journey, wrote, "O what a year it has been! O what a sweeping wind has gone over, and carried its thousands into the grave, while thousands of others have been tortured and scarcely survive. . . . The year past has been a year of spiritual darkness."[34]

Not only the journey itself, but the impact after the journey also proved to be devastating to all of the tribes who were force-marched from their ancestral homes. Several hundred Creeks died during the journey, and approximately 3,200 died from disease, malnutrition, and exposure after their arrival in Indian Territory. Disease also took a toll on the Chickasaw, who lost more than five hundred men, women, and children to smallpox. The Cherokee experience was perhaps the most severe. As many as one out of four Cherokees died because of their westward journey.[35]

For the Cherokee, Creek, Choctaw, Chickasaw, and Seminole tribes, the thread of the Doctrine of Discovery yielding the *M'Intosh* verdict moving towards the Indian Removal Act proved to be a brutal blow that decimated their people. The legal justification of Indian removal that allowed for the brutal and genocidal actions of the United States government not only found expression in the Trail of Tears, but also found expression in the areas of the country where Native tribes were being displaced. As Native bodies were pushed towards extinction with a brutal displacement in the southern states, Native bodies were also being slaughtered in lands further west.

NATIVE GENOCIDE AND WESTWARD EXPANSION

On January 24, 1848, gold was discovered in California. Over the next few years, more than 300,000 people flooded the state from both within the United States as well as from abroad. This sudden rush of people devastated the indigenous population of California, which at that time was estimated to have numbered approximately 150,000. Fewer than thirty years later that population was reduced to fewer than 30,000.[36] Native bodies had to be removed to make room for more worthy bodies in the state of California.

In 1851 in Shasta City, officials offered a bounty of five dollars for each California Indian head turned in. Several unsuccessful miners suddenly found a more lucrative living in murdering Indians, bringing in horses laden with as many as a dozen Native people's severed heads. Marysville and Honey Lake paid similar bounties on scalps. In places where no bounty was offered, freelance Indian killers often sought and received payment for services rendered from the state government.[37]

During the Gold Rush, California grew so fast and experienced so much prosperity that it was one of only a handful of states to bypass becoming a territory and jump directly to statehood. Even though California was admitted as a free state, in 1850 the newly established California legislature passed the Indian Indenture Act, which "establishes a form of legal slavery for the native peoples of the state by allowing whites to declare them vagrant and auction off their services for up to four months. The law also permits whites to indenture Indian children, with the permission of a parent or friend, and leads to widespread kidnapping of Indian children, who are then sold as 'apprentices.'"[38] The Pechanga Band of Luiseno Indians, one of the original California tribes, details this era of their history on their website. California created a state fund that

> paid $1 million for such services at prices said to range from 25 cents per scalp, to $5 per severed head. . . . Other practices encouraged under California state law . . . permitted the trafficking in Native people as slaves. The practice was understated as "authorizing [the white person] to have the care, custody, control and earnings of such [Indian] minor until he or she obtain the age of majority." In the late 1800's, more than 4,000 Native American children were sold into slavery—prices ranged from $60 for a boy, to $200 for a girl.[39]

The wanton killing, enslavement, and complete disregard for the lives of the California Indians was so pervasive that even California's first governor, Peter Burnett, acknowledged their demise in his State of the State Address in 1851: "That a war of extermination will continue to be waged between the races until the Indian race becomes extinct must be expected. While we cannot anticipate this result but with painful regret, the inevitable destiny of the race is beyond the power or wisdom of man to avert."[40]

On December 29, 1890, approximately 300 Lakota men, women, and children were slaughtered by the US Army. The event is known as the Massacre at Wounded Knee. In late 1890, the Lakota people and the US Army were in negotiations at Wounded Knee over the surrender of one of the Lakota chiefs. Neither side trusted the other, and tensions were high. Many weapons were present, and though no one knows exactly who fired the first shot, a shot was fired and chaos ensued.

> From the heights above, the army's Hotchkiss guns raked the Indian teepees with grapeshot. Clouds of gun smoke filled the air as men, women and children scrambled for their lives. Many ran for a ravine next to the camp only to be cut down in a withering cross fire. When the smoke cleared and the shooting stopped, approximately 300 Sioux were dead, . . . Twenty-five (US) soldiers lost their lives.[41]

The army had brought a battery of four Hotchkiss guns to Wounded Knee. These are forty-two-millimeter guns that shoot two pound rounds and have a range of nearly four-thousand yards. As the shooting started, the army began raining bullets from these cannons down on the Lakota people, many of them running into a ravine to seek shelter from the gunfire. The part of the Wounded Knee story that is often not told is that the US Army awarded eighteen medals of honor to soldiers who participated in the massacre. Three of these medals were given specifically for flushing the Lakota people out of the ravine. The citations read as follows:

> Austin, William G: "While the Indians were concealed in a ravine, assisted men on the skirmish line, directing their fire, etc., and using every effort to dislodge the enemy." Gresham, John C.: "Voluntarily led a party into a ravine to dislodge Sioux Indians concealed therein. He was wounded during this action." McMillan, Albert W: "While engaged with Indians concealed in a ravine, he assisted the men on the skirmish line, directed their fire, encouraged them by example, and used every effort to dislodge the enemy."[42]

The US Army website lists 425 Congressional Medals of Honor given to US soldiers between 1839–1898 for fighting in the Indian Wars. In 1840, roughly a third of the current number of states were established. By the end of the century, virtually all of the land now considered the continental United States had been settled and was either a US territory or an actual state. During the same period, the nineteenth century, the US population ballooned from 5.3 million to 76.2 million. But throughout this same period, the Native population dwindled from 600,000 to 237,196 as Manifest Destiny was completed and nearly thirty new states were added to the Union.

The displacement, decimation, and destruction of Native lives and communities were sanctioned and carried out by the US government. The narrative of white American exceptionalism that had been deeply internalized by the Western mind found expression in a dysfunctional legal system and genocidal military activity. The dysfunctional imagination that diminishes the humanity of Natives manifested in further acts of dehumanization, including the physical removal and death of Natives' bodies. Atrocities that reveal genocidal actions found a foundation in the Doctrine of Discovery, which would be used as legal justification in multiple Supreme Court rulings for these genocidal actions. The legal precedent set by the Marshall Supreme Court that relied upon the Doctrine of Discovery lived into the function of the founding documents of the United States—it protected the right of white male landowners. The legal system would perpetuate the narrative of white supremacy and provide the engine of oppression with the necessary fuel.

CHAPTER EIGHT

Genocide, the Impact of a Dysfunctional Theology

IN CONTRAST TO THE HORRIFIC HISTORY of the US revealing the reality of the dividing walls of hostility, God had originally intended unity and community for humanity. The elevation of one group of people as the standard and authority by which all others should be judged undermines the human community that reflects the image of God. Emil Brunner states that since "God . . . creates me in and for community with others . . . the isolated individual is an abstraction. . . . I am not 'I' apart from the 'Thou.'"[1] The I-thou relationship between one human with another reflects the image of God and the relationship found in the Trinity. The positioning of the other as less than—as asserted by the Doctrine of Discovery—breaks the community that God had intended.

God's desire was for relationship. He expressed that desire through the sending of his Son, Jesus, into the world. The Bible indicates a close connection between a people and their land that is based upon a relationship between God and his people. Relationship governs the connection between the people and the land. In the Old Testament, there are frequent references to a covenant agreement between God and his people that leads to the granting of land.

The sovereign Creator, therefore, is responsible for the establishment of a people upon the land. The people do not own the land, God does. Humanity, therefore, cannot be understood in isolation. Human identity arises out of one's connection to the land and to the surrounding environment. As Calvin Luther Martin asserts, "only a fool would imagine himself as somehow exclusively a human being. Through language and artifice one could recall and vivify the primal linkage (we might call it an evolutionary connection) to other forms of life, animal and plant."[2]

The formation of a people and the formation of a culture are not so easily separated from land and one's natural context. Given the importance of the connection of a people to the environment, the absence of that connection between the English colonists and the North American continent results in a growing insecurity by the white inhabitants of North America. If the land was improperly obtained, then that land is tenuously held. Willie Jennings asserts, "Humans are all bound to the earth. However, that articulated connection to the earth comes under profound and devastating alteration with the age of discovery and colonialism. . . . Whiteness replaced the earth as the signifier of identities. . . . With the emergence of whiteness, identity was calibrated through possession of, not possession by, specific land."[3]

One of the central mediating narratives of American society is the right to own property. It is one of the defining characteristics by which Americans can identify themselves as Americans. Those who are indigenous and the original occupants to the land could be seen as standing in the way of the assumption of the American right to own land. Our insecurity regarding our rights to the land is a result of the elevation of land ownership on an economic level, without a deep understanding of the theological value of land.

The acquisition of Native lands was often in violation of the colonists' own laws and revealed a usurping of land from the rightful owners. This usurping of land was accomplished under the guise of a political, social, spiritual, and moral superiority over the indigenous population. To the people whose claim to the land is based upon conquest and possession rather than a deep connection to the land, there is an implicit insecurity. The majority culture's rights to the land can be called into question, and therefore the myth of redemptive violence allows the majority culture to use violence to cement ownership of the land.

For Christians, there should be the awareness that usurping Native lands would be considered sin in the eyes of God. The accompanying acts of genocide should further generate significant insecurity before God. Given this insecurity, would the current occupants of the land feel the fullness of anxiety and fear when the tribes indigenous to the land reclaim their proper role within the land? Would that anxiety also extend towards any new people group that would arrive in North America? The insecurity of ill-gained and violently acquired land results in the fear of being brought down from a self-anointed space of superiority. The history of violence against Native peoples reveals how a dysfunctional theological imagination results in broken expressions of violence and injustice.

RICHARD PRATT AND THE INDIAN PROBLEM

In 1892, two years after the massacre at Wounded Knee, many tribes had been moved to reservations with great uncertainty about their future. Natives were not considered US citizens yet lived within the jurisdiction of the US borders. Native communities had a deep connection to the land and strong tribal affiliations as well as cultures, languages, and systems of governance. The American public was losing its stomach for these acts of outright genocide but still sought ways to keep the Native population subjugated. This moral dilemma was known as the "Indian Problem."

At the Nineteenth Annual Conference of Charities and Correction, retired army general Richard Pratt proposed his solution to the "Indian Problem." Pratt founded the first Indian boarding school, Carlisle Indian School, and helped to shape the system of boarding schools that would wreak havoc on Native communities for more than a century. His speech at the convention is famous for containing what became the theme for the Indian boarding schools: "Kill the Indian in him, and save the man."[4] Pratt articulated an argument for why these schools were both necessary and justified. Before he made his argument justifying boarding schools that abused and oppressed Native children, he first justified the nation's racist institution of chattel slavery: "Horrible as were the experiences of its introduction, and of slavery itself, there was concealed in them the greatest blessing that ever came to the Negro race— seven millions of blacks from cannibalism in darkest Africa to citizenship in free and enlightened America."[5]

Pratt began his argument by looking at the fruits he believed came from the oppressive and dehumanizing practice of slavery. He conceded that the institution of slavery was horrible but sought to justify it at the same time. Cannibals and savages would become civilized. The language of blessing, freedom, and enlightenment would be invoked as justification. Pratt believed that slavery was actually an act of benevolence that humanized the savages from out of the depths of Africa.

> They became English-speaking and industrious through the influences of association. . . . Under the care and authority of individuals of the higher race, they learned self-support and something of citizenship, and so reached their

present place. . . . Left in Africa, surrounded by their fellow-savages, our seven millions of industrious black fellow-citizens would still be savages.[6]

To the white supremacist mind, the most charitable act and the most benevolent blessing they can bestow is allowing those of the lower race to associate with them.

Theologian Willie Jennings best summarizes this perspective by revealing that salvific viability is often correlated with proximity to whiteness.[7] The high value for assimilation in the United States may be explained by this perspective. Assimilation seeks to make minorities or people of color more culturally similar to the majority (i.e., white) culture. The assumption of exceptionalism underlines attempts at assimilation. Pratt assumed that assimilation was the proper and appropriate goal for the other in the midst of a European American reality:

> As we have taken into our national family seven millions of Negroes, and as we receive foreigners at the rate of more than five hundred thousand a year, and assimilate them, it would seem that the time may have arrived when we can very properly make at least the attempt to assimilate our two hundred and fifty thousand Indians.[8]

Pratt's speech, therefore, reveals a blatant white supremacy. He not only asserts the superiority of the white body but also the superiority of the white mind and the product of the white mind, such as language and culture. He believes in the salvific work of white culture and society to civilize nonwhites through assimilation. Towards that end, the boarding schools would seek to assimilate (by any means necessary) the Native body and mind into the life of the white body and mind. His perspective reflects the social and theological imagination of its time.

The sin of this dysfunctional imagination is the assertion of dominion and superiority of whiteness over against others. If racism can be simply defined as the attempt by humanity to take God's rightful place of creation, then Pratt's speech reflects the belief that the human standards of rightness, as defined by whiteness, serve as the replacement of any standard established by God.

Pratt's words, therefore, may be seen as limited to one man's perspective, but Pratt reflected and helped to shape the social imagination of the times. Pratt's perspective led to policies that not only impacted individual Natives on a personal level but impacted the entire society. Pratt's human standard of white supremacy over against Natives elevated his personal standards in the place of God, resulting in the sinful expression of his dysfunctional theology into society. Pratt took God's place in creation and determined and judged what is good and what is bad from a godlike position of authority rooted in white supremacy. The elevation of white bodies, minds, language, and culture therefore presents a profound expression of human fallenness with its attempt to take the place of God's created order.

Dietrich Bonhoeffer examines this approach to sin in *Creation and Fall*. Bonhoeffer posits that "man's limit is in the middle of his existence, not on the edge. The limit which we look for on the edge is the limit of his condition, of his technology, of his possibilities. The limit in the middle is the limit of his reality, of his true existence."[9] Bonhoeffer explains sin as the human attempt to transcend "the limit." This limit defines and orders humanity rather than besmirches humanity. It is in the limit that there is true human existence.[10] Transcending that limit would be an essential element of the nature of sin. Racism, particularly as expressed as white supremacy, would be an example of transgressing the limit. It is an example of the human attempt to assert the human self as the standard in the place of God. The lie of white supremacy elevates the image of God in one people group and diminishes the image of God in others. The lie of white supremacy is embedded deeply in the diseased theological imagination of the American

Christian mind and serves as a foundation for the destructive sin of racism.

The goal of Richard Pratt's speech in 1892 was to articulate his vision for Indian boarding schools. Over the next seventy-five years, these boarding schools would be employed by both the US government and religious institutions as a way to convert and forcibly assimilate Native children to Western white American culture. Children were taken from their homes, they were punished for speaking their language, and beaten for practicing their culture. They were forced to eat, drink, sleep, learn, speak, and think like white people. Many were presented a gospel message but were required to become like a white American in order to receive it.

Pratt sought to justify the injustice of forced assimilation via the boarding school system by claiming success in civilizing the savages from "darkest Africa." If that goal was so quickly and thoroughly accomplished through the unintentional association that came through the institution of slavery, Pratt argued, how much more effective and quick would the same goal be achieved through intentional assimilation. Pratt claimed:

> The Indians under our care remained savage, because forced back upon themselves and away from association with English-speaking and civilized people, and because of our savage example and treatment of them. . . . We have never made any attempt to civilize them with the idea of taking them into the nation, and all of our policies have been against citizenizing and absorbing them. . . . We make our greatest mistake in feeding our civilization to the Indians instead of feeding the Indians to our civilization.[11]

Pratt's social imagination, which resulted in the proliferation of a severely oppressive and toxic boarding school system, was based upon a theological imagination of white supremacy, which pointed towards the spiritual benefit of proximity to whiteness. Assimilation would benefit the savage because it would allow the lesser entity to come in contact with and be positively shaped by the greater entity. The image of God in the superior white mind and body would become self-evident.

To the white supremacist mind, the most benevolent and charitable gift that can be given to the broader "subhuman" population is the privilege of association with and assimilation to the dominant culture. This implicit bias of white supremacy can be seen even in the language that is used today. Many authors, professors, pastors, and social justice leaders and organizations (both Christian and secular) who are considered to be on the forefront on the racial dialogue frequently use the term "white privilege." However, the word *privilege* suggests that the inequality that favors white people is actually a blessing which they must learn to share. The term white privilege perpetuates an implicit bias. Whiteness is neither a privilege nor a blessing to be shared, it is a diseased social construct that needs to be confronted.

THE RELENTLESS IMPACT OF THE DOCTRINE OF DISCOVERY

The implicit bias of white supremacy is rooted in the Doctrine of Discovery, articulated in the Declaration of Independence, established as a foundational principle in the US Constitution, and was repeatedly codified into US case law by the courts. The legal precedent established by the *M'Intosh* verdict has been in place for nearly two hundred years and was specifically referenced by the Supreme Court in 1954, 1985, and most recently in 2005.

The discovery doctrine continued its impact from the nineteenth into the twenty-first century as legal justification for the inhuman treatment of Native communities. As Robertson notes, "the federal courts have continued to follow the precedent of Johnson v. M'Intosh and have enforced the Doctrine of Discovery against the Indian nations and the states, and have continued to recognize the federal

Discovery power in dozens of cases since 1823."[12] To Robertson's point, the *M'Intosh* precedent and the discovery doctrine cited within the case would be referenced by the Supreme Court in 1954 (*Tee-Hit-Ton Indians v. United States*):

> It is well settled that . . . the tribes who inhabited the lands of the States held claim to such lands after the coming of the white man. . . . This is not a property right, but amounts to a right of occupancy. . . . This position of the Indian has long been rationalized by the legal theory that discovery and conquest gave the conquerors sovereignty over and ownership of the lands thus obtained [1 Wheaton's International Law, c. V]. The great case of Johnson v. McIntosh . . . confirmed the practice of two hundred years of American history "that discovery gave an exclusive right to extinguish the Indian title of occupancy, either by purchase or by conquest."[13]

The Doctrine of Discovery was cited again in 1985 in the *City of Oneida v. Oneida Indian Nation*:

> It was accepted that Indian nations held "aboriginal title" to lands they had inhabited from time immemorial. The "doctrine of discovery" provided, however, that discovering nations held fee title to these lands, subject to the Indians' right of occupancy and use.[14]

These court cases adjudicated in the twentieth century provide legal boundaries and guidelines around Native American agency and land ownership. *M'Intosh* created the possibility for the doctrine to be used as a legal precedent in dealing with Indian lands and Native peoples on an ongoing basis even into the twenty-first century.

As recently as 2005, the discovery doctrine is cited by the United States Supreme Court in the case *City of Sherrill, New York v. Oneida Indian Nation of New York*. In 1776, the aboriginal homeland of the Oneida Indian Nation "comprised some six million acres in what is now central New York State." In 1788, that land was reduced, by treaty, to a reservation of three hundred thousand acres. "In 1790, Congress passed the first Indian Trade and Intercourse Act . . . barring sales of tribal land without the Government's acquiescence." In the Treaty

of Canandaigua (1794), the United States guaranteed the Oneida
Indian Nation "free use and enjoyment" of their reserved territory.
However, the state of New York continued to illegally purchase lands
from the Oneida Indian Nation. Pressured by the removal policy,
many Oneidas left the state. Those who stayed continued to diminish
in number and during the 1840s sold most of their remaining lands
to New York. By 1920, the New York Oneidas retained only thirty-two
acres in the state.[15]

In 1997 and 1998, the Oneida Indian Nation purchased lands within
the limits of the city of Sherrill, New York. Their intention was to
reestablish their traditional sovereignty over these lands, meaning
they would not pay taxes on them. The City of Sherrill wanted tax
revenue from these lands, so they sued the Oneida Indian Nation in
the US District Court for the Northern District of New York and lost.
The City of Sherrill then joined with the county and appealed to the
US Second Circuit Court of Appeals, but the original ruling, in favor
of the Oneida Indian Nation, was upheld. They finally appealed to the
United States Supreme Court and the case was heard in 2005. While
the Supreme Court did not directly overturn the lower court's ruling,
they did make several reversals. In the first footnote of the opinion,
the Supreme Court referenced the Doctrine of Discovery: "Under the
doctrine of discovery, . . . fee title to the lands occupied by Indians
when the colonists arrived became vested in the sovereign—first the
discovering European nation and later the original States and the
United States."[16]

The opinion went on to recognize "the impracticability of returning
to Indian control land that generations earlier passed into numerous
private hands."[17] The court then places the burden on the Oneida
Indian Nation, concluding that they waited too long to seek legal
relief: "However, the distance from 1805 to the present day, the
Oneidas' long delay in seeking equitable relief against New York or its

local units, and developments in the city of Sherrill spanning several generations, evoke the doctrines of laches, acquiescence, and impossibility, and render inequitable the piecemeal shift in governance this suit seeks unilaterally to initiate."[18]

In the *M'Intosh* opinion written in 1823, John Marshall used the term "savages" in reference to the Native tribes of North America and also referenced the process of "civilization" as justification for denying indigenous tribes full rights to their lands. Marshall opines: "But the tribes of Indians inhabiting this country were fierce savages whose occupation was war and whose subsistence was drawn chiefly from the forest. To leave them in possession of their country was to leave the country a wilderness."[19]

In the 2005 opinion, the specific term "savages" was not used but the opinion employed the basic argument for civilization from the 1823 case. The 2005 opinion states that, "Moreover, the properties here involved have greatly increased in value since the Oneidas sold them 200 years ago. Notably, it was not until lately that the Oneidas sought to regain ancient sovereignty over land converted from *wilderness* [emphasis ours] to become part of cities like Sherrill."[20] Ultimately the US Supreme Court concluded in the 2005 case: "We now reject the unification theory of OIN and the United States and hold that 'standards of federal Indian law and federal equity practice' preclude the Tribe from rekindling embers of sovereignty that long ago grew cold."[21]

In this 2005 case, the Supreme Court first referenced the Doctrine of Discovery and the dehumanizing legal precedent for land titles established in 1823. The court then chastises the Oneida Indian Nation for waiting two hundred years to seek relief in court—disregarding the fact that for well over half of that period, Native people were not even considered citizens of the United States and for that entire period the indigenous tribes of Turtle Island were relegated to the inferior legal status of domestic dependents. (Turtle Island is the indigenous name for the land we now identify as the United States.) The court also seemed to forget that the original purpose of the US Constitution was to protect white landowning men and that Native peoples are explicitly excluded from rights outlined in the Constitution.

The court also fails to acknowledge that the state of New York illegally purchased the lands from the Oneida Indian Nation. New York State then washed its hands of responsibility because (white) people have since settled, sold, and purchased said lands. Next, the court reiterates the initial racist argument articulated by Justice John Marshall, that natives are savages and our wilderness lands have since been successfully converted to civilization. Finally, the Supreme Court restates, in case there is any doubt, that according to "standards of federal Indian law," which the very first footnote identifies as the Doctrine of Discovery and the 1823 *Johnson v. M'Intosh* ruling, "preclude the Tribe from rekindling embers of sovereignty that long ago grew cold."[22]

This 2005 opinion reveals a white supremacist legal opinion written by the United States Supreme Court that reiterates the highly problematic *M'Intosh* verdict written nearly two hundred years earlier. The opinion in the 2005 case, *City of Sherrill v. Oneida Indian Nation of N. Y.*, was written and delivered by the iconic progressive Supreme Court Justice, Ruth Bader Ginsburg.

The implicit bias of white supremacy is alive and well in the United States of America and is a bipartisan value that is perpetuated by nearly every US citizen (or at least every US citizen who owns, or hopes to own, land).

WHOSE HOMELAND?

In the early 2000s I (Mark) moved with my family from Denver, where I was serving as the pastor of a small church called the Christian

Indian Center, back to *Dinétah*, the traditional lands of our *Diné* people. We moved into a community that was located on a dirt road six miles off the nearest paved road, and we lived in a one-room traditional dwelling called a hogan, constructed of log walls and with a dirt floor. Our community, like many other remote communities throughout our reservation, had no running water or electricity. We were on a sheep camp and lived near a family who wove rugs and herded sheep for a living.

One day I was out herding sheep with one of the shepherds from that area. He was a boarding school survivor who had lived on the reservation his entire life and spoke our Navajo language fluently. George W. Bush was in office, and the discussion of immigration reform was just beginning to surface in the national dialogue. As we walked through the fields, I asked my friend for his thoughts on immigration reform. "Well," he said to me, "there are already so many of them here, perhaps we should not even worry about borders anymore."

Anywhere else throughout the country, it would be assumed that he was talking about the fourteen million undocumented immigrants who had crossed the southern border of the United States with Mexico. But because we were both Native, because we were on an Indian reservation, and because he was a boarding school survivor, I had to at least pause and ask: Was he referring to the fourteen million undocumented immigrants, or to the three hundred million undocumented immigrants who had been pouring into this continent since 1492?

After nearly a decade of national debate, in the spring of 2013, the Gang of 8, a bipartisan group of senators comprised of four Democrats and four Republicans put forth a bipartisan bill for immigration reform. Immediately, the Evangelical Immigration Table, a consortium of Evangelical Christians, leaders, and organizations who are supportive of comprehensive and just immigration reform, began working hard to move the bipartisan bill through Congress. One of the tools used by the Evangelical Immigration Table in their campaign was a list of forty Bible verses they compiled to demonstrate "God's Heart for Immigrants & Refugees." Twenty-six of the verses came from the Old Testament, and fourteen came from the New Testament. Many of the verses from the Old Testament included the sentiment that "you (Israel) had once been foreigners in Egypt," with the implication, "but now you are in your Promised Land."

One specific reference used by the Table was Jeremiah 7:5-7, where verses 5 and 6 read: "If you really change your ways and your actions and deal with each other justly, if you do not oppress the foreigner, the fatherless or the widow and do not shed innocent blood in this place, and if you do not follow other gods to your own harm . . ." These verses reveal an admonition to justice that all Christians should heed. However, verse 7 promises "then I will let you live in this place, in the land I gave your ancestors for ever and ever."

Through these verses, the Evangelical Immigration Table sought to build a biblical case for their efforts in enacting comprehensive and just immigration reform. However, because of the acceptance of the heresy of Christian empire by the entire American church (both liberal and conservative) and because the American church has co-opted God's Old Testament promise of land to Israel, the members of the Evangelical Immigration Table took this passage out of context. Jeremiah 7:7 was written and intended solely for the Old Testament nation of Israel. It does not apply to white Americans or the American church. The western church, the colonial nations of Europe, and the United States of America do not have a land covenant with the God of Abraham.

What most Americans miss regarding immigration reform is that without Natives at the table, the United States of America is incapable of comprehensively or justly reforming immigration law. Without Natives at the table, one generation of undocumented immigrants is trying to decide what to do with another generation of undocumented immigrants. There is no integrity in the dialogue. It does not matter if your plan is to build a wall to keep people out or if you are working to open the gate to let people in. Neither of those decisions is yours to make alone.

When you are in possession of stolen property, and the people you stole it from are right in front of you, the only just thing to do is give it back. Whether you are attempting to hoard it or to share it is irrelevant. Both actions are unjust. White Americans are not superior to anybody. Turtle Island is not Europe's promised land. And you cannot discover lands that are already inhabited.

CHAPTER NINE

Abraham Lincoln and the Narrative of White Messiahship

THE VICTORS WRITE THE HISTORY. And that is incredibly dangerous.

One of the imaginative challenges facing the United States is that the country has never lost a war that mattered. The US never lost a war that breached its borders and physically threatened the security of the homeland. The US has never been forced into a position of surrender by another nation or group of nations. The Revolutionary War, the War of 1812, the Mexican-American War, Spanish-American War, World War I, and World War II all concluded with decisive victories that not only protected the borders but in many cases physically expanded them. Each of these victories worked to solidify the reputation of unquestioned military might and of increasing colonial dominance to the rest of the globe. The 1950s, '60s, and '70s may have caused some anxiety, but officially the Korean War never ended and the US did not surrender after the Vietnam War. Most recently, the US-led coalition won the Gulf War. Kuwait was "liberated," and the oil interests of the United States were protected.

Because the US has won virtually every major war and has never been forced into a position of surrender, the country has not had a political, economic, military, and philosophical change mandated by the global community. When a nation loses a war, it endures the scorn and shame of that community. Political leadership changes, economic controls are imposed, and military leadership and weapons are removed. These types of challenges can lead to transformations, such as those that occurred in Germany and Japan following World War II. Other times, a postwar transition may prove to be less successful, such as Iraq after the two Gulf Wars, when a dictator was overthrown, but the rebuilding and eventual withdrawal did not result in regional peace.

The US has always been the victor, and the victors write the history. The social imagination of American exceptionalism and triumphalism, therefore, has grown unchecked. While this situation may sound like a blessing, never losing a war can be incredibly dangerous. Every empire commits evil actions. Every empire oppresses. Every empire exploits. When one nation is able to control the telling of their own history for hundreds of years, a mythology forms that allows injustice, oppression, exploitation, and even war crimes to be seen as benign and even to possibly be honored and celebrated. Even as their mythological history grows and their dominant military and economic oppression mounts, every empire eventually falls.

A Tale of Two Men

In the early twentieth century, two men were born just five years apart. Oskar Gröning was born in Nienburg, Germany, in 1921. Oskar served as a German SS junior squad leader and was stationed at the Auschwitz concentration camp. His responsibilities included counting and sorting the money taken from prisoners who arrived there. While serving at Auschwitz, Gröning occasionally witnessed the abuse, murder, and gassing of the Jewish prisoners. This made him uncomfortable, and he even requested a transfer, but when it was denied, he continued working his job. Returning to work day after day, he delivered an accounting of stolen belongings to the Nazi regime. He was eventually transferred out of Auschwitz to a unit fighting on the front where he was captured by the British and served time in a forced labor camp. After the war he returned to a quiet life in Germany and was reluctant to mention his duties at Auschwitz.

In the early 2000s however, when the Holocaust denial movement began to gain traction in Germany, he started speaking out about his service. Not because he was proud of it but to silence those who denied the Holocaust. In 2014, not long after a particularly in-depth interview with the BBC, Gröning was arrested and charged by German prosecutors as an accessory to the murder of three hundred thousand Jews for his role as an accountant at the Auschwitz concentration camp.

After the state prosecutor, Jens Lehmann, read the charges, Mr. Gröning spoke for an hour, then turned to Judge Franz Kompisch and said: "It is beyond question that I am morally complicit. This moral guilt I acknowledge here, before the victims, with regret and humility." He asked for forgiveness. "As concerns guilt before the law," he told the judge, "you must decide."[1]

At the conclusion of the trial, Judge Franz Kompisch ruled that "the defendant is found guilty of accessory to murder in 300,000 legally connected cases." Judge Kompisch went on to say that Gröning had willingly taken a "safe desk job" in "a machinery designed entirely for the killing of humans," a system that by any standard was "inhumane and all but unbearable for the human psyche."[2] At the age of ninety-four, Oskar Gröning was sentenced to four years in prison. He died two years later, a condemned war criminal.

Robert McNamara was born in 1916 in San Francisco, California. He graduated from U.C. Berkeley and Harvard Business School.

McNamara went on to serve during World War II as a statistician in Guam with the US Air Force, under General LeMay. In the 2003 documentary *The Fog of War*, he described his role in General LeMay's decision to firebomb densely populated Japanese cities in 1945. Specifically, McNamara was involved in "Operation Meetinghouse," the firebombing of Tokyo on March 9, 1945, which killed more civilians than either Hiroshima or Nagasaki.

> Robert McNamara: "I was on the island of Guam. In his command. In March of 1945. In that single night we burned to death 100,000 Japanese civilians in Tokyo, men women and children."
>
> Question: "Were you aware this was going to happen?"
>
> Robert McNamara: "Well I was part of a mechanism that in a sense recommended it. I analyzed bombing operations and how to make them more efficient. . . . Now I don't want to suggest that it was my report, that led to, I'll call it the firebombing, it's not that I'm trying to absolve myself of blame for the firebombing, I don't want to suggest that it was I that put in LeMay's mind that his operations were totally inefficient and had to be drastically changed. But anyhow, that's what he did. . . . Tokyo was a wooden city, and when we dropped these firebombs, and he just burned it."[3]

Robert McNamara completed his active duty in 1946 and was awarded the Legion of Merit, which is awarded for "exceptionally meritorious conduct in the performance of outstanding services and achievements."[4]

Fifteen years later, President John F. Kennedy asked Robert McNamara to serve as Secretary of Defense, which he did from 1961 to 1967. During much of his tenure, the US was embroiled in the Vietnam conflict. The conflict defined McNamara's legacy as secretary. He was seen as one of the primary architects of the Vietnam War, including the responsibility for the development and use of Agent Orange, a part of the US herbicidal warfare program to destroy foliage and food growth in South Vietnam.

Operation Ranch Hand . . . began in January 1962. Gradually limitations were relaxed and the spraying became more frequent, and covered larger areas. By the time it ended nine years later, some eighteen million gallons of chemicals had been sprayed on an estimated twenty percent of South Vietnam's jungles.[5]

Agent Orange contained the poison dioxin. Because of its heavy concentration and widespread use, over four million Vietnamese people, including civilians, were exposed and up to three-fourths of them suffered health and medical problems. Many died as a result.

In the documentary *The Fog of War*, McNamara addresses the authorization and use of Agent Orange. He reveals the internal moral conflict he felt as a decision and policymaker in the machinery of war. Secretary McNamara concludes:

> Any military commander who is honest with himself will admit that he has made mistakes in the application of military power. He has killed people unnecessarily—his own troops or other troops—through mistakes, through errors of judgement. Hundreds or thousands or tens of thousands or maybe even one hundred thousand. . . . Now the conventional wisdom is, "Don't make the same mistake twice, learn from your mistakes." And we all do, maybe we make the same mistake three times, but hopefully not four or five.[6]

Robert McNamara served as Secretary of Defense until 1968 and was awarded the Medal of Freedom by President Lyndon Johnson on February 28, 1968, for his service.

What is the difference between Oskar Gröning and Robert McNamara? They are two men born into the same era of history. One grew up in Germany and served as a soldier in the Nazi death machine. The other grew up in the United States and served in the opposing military. The former was tracked down, tried, and convicted for accessory to the murder of three hundred thousand Jews. The latter was awarded the Legion of Merit for his service in World War II that resulted in the murder of three hundred thousand Japanese civilians. Oskar died a convicted war criminal, and Robert was buried with honors at Arlington National Cemetery. Why was the service of the first condemned while the service of the second was celebrated?

In *The Fog of War*, Secretary McNamara wrestles with the morality of his actions in Japan. He says, "The human race prior to that time, and today, has not really grappled with the rules of war. Was there a rule that said you shouldn't burn to death one hundred thousand civilians in a night? [pause] LeMay said, 'If we lost the war, we'd all have been prosecuted as war criminals.' And I think he's right. He and, I'd say I, were behaving as war criminals."[7]

The difference between the two men is not a matter of legal guilt or innocence. Nor is it an issue of morality or immorality. It is not even a matter of right or wrong. The difference is between winning and losing. The difference is in who writes the history. Oskar's side lost, and seventy years later he was convicted as an accessory to murder and branded a war criminal. Robert's side won and to this day, he is celebrated as a war hero. The victors write the history, and that is incredibly dangerous.

THE WAR OF DISCOVERY AND MANIFEST DESTINY

Imagine that Nazi Germany won World War II. How would the German history books have treated Adolf Hitler? As a hero, perhaps even as the nation's savior? If Nazi Germany won World War II, how would they have recorded the Holocaust? Perhaps as a necessary cleansing or maybe even ask, "What Holocaust?" The victors write the history.

While the United States of America has fought and won many wars, one war is almost never mentioned: the war of discovery and Manifest Destiny. The foundations for this war were rooted in the Doctrine of Discovery, which is based on the lie of white European Christian supremacy. This war traces back to Christopher Columbus and his "discovery" of America on behalf of Spain. Later, England, France, the Netherlands, and even Russia staked their claims on the North American continent. The most enduring claim emerged from the Puritans, who misappropriated the promises of the Hebrew Scriptures and claimed Israel's theology of promised lands in North America, seeking to establish a city on a hill, built by superior and exceptional white people of European descent. The thirteen American colonies assumed the right of discovery from England, and then subsequently as victors of the Revolutionary War.

In 1803 through the Louisiana Purchase, the young United States purchased the rights to lands "discovered" by France. The US further defined their borders with Great Britain and Canada in the War of 1812. In 1845, the term "Manifest Destiny" was introduced, and the quest for land was further defined in theological terms. The Civil War did not slow down progress in the war of discovery and Manifest Destiny as both the North and the South shared a value for excluding Natives from their Constitution and adding Native lands to their borders. In 1848, the United States defeated Mexico and much of the Southwest lands that were "discovered" by Spain were added to the US.

On May 10, 1869, the war of discovery and Manifest Destiny reached one of its most important shared milestones. With the driving of the golden spike at Promontory Summit in the Territory of Utah, the transcontinental railway as well as a telegraph line were completed, and the genocidal war of discovery and Manifest Destiny was mostly won. The "savage" New World that Christopher Columbus discovered in 1492 had officially been tamed. The white supremacist nation known as the United States of America had extended its boundaries from sea to shining sea.

The US thirst for expansion was still not satiated with the fulfillment of a coast-to-coast Manifest Destiny. In 1867 the United States of

America purchased the right of discovery, from Russia, over what would become the state of Alaska. In 1893 the annexation of the Kingdom of Hawai'i by US businessmen and politicians occurred, and the illegal takeover of the Kingdom of Hawai'i was completed in 1895. The Philippines, Puerto Rico, and Guam were added after the Spanish-American War concluded in 1898. And the United States claimed parts of the Samoan Islands in 1899 and officially renamed them American Samoa in 1911.

As in all wars, this war had heroes and villains. Today, many identify Christopher Columbus as a villain, as several states and municipalities have moved to no longer celebrate Columbus Day. But that is by no means a consensus. Andrew Jackson is also viewed by many as a villain, as a slave owner who signed the Indian Removal Act and initiated the Trail of Tears. But his status is also not a national consensus, as many Americans, including President Donald Trump, consider Andrew Jackson one of their role models.

Heroes are a bit easier to come by. George Washington is viewed by most as a hero for establishing the office and the role of the president. However, he is not identified as one who confronted the uglier parts of our history, specifically the institution of slavery and the policy of Indian removal. Abraham Lincoln comes closest to a consensus on the status as national hero. President Lincoln is credited with emancipating the slaves, unifying the nation, believing in the dignity of all men, abolishing the institution of slavery, and ultimately, losing his life for his work towards equality. His face is carved on Mount Rushmore, and his monument is the grandest in all of Washington DC. His birthday is celebrated as President's Day, and even Black History Month was designated in February in part because of his birthday.[8]

Most Americans agree on some level that our Founding Fathers were flawed. We recognize that when they said "We the People," they didn't actually mean all the people. But we believe that Abraham Lincoln led us down the path to equality. He is the president who solidified the United States as a government "of the people, by the people and for the people."[9] He redeemed our nation, corrected our faults, and preserved our union. Our nation's love for Lincoln even crosses party lines.

In 2008, Barack Obama, the first black president in the history of the United States, chose to be sworn into office with his hand on the Lincoln Bible. In the course of his 2016 presidential campaign, Donald Trump was endorsed by David Duke, a known white supremacist and former KKK Grand Wizard. After Trump declined to distance himself from this controversial endorsement, the Republican House Majority Leader, Paul Ryan, called the candidate out in a press conference:

> If a person wants to be the nominee of the Republican Party, there can be no evasion and no games. They must reject any group or cause that is built on bigotry. This party does not prey on people's prejudices. We appeal to their highest ideals. This is the party of Lincoln. We believe all people are created equal in the eyes of God and our Government. This is fundamental. And if someone wants to be our nominee they must understand this.[10]

Both Democrats and Republicans alike honor, respect, and celebrate the life, legacy, and history of President Abraham Lincoln. But we must not forget that the victors write the history, and that is often how mythology is born.

ABRAHAM LINCOLN'S POLITICAL CAREER AND THE SOCIAL IMAGINATION OF HIS TIMES

In the fall of 1858, Abraham Lincoln fought a brutal campaign for the US Senate against Judge Stephen Douglas. Prior to the debates, Abraham Lincoln was on record as being against the institution of slavery. Lincoln, therefore, had to work doubly hard to assure the voters where he stood. These debates were in a different format than they are today. Each debate consisted of a series of three speeches. One candidate began with a forty-minute speech. The other responded with a seventy-minute speech, and the first candidate concluded with another thirty-minute speech. Starting with their first debate, towards the beginning of his first speech, Abraham Lincoln sought to assure the white voters of exactly where he stood in regard to slavery and racial equality:

> I have no purpose, directly or indirectly, to interfere with the institution of slavery in the States where it exists. . . . I have no purpose to introduce political and social equality between the white and the black races. There is a physical difference between the two, which, in my judgment, will probably forever forbid their living together upon the footing of perfect equality, and inasmuch as it becomes a necessity that there must be a difference, I, as well as Judge Douglas, am in favor of the race to which I belong having the superior position.[11] (Abraham Lincoln - First Lincoln-Douglas Debate—August 21, 1858—Ottawa, Illinois)

Several weeks later, during his fourth debate with Stephen Douglas, Abraham Lincoln reiterated his stance on both slavery and race, almost verbatim:

> I am not, nor ever have been, in favor of bringing about in any way the social and political equality of the white and black races, [applause] that I am not nor ever have been in favor of making voters or jurors of negroes, nor of qualifying them to hold office, nor to intermarry with white people; . . . there is a physical difference between the white and black races which I believe will forever forbid the two races living together on terms of social and political equality. . . . There must be the position of superior and inferior, and I as much as any other man am in favor of having the superior position assigned to the white race.[12] (Abraham Lincoln - Fourth Lincoln-Douglas Debate—September 18, 1858—Charleston, Illinois)

In their seventh debate, Judge Douglas accused Abraham Lincoln of applying the Declaration of Independence to "negros." This prompted Lincoln to reply: "I think the authors of that notable instrument intended to include all men, but they did not mean to declare all men equal in all respects. They did not mean to say all men were equal in color, size, intellect, moral development or social capacity."[13]

Lincoln is not referring to individual people. He is not saying that some individuals have more intellect and other individuals less. Nor is he saying that some individuals are more moral and other individuals less. Abraham Lincoln is referring to race, specifically the white and black races. He is restating what he stated clearly throughout these debates, that he believes the white race to be superior.

Abraham Lincoln lost that election. Remarkably, two years later he went on to win the 1860 presidential election. Before his inauguration, the southern slave-owning states moved quickly to organize their opposition to his presidency. In his State of the Union address on December 3, 1860, outgoing president James Buchanan recommended a course "in order to obtain an 'explanatory amendment' of the Constitution on the subject of slavery."[14] On December 20, 1860, South Carolina became the first state to secede from the Union. On March 4, 1861, just hours before the inauguration of President Abraham Lincoln, the US Senate passed the Corwin Amendment.[15] This amendment was a last-ditch effort by the US Congress to avert the secession of the southern states and a Civil War by constitutionally protecting the institution of slavery in states where it already existed.[16]

Later that day, in his inauguration address, President Lincoln reminded the nation of his position regarding the question of race and slavery. He reiterated his intention to not free the slaves in states where it already existed and reiterated his thoughts on race as he referenced the Douglas debates:

Apprehension seems to exist among the people of the Southern States that . . . their peace and personal security are to be endangered. . . . Indeed, the most ample evidence to the contrary has all the while existed and been open to their inspection. It is found in nearly all the published speeches of him who now addresses you. I do but quote from one of those speeches when

I declare that—I have no purpose, directly or indirectly, to interfere with the institution of slavery in the States where it exists. I believe I have no lawful right to do so, and I have no inclination to do so.[17]

Towards the end of his inauguration address, President Lincoln sought to build bipartisan support for the Corwin Amendment, which had already been signed by the outgoing Democratic president, James Buchanan. Lincoln referenced the amendment and expressed no objection to embedding the protection of slavery in constitutional law.

I understand a proposed amendment to the Constitution, which amendment, however, I have not seen, has passed Congress, to the effect that the federal government shall never interfere with the domestic institution so the States, including that of persons held to service. To avoid misconstruction of what I have said, I depart from my purpose not to speak of particular amendments, so far as to say that holding such a provision to now by implied constitutional law, I have no objection to its being made express and irrevocable.[18]

On March 16, 1861, even though the office of the president has no formal role in the process of amending the Constitution, Abraham Lincoln took it upon himself to send signed letters to all thirty-four state governors asking them to ratify the Corwin Amendment.[19]

THE PRAGMATISM, NOT THE HEROISM
OF ABRAHAM LINCOLN

On August 19, 1862, Horace Greeley, the editor of the *New York Tribune,* wrote an op-ed calling for the immediate emancipation of the slaves. President Lincoln had already written the Emancipation Proclamation but was not yet ready to issue it. He was concerned about the political fallout from the slave-owning states in the North. The states of Missouri, Kentucky, Maryland, and Delaware allowed slavery but had not seceded from the Union, and Lincoln wanted to assure the slave owners and political leaders from those states of his true intentions and beliefs regarding the black race. So Lincoln responded to Greeley's op-ed with a letter that stated:

> My paramount object in this struggle is to save the Union, and is not either to save or to destroy slavery. *If I could save the Union without freeing any slave I would do it, and if I could save it by freeing all the slaves I would do it; and if I could save it by freeing some and leaving others alone I would also do that* (emphasis ours).[20]

The latter half of this quotation is engraved on a marble plaque that today hangs in the museum at the base of the Lincoln Memorial in Washington, DC. President Abraham Lincoln declared to the slave owners in the northern states, and to anyone who enters the museum today, that he firmly believed that black lives do not matter.

On January 1, 1863, the Emancipation Proclamation went into effect. The wording of the Emancipation Proclamation was specific to limit the states, parishes, and counties from which slaves were to be freed.

> Arkansas, Texas, Louisiana, (except the Parishes of St. Bernard, Plaquemines, Jefferson, St. John, St. Charles, St. James Ascension, Assumption, Terrebonne, Lafourche, St. Mary, St. Martin, and Orleans, including the City of New Orleans) Mississippi, Alabama, Florida, Georgia, South Carolina, North Carolina, and Virginia, (except the forty-eight counties designated as West Virginia, and also the counties of Berkley, Accomac, Northampton, Elizabeth City, York, Princess Ann, and Norfolk, including the cities of Norfolk and Portsmouth[)], and which excepted parts, are for the present, left precisely as if this proclamation were not issued.[21]

The Emancipation Proclamation exempted many areas and counties throughout the Confederate states and never mentioned freeing slaves from the Union states where slavery was legal (Missouri, Kentucky, Maryland, and Delaware). Lincoln adhered to his own words by freeing only the slaves he had to free to preserve the Union. The slaves in the northern states would not be freed until after the death of Abraham Lincoln in 1865. Lincoln's conviction regarding the value of black lives would be evident not only in the wording of the Emancipation Proclamation, it would be evident in one of his lasting legacies, the Thirteenth Amendment.

On February 1, 1865, President Lincoln signed a joint resolution submitting the Thirteenth Amendment to the states for ratification. This amendment would cement his legacy as the President who freed the slaves and would become the capstone of his political career, out of which his reputation of being a president who believed in the equality of all people would grow.

In 1865, however, Lincoln was in a bind. He wanted to end chattel slavery but did not really believe that black lives mattered. He did not believe that black people should be judges, jurors, or even be allowed to vote. The Civil War was over, and he was the white president of a white supremacist nation that stood united around the narrative of white American Christian exceptionalism and triumphalism. He had to figure out what needed to happen to these inferior black people (along with other people of color) in a society, government, and Constitution that had been built for white landowners.

Abraham Lincoln's grand political solution was to use the Thirteenth Amendment to keep white supremacy alive beyond the grotesque institution of slavery, by creating a second-tier level of citizenship, specifically for people of color: "Neither slavery nor involuntary servitude, *except as a punishment for crime whereof the party shall have been duly convicted*, shall exist within the United States, or any place subject to their jurisdiction" (US Constitution, amendment XIII, emphasis ours). This clause in the Thirteenth Amendment meant slavery was never abolished; it was simply redefined and codified under the jurisdiction of law enforcement officers and the courts.

In the Lincoln-Douglas debates, his inauguration address, through his letter to Horace Greeley, and his exclusions in the Emancipation

Proclamation, Lincoln states and restates his commitment to protect the institution of slavery where it already exists. The Thirteenth Amendment, which cemented his legacy, protected the institution of slavery but in a new system. This clause constitutionally makes the freedom, civil liberties, and ultimately the citizenship of nonwhite people subject to the will and whim of a white US judicial system—a judicial system that Lincoln himself promised in the debates would never include black jurors, judges, or even voters.

This system of a second-class tier of citizenship was such an effective constitutional tool to maintain white supremacy that it was used again in the Fourteenth Amendment. The Fourteenth Amendment extended the right of citizenship to "All persons born or naturalized in the United States, and subject to the jurisdiction thereof." But Section II, which regulated voting rights, still specifically excluded Indians, young people, and women:

> Representatives shall be apportioned among the several states according to their respective numbers, counting the whole number of persons in each state, *excluding Indians not taxed*. But when the right to vote at any election for the choice of electors for President and Vice President of the United States, Representatives in Congress, the executive and judicial officers of a state, or the members of the legislature thereof, is denied to any of the *male inhabitants* of such state, being twenty-one years of age, and citizens of the United States, or in any way abridged, *except for participation in rebellion, or other crime*, the basis of representation therein shall be reduced in the proportion which the number of such *male citizens* shall bear to the whole number of *male citizens* twenty-one years of age in such state (emphasis ours).[22]

And because it contained the clause "except for participation in rebellion, or other crime," it also reaffirmed the white courts as the ultimate gatekeeper for the newly established voting rights of people of color.

Abraham Lincoln is celebrated as the greatest president in US history because he threaded the proverbial needle between maintaining the lie of white supremacy and removing the increasingly unpalatable institution of chattel slavery. While Lincoln tore down the evil system of institutional slavery, the narrative of white supremacy was retained, allowing for Jim Crow laws to rise up. Even when the Civil Rights Movement tore down the institution of Jim Crow, another system identifiable as the New Jim Crow served the narrative of white supremacy. Lincoln provided the tools that allow the establishment of mass incarceration as normative in our society today. The elevation of Lincoln as the hero and savior of the republic reveals the underlying narratives that fuel dysfunctional systems, even as we seek to canonize those who serve the narrative that continues on in multiple expressions.

CHAPTER TEN

Abraham Lincoln and Native Genocide

NOT ONLY DID ABRAHAM LINCOLN reveal the social imagination that black lives do not matter in his speeches, his writings, and his actions as president, he also revealed a blatant disregard for Native lives. Living into the expectation of the US Constitution to protect the rights and privileges of white male landowners, Lincoln's policies prioritized the flourishing of white landowners while disregarding the value of Native lives. Lincoln did not believe that Native lives mattered either.

In May of 1862, Abraham Lincoln signed the Homestead Act, which "provided that any adult citizen, or intended citizen, who had never borne arms against the U.S. government could claim 160 acres of surveyed government land. Claimants were required to 'improve' the plot by building a dwelling and cultivating the land. After 5 years on the land, the original filer was entitled to the property, free and clear, except for a small registration fee."[1] In July of 1862, President Lincoln signed the Pacific Railway Act.[2] This act "designated the 32nd parallel as the initial transcontinental route and gave huge grants of land for rights-of-way. The act was an effort to aid in the construction of a railroad and telegraph line from the Missouri River to the Pacific Ocean and to secure the use of that line for the United States government."[3]

In the fall of 1862, the Dakota tribe in Minnesota found themselves in dire straits. They had signed a treaty with the US government, ceding some of their lands in exchange for the promise of money and supplies. The winter of 1861–1862 was particularly harsh and the US government was not meeting their treaty obligations to the Dakota people. Throughout the summer and into the fall of 1862, the Dakota were not able to adequately prepare for the upcoming winter. Much of their land had been taken, and the promised funds and provision were not forthcoming.

On Sunday August 17, four young Dakota warriors came across a white settlement. A few of them entered the settlement to steal some eggs, which tragically resulted in the killing of some of the settlers. They returned home to Rice Creek and reported what they had done. After deliberation among several of the Dakota chiefs, some who favored war and others peace, Chief Little Crow, who favored peace, reluctantly agreed to go to war alongside the young warriors.[4] A short period of bloody conflict ensued between some of the Dakota people, white settlers, and the US military. After little more than a month, several hundred of the Dakota warriors surrendered and the rest fled north to Canada. Even after the surrender, violence against the Native tribes continued. Author Colette Routel writes, "following the end of hostilities in 1862, General John Pope, the commander of the U.S. Military's Department of the Northwest, directed Henry Sibley to offer a $500 reward for Taoyateduta 'dead or alive' and a $50 reward 'for each principal Chief of his band.'"[5]

The Dakota who surrendered were quickly tried in military tribunals and 303 of them were condemned to death. Historian Carol Chomsky describes the unfairness of the trial of the Dakota warriors:

> The evidence was sparse, the tribunal was biased, the defendants were unrepresented in unfamiliar proceedings conducted in a foreign language, and authority for convening the tribunal was lacking. More fundamentally, neither the Military Commission nor the reviewing authorities recognized that they were dealing with the aftermath of a war fought with a sovereign nation, and that the men who surrendered were entitled to treatment in accordance with that status.[6]

Because these were military trials and because so many prisoners were condemned, General Sibley deferred the execution order to General Pope, who in turn deferred the decision to the Commander in Chief, Abraham Lincoln. President Lincoln was reluctant to sign such an obviously genocidal order. Although any close examination of these trials would expose them as legal shams, Lincoln did not order retrials. Instead he simply modified the criteria by which charges warranted a death sentence as he explained in a letter to the US Senate on December 11, 1862: "Anxious to not act with so much clemency as to encourage another outbreak on the one hand, nor with so much severity as to be real cruelty on the other, I caused a careful examination of the records of trials to be made, in view of first ordering the execution of such as had been proved guilty of violating females."[7]

However, under his new criteria, only two of the Dakota warriors were sentenced to die. That small number seemed too lenient, and President Lincoln had to be concerned about the uprising by his white settlers in Minnesota, which was already taking place. "While President Lincoln was reviewing the records . . . a mob of citizens that included many women attempted 'private revenge' on the prisoners with pitchforks, scalding water and hurled stones."[8] And in another attack, many of the prisoners, most of whom were Dakota women and children "were assaulted by angry white citizens. Many were stoned and clubbed; a child was snatched from its mother's arms and beaten to death."[9]

Meanwhile, for a second time, instead of ordering retrials, President Lincoln simply changed the criteria of what charges warranted a death sentence, admitting in his own words, "Contrary to my expectation, only two of this class were found. I then directed a further examination and a classification of all who were proven to have participated in massacres, as distinguished from participation in battles. This class numbered forty, and included the two convicted of female violation."[10]

Ultimately, thirty-nine Dakota men were sentenced to die. On December 26, 1862, by order of President Lincoln, with nearly four thousand white American settlers looking on, the largest mass execution in the history of the United States took place with the hanging of the Dakota 38.

In February of 1863, President Lincoln signed into law a bill which nullified the treaties of the Dakota and Winnebago tribes in Minnesota. This law released the United States from any future obligation and forfeited lands from the Indians to the United States.[11] On the heels of this abrogation of existing treaties, Abraham Lincoln signed a bill in March of 1863 that gave him the authority to physically remove the tribes from the state of Minnesota. Specific Minnesota tribes were named to be removed to "unoccupied land outside the limits of any state."[12]

Later in March 1863, the decision was made to remove the Dakota and the Winnebago to an area along the Missouri River in the Dakota Territory. By April the removal had begun. Members from both tribes were rounded up and imprisoned at Fort Snelling near Minneapolis while they awaited transport out of the state of Minnesota. By June, the "previously uninhabited area near the mouth of Crow Creek was transformed into one of the largest population centers in the [Dakota] territory."[13] One thousand five hundred Dakota people and nearly as many Winnebago were crowded onto boats and barges and crammed into train cars, often without adequate food and drinking water. Many died along the journey to their reservation near Crow Creek. That winter (1863–1864), without adequate food, clothing or shelter, many more perished while "imprisoned" at Fort Thompson.[14]

For those Dakota who managed to avoid capture and remain in Minnesota, they were faced with the threat of physical violence and death as the state took extraordinary measures to complete the ethnic cleansing. The governor of the state appointed Colonel Henry Sibley to lead the forces against the Dakota. Sibley organized a corps of volunteer scouts for a period of sixty days. They were each paid $1.50 per day and $25 for every Dakota scalp they collected. The state also encouraged individual citizens to take part in the ethnic cleansing by offering a $75 bounty paid to any non-militia member who collected an Indian scalp.[15]

On July 20, the daily rate of pay was increased to $2 per day and the bounty paid to scouts was increased to $75 per scalp. On September 22, 1863, after the course of the corps of volunteers had finished, the adjutant general increased the bounty offered to independent scouts to $200 for each confirmed killing of a Dakota warrior.[16] The orders of the adjutant general were never repealed.

Less than a year after President Abraham Lincoln ordered the hanging of the Dakota 38 and less than six months after he nullified the Dakota treaties in Minnesota and granted himself the permission to remove them out of the state, virtually the entire populations of the Dakota and Winnebago people had been successfully removed and ethnically cleansed from the state of Minnesota.

In October of 1863, just a few months after the removal of the Dakota people was completed, President Lincoln issued a proclamation for the final Thursday of November to be commemorated as a national day of Thanksgiving. In his proclamation he acknowledged the death and violence against white people and by white people in the Civil War, but regarding the war of discovery and Manifest Destiny he stated: "Needful diversions of wealth and of strength from the fields of peaceful industry to the national defence, have not arrested the plough, the shuttle, or the ship; the axe had enlarged the borders of our settlements, and the mines, as well of iron and coal as of the precious metals, have yielded even more abundantly than heretofore."[17]

According to this statement, Lincoln viewed westward expansion through an optimistic and positive expression that focused on the assumed triumph of an exceptional people. He failed to recognize how those very policies meant the annihilation of entire people groups. Lincoln's policy towards Native Americans revealed a social imagination of white supremacy. White settlers had preeminence over the long-term claims of the indigenous population. The US government possessed the right of discovery, expansion, and dispossession, with minimal consideration of the genocidal impact on the Native people.

THE LONG WALK AND AMERICAN DEATH CAMPS

The genocide of the Native people initiated by the Lincoln administration and evident in Minnesota would have an even more profound impact upon the *Diné* in the Southwest. Throughout the fall and winter of 1863, on the orders of General Carleton, US Army Officer Kit Carson began ethnically cleansing the Navajo people from the territory of New Mexico. His orders were that "every Navajo male is to be killed or taken prisoner on sight. . . . Say to them 'Go to the

Bosque Redondo or we will pursue and destroy you. . . . We will not make peace with you on any other terms. This war shall be pursued until you cease to exist or move.'"[18]

The strength and numbers of the Navajo had already been depleted. Most of the crops were burned and livestock were killed. Raymond Friday Locke in *The Book of the Navajo* recounts the methodical steps of the operation. The US Army kept the Navajo people on the move, crisscrossing traditional lands, never allowing the Navajo to stay in place more than a few days at a time and thereby forcing them to survive without sufficient food, shelter, and clothing. Locke wrote:

> By the middle of December most of the weak and aged had died. There is hardly a Navajo family that cannot remember tales of an aged grandfather, a pregnant mother, or a lame child who had to be left behind when the camp had to be quickly deserted. The patrols were not interested in taking captives; it was too much trouble to transport them back to the forts. Any Navajo they saw was shot on sight. Mothers were sometimes forced to suffocate their hungry, crying babies to keep their families from being discovered and butchered by an army patrol or taken captive by the slave raiders.[19]

On January 15, 1864, President Abraham Lincoln approved the creation of the Bosque Redondo Indian Reservation in the southeast corner of the New Mexico territory.[20] After the fields, homes, and livestock of the Navajo people had been destroyed by Kit Carson, nearly ten thousand Navajos were rounded up by President Lincoln's army and marched to his newly created reservation. The term "reservation" is used loosely because for all ten thousand *Diné* marched there, Bosque Redondo would be their prison for the next three to five years and for nearly a quarter of the people, Bosque Redondo would be their death camp. In *Diné* this place is called *Hwéeld,i* and the removal is known as "The Long Walk." Throughout the forced marches to Bosque Redondo, hundreds of Navajo people died at the hands of the US soldiers, as well as from exposure and starvation. Those who survived the march and arrived at Bosque Redondo found no comfort or relief. Their pain and suffering had only just begun.

In the book *Bury My Heart at Wounded Knee*, author Dee Brown describes the conditions at Bosque Redondo. He reports that even the US government deemed the land as "unfit for cultivation of grain because of the presence of alkali"[21] in the soil. The water was dark and brackish, and the Navajo people were fed "meal, flour, and bacon which had been condemned as unfit for soldiers to eat."[22] Brown further describes the wretched conditions facing the Navajo people:

> The soldiers prodded them with bayonets and herded them into adobe-walled compounds. . . . Only roots were left for firewood. To shelter themselves from rain and sun they had to dig holes in the sandy ground, and cover and line them with mats of woven grass. They lived like prairie dogs in burrows. With a few tools the soldiers gave them they broke the soil of the Pecos bottomlands and planted grain, but floods and droughts and insects killed the crops, and now everyone was on half-rations. Crowded together as they were, disease had begun to take a toll of the weaker ones. It was a bad place, and although escape was difficult and dangerous under the watchful eyes of the soldiers, many were risking their lives to get away.[23]

Ultimately, nearly one quarter of the people, over 2,300, died while imprisoned at the Bosque Redondo death camp.

The Massacre at Sand Creek

In July 1864 President Lincoln signed the second Pacific Railway Act. This act doubled the amount of land set aside for the transcontinental railway and reversed the exception for mineral lands, meaning the railway companies could now also procure lands containing iron and coal in their government land grants.

Later that same year in November of 1864, the US Army, still under Commander-in-Chief Abraham Lincoln, committed the Massacre at Sand Creek in Colorado. In 1851 the United States signed a treaty with the Cheyenne and Arapaho tribes, establishing much of what today is eastern Colorado, western Kansas, southern Wyoming, and southwest Nebraska as their treaty lands. In 1858 gold was discovered in the Rocky Mountains, and over the next three years, Cheyenne and Arapaho lands were overrun with more than one hundred thousand prospectors and settlers.

In February of 1861, less than one month before the inauguration of President Lincoln, the US signed another treaty with the Cheyenne and Arapaho at Fort Wise, Colorado. The Treaty of Fort Wise was suspect because it was signed only by a minority of the Cheyenne Chiefs and the Eastern Arapaho Chiefs and was never given consent by the broader tribes. In the Treaty of Fort Wise, "the Indians settled for a tract between Sand Creek and the Arkansas River, less than one-thirteenth the size of the 1851 reserve."[24]

With the treaty not having received approval from all of the tribes, certain Cheyenne and Lakota tribes opposed white settlers moving into their lands. In 1864, a group of Civil War soldiers under the command of Colonel John Chivington, a Methodist minister, began to attack several Cheyenne tribes.[25] Two chiefs attempted to establish a truce by setting up camp near Fort Lyon as a friendly gesture. They were advised to fly an American flag as an expression of their peaceful intentions. Colonel Chivington, however, ordered the slaughter of the camp while the majority of the males were out hunting.

On November 29, 1864, approximately 675 United States soldiers under the command of Colonel John Chivington killed more than 200 Cheyenne and Arapaho villagers, mostly elderly men, women, and children, approximately 180 miles southeast of Denver near Eads, Colorado. Despite assurance from American negotiators that they would be safe, and despite Cheyenne Chief Black Kettle raising both a United States flag and a white flag as symbols of peace, Colonel Chivington ordered his troops to take no prisoners and to pillage and set the village ablaze, violently forcing the ambushed and outnumbered Cheyenne and Arapaho villagers to flee on foot. Colonel Chivington and his troops paraded mutilated body parts of men, women, and children in downtown Denver in celebration of the massacre.[26]

Initially this massacre was celebrated, but after the gruesome details became public, an investigation was eventually initiated by the military into Colonel Chivington's actions. He was reprimanded but then allowed to retire. Within eighteen months after the Massacre at Sand Creek, the Cheyenne and Arapaho were completely removed from Colorado to a reservation in Oklahoma.

During his annual addresses to Congress in December of 1864, President Lincoln announced that a total of 1.5 million acres had been successfully homesteaded through the Homestead Act. Regarding the transcontinental railway, he reported that "the great enterprise of connecting the Atlantic with the Pacific States by railways and telegraph lines has been entered upon with a vigor that gives assurance of success."[27] Both of these acts were hugely symbolic in the quest to fulfill the nation's self-proclaimed Manifest Destiny.

The transcontinental railway had several proposed routes. The primary route was to take the railway from Omaha, Nebraska, to San Francisco, through the lands of southern Wyoming and northern Colorado. And of the next four routes to be completed, a northern route was proposed that ran from Duluth through the state of Minnesota to the coast of the Pacific Northwest near Tacoma, Washington. And of the southern routes, one was proposed to run directly through the territory of New Mexico toward Los Angeles. Within three years of signing the first Pacific Railway Act in 1862, President Abraham Lincoln had ethnically cleansed the Dakota and Winnebago from Minnesota (northern route), the Cheyenne and Arapaho from Colorado and Wyoming (central route), and the

Navajo and some Apache from the Territory of New Mexico (southern route).

The expansion of the Americas could now progress unimpeded. The Homestead Act and the explicit goal of completing the transcontinental railway had generated concrete ways by which the imagination of Manifest Destiny could be enacted. The legal action stemming from this deeply embedded social imagination found expression under the administration of Abraham Lincoln. Acts of Congress, executive orders, broken treaties, and military actions enacted under Abraham Lincoln would serve to remove the most significant obstacle to westward expansion and Manifest Destiny. It would also mean that President Abraham Lincoln is responsible for some of the most significant negative impact on the Native American population in US history. Abraham Lincoln's actions, both direct and indirect, resulted in the ongoing and intentional genocide of the Native peoples. Native lives did not matter to Abraham Lincoln.

THE MESSIAHSHIP OF ABRAHAM LINCOLN

Despite Abraham Lincoln's horrific record on the systematic genocide of Native peoples, he is still regarded as one of the greatest presidents in US history. He is viewed as a near messianic figure who lost his life because of his commitment to the causes of freedom. The fact that his assassination occurred on Good Friday, 1865, appears to be a divine confirmation of his legacy as the savior of our nation.

But this legacy is a mythology. The mythology ignores his deliberate actions that led to his attempted extermination of Native peoples. The mythology also ignores his own words, which betray that his social imagination did not accept the equality of the races, but instead sought to preserve the union at all costs. The full record of Abraham Lincoln reveals a president who directly contributed to the genocide of the Native community and perpetuated the dehumanization of the African American community.

In 1863, Abraham Lincoln delivered a speech which many hail as the most significant 272 words spoken in American history. The Gettysburg Address begins with a reference to the Declaration of Independence that "all men are created equal" and concludes with the often-quoted line, "and that government of the people, by the people, for the people, shall not perish from the earth."[28] Many believe this speech to be the perfect capstone to his life and political career. But, like the inclusive language used by the authors of the Declaration of Independence ("all men") and the US Constitution ("We the people"), Lincoln does not, in the immediate context of his words, define who he is including when he refers to all men and people. His mythology argues that he transformed the definition of "all men" and "we the people" to include "all the people." But a close examination of his life, his speeches, his policies, and his legacy paints an extremely different picture.

We cannot forget that the victors write the history, and this is incredibly dangerous. Prior to and throughout World War II, Nazi Germany celebrated Adolf Hitler as a God-ordained ruler who was making Germany great again. In the twenty-first century, Nazis and neo-Nazis deny that the Holocaust ever happened and glorify the exploits of Adolf Hitler and Nazi Germany. As Americans, we credit Abraham Lincoln with winning the Civil War, preserving our Union, and reestablishing the United States of America as a God-ordained beacon of freedom and equality. But that is a myth. The war Abraham Lincoln actually won was the war of discovery and Manifest Destiny.

The Civil War was an internal spat between the North and the South, who could not agree on the best way to keep white supremacy intact. Lincoln stated this priority in his debates with Douglas: "What is it that we hold most dear amongst us? Our own liberty and prosperity. What has ever threatened our liberty and prosperity save and except this institution of Slavery?"[29] Lincoln was concerned that the issue of slavery was pitting sides of the superior white race against one another and that conflict had the possibility of destroying their carefully constructed union.

Had Lincoln won the Civil War but not been able to ethnically cleanse the Dakota and Winnebago from Minnesota, the Cheyenne and Arapaho from Colorado, and the Navajo and Apache from New Mexico—which cleared the path for the transcontinental railway and the fulfillment of Manifest Destiny—he may have been deemed a failure. Had he kept the union together in spite of emancipating some of the slaves but not developed the constitutional tool of mass incarceration (a tool perfected by presidents Ronald Reagan and Bill Clinton) to keep in check the civil liberties enjoyed by people of color, he may have been a similar unknown with benign historical significance as that of his predecessor James Buchanan, or of his successor Andrew Johnson.

The Lincoln Memorial refers to itself as a temple and shares many striking architectural similarities to the temple to the goddess Athena in Greece. This temple has been among the most visited monuments of all the US national memorials. Lincoln's face was selected to be among those this nation used to desecrate the sacred mountain of the Lakota people. Lincoln looks over the United States from his exalted position at Mount Rushmore, his temple in Washington, DC, in movies and pop culture, and in the history books as the greatest president to whom the nation owes a great debt. He serves as a messianic figure for the American narrative of exceptionalism and triumphalism.

As Eusebius demonstrated in the fourth century, in order to effectively promote the heresy of Christendom, one first has to remove Christ. Eusebius constructed a mythology of the emperor Constantine as a God-ordained ruler for such a time as his. Eusebius effectively wrote Christ out of ecclesiastical history and replaced him with the mythology of Constantine. Thirteen years later, Constantine embraced that mythology and related a tale to Eusebius of a fantastic vision, where Christ himself told him that he would triumph over his enemies beneath the symbol of the cross. Eusebius in his book *The Life of the Blessed Emperor Constantine* affirms this triumphalistic Christendom narrative with chapters titled, "He was the servant of God and the conqueror of nations," and "He conquered nearly the whole world." The church affirmed Christendom and replaced the messiahship of Jesus with the messiahship of Constantine.

Jesus opposed the creation of a Christian Empire. The role of the Messiah was not to establish another worldly kingdom. The heresy of Christendom rejects the teachings of Jesus of Nazareth regarding the role of the Messiah and, therefore, Christendom cannot coexist with the teachings of Jesus. In order to promote Christendom, Jesus the Messiah must be rejected and a new messiah must take his place. As the United States fully embraced the narrative of exceptionalism and triumphalism, the Jesus of the Bible was no longer sufficient. Instead, a new messiah needed to emerge to cement the Christendom stature of the United States. At the conclusion of his Gettysburg Address, Abraham Lincoln embraced his budding mythology as the savior of the Union as well as embracing the heresy of Christian empire when he said "that this nation, under God, shall have a new birth of freedom."[30] The mythology of Abraham Lincoln has subsequently grown unchecked as the messianic figure of Lincoln continues to loom over the triumphant history of America since the Civil War. This messianic assignation continues despite the known words, rhetoric, actions, and impact of Abraham Lincoln.

In 1492, at the start of the war of discovery and Manifest Destiny, the estimated Native population of Turtle Island (North America) ranged between 1.2 million and 20 million. For the sake of argument, we will use the median of the two numbers, which is 9.4 million. Then excluding the approximately three to four million who lived in what is now Canada and Alaska, we will estimate the Native population of the lower continental United States in the year 1500 to be six million people. Between 1492 and 1900 the estimated population of indigenous peoples in the continental United States dropped to 237,000. That gives the war of discovery a 96 percent rate of genocide (i.e., 96 percent of the Native population was wiped out during the ongoing war). From 1800 to 1900, often referred to as the century of expansion, the indigenous population of Turtle Island was depleted from 600,000 to 237,000, giving the war of discovery and Manifest Destiny a genocide rate of 60 percent. And from 1860 to 1870, the decade which included the presidency of Abraham Lincoln, the actual number in the US Census of off-reservation, taxpaying, assimilated American Indians living in the United States fell from 44,000 to 25,713, a decrease of 41 percent. Nearly half of that drop came from the population in New Mexico, where Abraham Lincoln marched ten thousand Navajo men, women, and children to what for nearly a quarter of them was a death camp, which he approved, called Bosque Redondo.

By comparison, Nazi Germany had a genocide rate for the Jewish people of 35 percent.

It may be challenging enough to draw a comparison between Robert McNamara and Oskar Gröning. It would be even more challenging to even hint of a comparison between Abraham Lincoln and Adolf Hitler. But an objective comparison of their words, rhetoric, action, and impact may reveal a different story. However, the most challenging comparison is that we—the United States of America, the leaders of the modern-day heretical kingdom of Christendom, one exceptional nation that for centuries has been thriving, growing, and expanding (supposedly) under God—are not that dissimilar from Nazi Germany.

The United States of America does not hold a morally exceptional position greater than Nazi Germany. We are not more just. Our sense of equality is not any superior. Our nation has never been Christian. We have just won our wars. And therefore, for centuries, we wrote our own history. And that has proven to be incredibly dangerous.

CHAPTER ELEVEN

The Complex Trauma of the American Story

ONE OF THE HARDEST periods of my life (Mark) began in the fall of 1988. I was a senior in high school, traveling with my brother to see my grandparents for their fiftieth wedding anniversary in Denver. I was driving, my brother was the passenger, and we were following our parents, who were in their car a few miles ahead of us. We stopped for breakfast and to get gas in Albuquerque, New Mexico. From that moment I lose my memory. I remember joining the family for breakfast. I remember stopping at the gas station near the interstate on-ramp. I even remember pulling away from the gas station, but I have no memory of getting on the highway about half a mile later.

What I've been told is that we drove another hour almost to Santa Fe. Witnesses reported that our car switched lanes to pass another car but then kept going off the road. We hit a sign in the median, the car flipped, and my brother was killed instantly. My life was spared because coming toward us in the opposite direction was someone who was medically trained. They were one of the first people on the scene of the accident. I had a massive head injury, which should have killed me, but they knew exactly what to do. Had they not been there, I probably would have bled to death. They stabilized me until an ambulance arrived and brought me to a nearby hospital.

I was awake and alert. I answered questions at the accident site, but even that caused further confusion as I incorrectly told the emergency responders that the passenger was my best friend from high school, instead of my brother. But I have no memory of any of that. In fact, my memory didn't return until about three to four days later, slowly and in pieces.

The experience was almost like waking up slowly out of a foggy dream. The type of dream where the exact moment between being asleep and waking up is nearly impossible to discern. My memory did not return all at once but came back in pieces, a few moments here and a couple moments there.

I never had the conscious shock of one minute my brother being alive and the next minute dead. I was never overwhelmed with emotion or burst into tears regarding the sudden news of his passing. I just slowly became aware while I was in the hospital, and over a period of several days, that something traumatic had happened and that my brother was no longer with us. As I recovered physically, I didn't know what to do about my lack of an emotional response. In the weeks and months that followed, I asked many questions about what happened. I could talk openly about the accident and tell people the stories I was told about it. But emotionally I was very disconnected from the entire experience. It was as if I was relaying details of a story that I read in a newspaper.

I asked those around me why I had not cried. Perhaps, it was suggested, if I visited the scene of the accident, I might cry there. I made the pilgrimage to the accident site but—nothing. I also went to look at the totaled car, but it brought up no emotion. Some suggested I might cry on the first anniversary of the accident. But that date came and went with no tears. I figured I was dealing with trauma and probably had some level of posttraumatic stress disorder (PTSD), but I didn't know what to do about it.

So I went on with my life. I graduated from high school and went to college. I did not realize it at the time but throughout my senior year of high school, I began cutting myself off emotionally and isolating myself relationally. I was unaware of this, but I began to keep an inventory of how I would be affected if another one of my friends or family members died, and then disconnected myself emotionally from those whose passing would cause me pain. I thought going to college would give me a second start relationally, since, by the end of my senior year I had cut off most of my close high school friends. In college I began building new friendships, and by the time sophomore year rolled around I had a close-knit group of friends whom I cared about. But that year, an emotional can of worms was opened that I had no idea what to do with.

Some mornings I would wake up scared to go outside because I was convinced God was going to kill me. Other days I would sit in my apartment, terrified and not sure what to do as so much guilt, shame, and overwhelming emotion came upon me. I couldn't concentrate on my studies anymore, so I withdrew from school. I went to counseling to try to figure out what was wrong with me. On a cognitive level, I knew my current mental state had something to do with the death of my brother, but the emotions I was feeling were completely disconnected from the accident.

Since the accident, I wondered about the specifics of what caused it. But because it was a single car accident, and it was a family member who died with no one pressing charges, there was no legal conclusion as to what caused it. Whenever I brought it up, I was quickly told by well-intentioned and loving people that it wasn't my fault. No one ever got mad or screamed at me for my negligent driving. No one ever accused me of falling asleep at the wheel or getting distracted. Nor did anyone ever conclusively prove that it was a mechanical problem. I was just told, over and over, that it wasn't my fault and this was God's timing.

But emotionally, deep down, those words didn't comfort me. If it wasn't my fault, whose fault was it? I was the driver of the car and it was a single-car accident. I knew there was a good chance this accident was my fault. As the driver of the car, it was highly probable that something I did or didn't do resulted in the death of my brother. I didn't know how to process this, and no one gave me the emotional space to deal with it.

The summer after my sophomore year of college, I was attending a weeklong Bible conference on Catalina Island, off the coast of Long Beach. I was involved in a seminar on prayer. As we were praying one day toward the middle of the week, one of the leaders asked if there was anyone in the room who needed prayer for forgiveness—specifically, if someone needed prayer to forgive another person in their life. They invited those who felt they needed to seek forgiveness from someone else to stand up so they could be prayed for. The moment that offer was extended, my mind began racing. I knew I had to stand up but didn't know why.

My mind paged through all of my relationships, but I couldn't think of anyone mad enough at me to warrant standing up and getting prayed for. Finally, the thought occurred to me that I had never forgiven *myself* for being the driver of the car that killed my brother. I had no emotion connected to that thought, it was purely cognitive. But relieved, I stood up. From the moment I got to my feet, it felt like I was dragging a melon up from my gut, through my chest, and out of my mouth. Within three to four minutes I was lying flat on the floor, weeping for the first time in nearly three years. All of the guilt, all of the pain, all of the shame that I had kept bottled in for so long was finally coming out. It felt like I was lying in Jesus' arms and he was holding me. It was one of the most terrible yet beautiful moments I had ever experienced. That prayer time started a journey where I began to acknowledge that something I did or didn't do that morning in October 1988 resulted in the accident. It was a journey of learning to live with myself, knowing that I could very well be responsible for the death of my brother.

That journey took years, and occasionally things will still come up that I have to sort through; feelings of guilt that I must deal with and emotions that I must process. God began a healing journey. It didn't happen overnight. But he started something in that prayer session—a confrontation of my denial, an ongoing encounter with my bro-kenness, and a journey toward healing that is still going on in my life today.

UNDERSTANDING TRAUMA

Many are familiar with the term posttraumatic stress disorder, or PTSD. PTSD is defined as a "mental health condition that's triggered by a terrifying event—either experiencing it or witnessing it. Symptoms may include flashbacks, nightmares and severe anxiety, as well as uncontrollable thoughts about the event."[1] PTSD is an indi-vidual diagnosis for a person who has experienced a horrifying event. Soldiers returning from the battlefield, abuse victims, accident sur-vivors, gunshot victims, people who are mugged, robbed, raped, or violently threatened may experience varying degrees of post-traumatic stress or even PTSD. It is usually identified as a condition that afflicts individuals.

On the corporate and communal level there is another form of trauma called historical trauma. "Historical trauma refers to cumu-lative emotional and psychological wounding, extending over an individual lifespan and across generations, caused by traumatic experiences. The historical trauma response (HTR) is a constellation of features in reaction to this trauma."[2] Unlike PTSD, HTR is not an individual diagnosis. HTR is how psychologists understand dis-ease and dissatisfaction within a broad community.

The tribes of the Cherokee, Chickasaw, and the Choctaw were afflicted with historical trauma after the Trail of Tears. The Navajo, Cheyenne, Arapaho, Dakota, and Winnebago people who survived the ethnic cleansing policies of Abraham Lincoln including the hanging of the Dakota 38, the Massacre at Sand Creek, and the Long Walk were afflicted with historical trauma. The hundreds of tribes that experienced nearly a century of horror as their children were stolen and imprisoned in government- and church-run boarding schools so their culture and language could be beaten out of them display symptoms of historical trauma. The diagnosis HTR was developed by Maria Yellow Horse Brave Heart, a Lakota woman and social worker among her people in South Dakota.[3] She was working to better understand the prevalence of dissatisfaction that she observed in Native communities.

HTR and HTR-type symptoms can also be observed among African Americans (the progeny of slaves), Japanese Americans (after the internment camps), and Jewish communities (as a result of the Holocaust). Any group that has endured widespread and prolonged oppression on the communal level can display symptoms of HTR. Historical trauma does not end with the generation that was traumatized. HTR is part of a classification of trauma diagnosis known as transgenerational trauma. This is "trauma that is transferred from the first generation of trauma survivors to the second and further generations of offspring of the survivors via complex post-traumatic stress disorder mechanisms."[4]

While attempting to understand the psychological condition of survivors of prolonged abuse, psychologist Judith Herman observed,

"Even the diagnosis of 'Post Traumatic Stress Disorder,' as it is presently defined, does not fit accurately enough. The existing diagnostic criteria for this disorder are derived mainly from survivors of circumscribed traumatic events. They are based on the prototypes of combat, disaster and rape. In survivors of prolonged, repeated trauma, the symptom picture is often far more complex." These observations led her to conclude that the syndrome resulting from prolonged, repeated trauma needed its own name, which she called "complex post traumatic stress disorder."[5]

A 2003 study observed that the grandchildren of Holocaust survivors "were overrepresented by 300% among the referrals to a child psychiatry clinic, in comparison with their representation in the general population."[6] This transgenerational manifestation of trauma matches the experience and observation of anyone who has spent significant time on an Indian reservation with a tribe that endured the ethnic cleansing and genocide removal policies of the US government and the horrors of boarding schools. It is evident in the inner city neighborhoods comprised of descendants of African slaves, lynching victims, survivors of Jim Crow laws, segregation, and mass incarceration. While most everyone is aware of the individual diagnosis of PTSD, fewer people have heard about the condition known as historical trauma.

Historical trauma can be understood as a transgenerational, communal manifestation of PTSD and complex posttraumatic stress disorder (C-PTSD). We may not understand exactly how it works, but transgenerational trauma can be observed in communities past the one that experienced the oppression firsthand. The vast amount of research into PTSD, C-PTSD, transgenerational trauma, and historical trauma provides language and frameworks to engage communities of color in dialogue regarding our nation's unjust history. These diagnoses and their concomitant symptoms do not exist in isolation.

For example, on the Navajo reservation, anyone over the age of fifty is most likely a boarding school survivor who endures the symptoms of PTSD and C-PTSD from that experience. Nearly every Navajo can recall the name and even specific stories about a parent who survived the boarding schools or a grandparent or great-grandparent who experienced and were even killed during the Long Walk. A generation of elders still reels from the PTSD and C-PTSD of boarding schools, while simultaneously struggling with the transgenerational and communal symptoms of HTR from the Long Walk. Repeated, complex traumas are being passed down and manifest in the form of historical trauma to the younger generation.

The experience of the Navajo tribe is not unique. The Indian Removal Act and the Trail of Tears occurred less than two hundred years ago. The ethnic cleansing policies of President Abraham Lincoln that resulted in multiple massacres took place within the last 155 years. The first boarding school opened 130 years ago, and many were still fully operational into the 1980s. As a result, many tribes have multiple generations experiencing symptoms of both C-PTSD and HTR.

PTSD and C-PTSD affect individuals who endured horrifying events. Trauma, however, often moves beyond merely the individual's experience. Therefore, those who come to the reservation from the outside in hopes of seeking racial reconciliation and healing through an individualistic framework may not fully comprehend the corporate nature of trauma. The elders of the community may still struggle with unresolved issues stemming from their boarding school experience, triggering negative responses to these well-intentioned but inadequate attempts. Those who do not understand the deep pain arising from historical trauma are likely to do or say something that will trigger a negative reaction, resulting in significant disruption of good intentions.

Understanding the trauma of people of color, both individual and communal, is crucial for anyone who hopes to engage a conversation regarding our nation's tainted history around race relations. Stolen lands, broken treaties, slavery, Jim Crow laws, lynchings, Indian removal, boarding schools, segregation, internment camps, and families separated at our borders all contribute to a historical trauma that impacts current conversations on race. But those who have done significant work in the area of racial conciliation and healing recognize that it is not always the trauma experienced by people of color that is derailing these conversations.

THE TRAUMA OF WHITE AMERICA

The authors have engaged in many different conversations on race, offering teaching and historical examples that reflect the content of this text. Two different responses can be observed. On one end of the spectrum, people of color resonate powerfully with the content. They find validation of their experiences and their theories on the deep and systemic nature of these injustices. Often they express that this content offers words to what they have been feeling for years. On the other end of the spectrum, some white people may have glazed, blank looks upon their faces. Some may actually appear panicked or in shock. They may state, "I had no idea the history was that bad," often followed by the words, "Please, tell me how to fix it."

The response of many of the shell-shocked whites seems to indicate a sort of trauma. PTSD, C-PTSD, and HTR are helpful in dealing with the trauma experienced by people of color in the United States. However, could whites, even as perpetrators and beneficiaries of trauma inflicted upon people of color, also experience a trauma that is distinct from the trauma experienced by people of color? Could white Americans, privileged and empowered, be responding to the reality of trauma in their lives? There are, however, no handles or language that deal with the traumatized white person.

In the conversation around race, white Americans are often placed into one of two categories. The first category is the presumption of individual racism with the blanket statement: "All white people are racist." This perspective actually addresses an important aspect of the conversation, which needs in more healthy ways to incorporate concepts of corporate responsibility. This statement, however, can often impede further conversation.

The assumption that all individual white people are racists does not allow for individual agency and the call to move individuals out of that place of racism. If all white people were racist in the individual sense of the word, every time a white person raises a question or a challenge, he or she may be labeled a threat. Treating every individual white person as a racist necessitates a defensive response to their presence. If every individual white person could be labeled a racist simply because of a lack of pigmentation in their skin, there would be no room for white people in the dialogue. This perspective ends any opportunity for healing in conversations on race.

The second perspective asserts that white people are fragile. Robin DiAngelo defines white fragility as "a state in which even a minimum amount of racial stress becomes intolerable, triggering a range of defensive moves. These moves include the outward display of emotions such as anger, fear, and guilt, and behaviors such as argumentation, silence, and leaving the stress-inducing situation. These behaviors, in turn, function to reinstate white racial equilibrium."[7] DiAngelo's work on white fragility provides deep and extremely helpful insight into both the psychology and behavior of white people in racial dialogues. However, the paradigm of fragility limits the responses that can be taken towards white people to either dismissiveness or walking on eggshells around them.

If a mover sees a box marked "fragile," he or she has one of two choices. The mover can trust the label and treat the items inside the box with extreme care. Damaging the contents would surely incur the wrath of the one who hired the movers. The second choice would be for the mover to dismiss the label. "I saw them pack this box. Its contents are not fragile." The mover may throw the box into the back of the moving van, breaking the fine china that was carefully packed beneath the folded towels and blankets. The language of fragility can limit engagement on the topic of race as it requires dismissing the feelings of white people or walking on eggshells around white people.

As I (Mark) struggled with observing trauma in the response of whites to racial dialogue and conversation, I was convinced that I knew what I was seeing, and I was certain I had seen it before. But where? Finally it dawned on me that I had seen it in myself. The same glazed look in the eyes, the same emotional unbelief—I experienced all of these symptoms when I was triggered in college over my brother's death and felt terrified to walk out of my apartment for fear that God would kill me. The response of many white people reflected symptoms of classic trauma. Initially, there was flat-out denial. "You're lying. The Declaration of Independence doesn't say that. . . . Our nation didn't do that." Second, there was a brief acknowledgement of sorrow followed immediately with the impulse to flee or to quickly solve the problem. "Please forgive me. . . . Tell me now, what can I do to fix it?" The quick and impulsive response reveals a trauma that has been experienced but never addressed.

Psychologist Rachel McNair in her book *Perpetration-Induced Traumatic Stress: The Psychological Consequences of Killing* "introduces the concept of Perpetration-Induced Traumatic Stress (PITS), a form of PTSD symptoms caused not by being a victim or rescuer in a horrifying event but by being an active participant in causing the event. Sufferers include soldiers, executioners, or police officers, where it is socially acceptable or even expected for them to kill."[8] When considering the impact of trauma, we typically focus on trauma experienced by the victims of violence. In wartime, individuals who lost their home, witnessed the murder of loved ones, or experienced torture are all easily identifiable as victims of trauma and likely to exhibit PTSD. But a drone operator, bomber pilot, or even the soldier that set fire to the village also experiences a form of trauma.

McNair draws her conclusions from a comprehensive study on Vietnam veterans. She defines PITS as involving "any portion of the symptomology of PTSD at clinical or sub-clinical levels that results from situations that would be traumatic if someone were a victim but situations for which the person in question was a causal participant."[9] McNair's work can be summarized with a citation of Socrates that "the doer of injustice is more miserable than the sufferer."

Ever since the death of my brother in 1988, I had assumed I was personally dealing with posttraumatic stress caused by the accident. PTSD helped explain the three years of emotional denial as well as the relational triggers I experienced when I began building more meaningful relationships my second year in college. But PTSD did not fully explain the guilt I felt as the driver of the car. Some people called it survivor's guilt, but I knew it was deeper as I was most likely the person that caused the accident which killed my brother.

PITS, on the other hand, made sense not just on a cognitive level but on an emotional and psychological one as well. If PTSD has a more complex version known as complex posttraumatic stress disorder that resulted from prolonged exposure to trauma, could there be a more complex form of PITS? C-PTSD affects the children, grandchildren, and great grandchildren of those exposed to prolonged and repeated trauma. C-PTSD, experienced on a larger societal level, results in the transgenerational and communal diagnosis of historical trauma (HTR).

Is it possible that PITS also has a complex version for people who lived their entire lives perpetrating dehumanizing violence against people of color? This version would include slave owners, soldiers participating in genocidal battles against Native peoples, and white settlers moving west and pushing the removal, and even extinction, of indigenous tribes. C-PITS could express a transgenerational and communal manifestation, which was the traumatized behavior many whites expressed in the context of difficult conversations on race. In short, are whites experiencing the phenomena of a generational trauma that can be labeled "the trauma of white America"? White America could not perpetrate five hundred years of dehumanizing injustice without traumatizing itself.

These categories are an attempt to initiate a conversation on race that allows for the full participation of all people groups. The goal is not to force a label on white America, but instead, to offer people of color the opportunity to view white Americans from a fresh perspective. In treating white people as a traumatized people, people of color have the authority to maintain their own agency and humanity in a way that has not been accessible before. Oftentimes, in conversations on race, whites are viewed as those with power who should initiate the seeking of forgiveness and initiate the process of reconciliation and healing. Instead, by treating white Americans as a traumatized people, we are called to an equality in our mutual brokenness and trauma.

If we understand white Americans as another group of traumatized people, it is easy to identify the symptoms. The American Psychological Association (APA) defines trauma as "an emotional response to a terrible event like an accident, rape, or natural disaster. Immediately after the event, shock and denial are typical. Longer term reactions include unpredictable emotions, flashbacks, strained relationships, and even physical symptoms like headaches or nausea."[10]

One of the first symptoms of trauma is denial. Denial is often evident in white America's engagement around race issues. For example, both the states of Texas and Oklahoma, where a majority of school textbooks are printed, have proposed and passed laws stating that you can only teach patriotic history. They are even trying to remove references to the word *slavery* in their textbooks. This response reveals an unresolved trauma. Institutions established by whites are so ashamed of their own past that they are unable to even publish accurate history.

CHAPTER TWELVE

The Christian Worldview and the Failure of Re-conciliation

MANY PTSD PATIENTS EXPERIENCE TRIGGERS. Triggers can be a sight, a sound, or a smell which launches the patient out of reality and back into the moment of emotional and psychological chaos of when the trauma occurred. One of my triggers regarding the accident and the death of my brother was the relationships I began to build during my years in college. For a veteran soldier experiencing PTSD from the battlefield, it may be the backfire of a muffler. For the victim of abuse, it may be a brush of the skin or a particular scent. Even music can be a trigger. Once triggered, the patient reverts to fight or flight instincts. Often, the patient is unaware that this is taking place. They feel nervous, they feel tense, they feel trapped, but they don't know why. Because of the state of denial that frequently accompanies trauma, the patient may be the last person to see or understand their triggers. Often, it is their family, friends, and coworkers who identify them first.

If we understand white America to be a traumatized people, triggers may be more easily identified. For a nation with a white supremacist Declaration of Independence, a white supremacist Constitution, and a white supremacist Supreme Court, eight years of a black president was a trigger. From 2008 through 2016, many white Americans and white Evangelical Christians did not know what to do with the optic of a black man governing from an office that historically had been reserved for white landowning men. The election of Donald J. Trump as the forty-fifth president of the United States of America was a triggered reaction to eight years of President Barack Obama.

Traumatic triggers may also explain the varied responses by the American church to the Doctrine of Discovery. In 2013, following the trend among several Christian denominations, the synod of the Christian Reformed Church of North America (CRCNA) voted to establish an official task force to examine the Doctrine of Discovery and what influences it may have had on the CRCNA. I was serving as a member of the board of trustees for the CRCNA and was appointed as a member of the study committee. For three years we researched the Doctrine of Discovery as well as the history of our missions agency. We closely examined the narrative of "Heathen Missions" in the CRC and heard from boarding school survivors.

The report submitted to the board of trustees in 2015 offered a sharp critique of the Rehoboth Christian Boarding School and included the firsthand account of two boarding school survivors. One of the survivors attended a BIA Boarding School and the other survivor attended Rehoboth, the boarding school of the CRCNA. (Full disclosure: I attended Rehoboth Christian High School as a day school student for twelve years during the period it was transitioning from a boarding school to a day school. Further disclosure: My term of service on the CRCNA board of trustees concluded the year prior to the submission of our report.)

When the report was released publicly to the CRC, our task force was dismayed to learn that the board of trustees had voted to remove the story of the Rehoboth boarding school survivor from the public version of our report. We were told this was done for "pastoral reasons." However, this public denial revealed a multigenerational and communal manifestation of their perpetration-induced traumatic stress. This sanitized version of the report was included in the agenda for the 2016 Synod. The day the report was scheduled to be discussed at Synod, I was asked to open the session in prayer. Expecting that the discussion of this report was going to be extremely contentious and would probably trigger the trauma of white America, I included in my prayer a reminder that as "reformed" Christians, we believe in the depravity of all people and we believe that our salvation comes from our faith rather than through our works. It was an effort to create a theological space for my white brothers and sisters to wrestle with this systemic, multigenerational, and communal sin.

Article 70 was the first article dealt with by Synod. The article stated: "That synod acknowledge that the existing Doctrine of Discovery is a heresy and we reject and condemn it. It helped shape western culture and led to great injustices."[1] Synod got off to a good start as it voted to adopt Article 70. The CRCNA included member churches from both the United States and Canada. In response to a lawsuit brought by residential school survivors the Canadian government and many churches reached the Indian Residential School Settlement Agreement, which established a national Truth and Reconciliation Commission (TRC).

> Between 2007 and 2015, the Government of Canada provided about $72 million to support the TRC's work. The TRC spent 6 years travelling to all parts of Canada and heard from more than 6,500 witnesses. The TRC also hosted 7 national events across Canada to engage the Canadian public, educate people about the history and legacy of the residential schools system, and share and honour the experiences of former students and their families.[2]

As a result, the Canadian delegates to Synod came into the conversation with some awareness of the issues of injustice that were on the table.

However, the good start was reversed rather quickly. After Article 70 was adopted, the room abruptly pivoted and entered into twenty minutes of sharing about the great and positive contributions of the CRCNA missionaries who both established and ran the Rehoboth boarding school. A second article was proposed and adopted that stated an affirmation for CRC missionaries: "That synod, nevertheless, recognize also the gospel motivation in response to the Great Commission, as well as the love and grace extended over many years by missionaries sent out by the CRCNA to the Indigenous peoples of Canada and the United States. For this we give God thanks, and honor their dedication."[3]

Mere minutes after rejecting and condemning the Doctrine of Discovery as heresy, the synod of the Christian Reformed Church was affirming our missionaries who ran a boarding school for nearly ninety years as being motivated not by the Doctrine of Discovery but by the Great Commission.

In 1896, after failing to successfully plant an "Indian mission" among the Sicangu Oyate on the Rosebud Reservation, the Christian Reformed Church set its sights on the tribes of the Southwest. In the early 1900s the CRC purchased lands in the territory of New Mexico. The lands we purchased had been ethnically cleansed of Navajo people in the 1860s. This act of genocide was perpetrated via the Long Walk as part of the Indian Removal policies of the Lincoln administration to clear lands for the transcontinental railway. The CRCNA purchased land directly east of Gallup and planted a new "Indian Mission." On the mission compound we built a church. In 1903 the Christian Reformed Church opened an Indian boarding school with an enrollment of six Native students.

The narrative of Manifest Destiny and the Doctrine of Discovery was embedded in the social imagination and worldview of the CRC, and therefore we were able to ignore the genocidal policies that were enacted by the US government to ethnically cleanse those lands just forty years prior. We even named our mission "Rehoboth." This name comes from the book of Genesis 26 where it states, "Now the LORD has given us room and we will flourish in the land" (v. 22). The CRCNA continued our boarding school operations until the early 1990s.

Because I was not a delegate to Synod and I was not the chair of our task force, I did not have the privilege of the floor and lacked the right to directly address Synod. So I sat through the remainder of the discussion that had been co-opted by a group of traumatized white people who were more concerned with protecting their mythological legacy on the mission field than they were with hearing the stories of the people our denomination had oppressed.

The contents of our report were good, but the way the report was written treated the denomination as fragile rather than as traumatized. Treating the audience as fragile necessitated the need for positive affirmation when it was not appropriate. Treating the audience as fragile meant that certain voices, particularly the voices of the victims, could not be included in the report since it would shatter perceptions of exceptionalism by fragile people.

The CRC synod was treated as a fragile people, even though they were clearly flailing about in their trauma. They were disgusted by the idol of Christendom but lacked the psychological wherewithal and the theological acumen to experience the blood of Christ in this area of systemic, transgenerational, and communal sin. The rich Reformed theology of the CRC should have directed Synod towards the profound theology of human depravity. Yet when confronted with systemic sin and transgenerational human brokenness, the CRC did not move towards the appropriate response of confession and lament but instead sought to justify our religion by works. The hyper-individualism of Western culture and the heresy of Christian empire had replaced a theology of communal grace, mercy, and forgiveness from a sovereign God with an individual theology of works that relied on the power of a self-perceived exceptionalism that required us to secure our own salvation.

THE PERVASIVE POWER OF A CHRISTENDOM WORLDVIEW

While confronting traumatized conservative white Evangelicals with the truth of biblical justice can be a significant challenge, sometimes engaging the trauma of white liberal Christians who believe they are "woke" can be just as challenging. This group will affirm the calling out of racial biases and can identify many of the expressions of systemic racism and sexism in society today. However, they may also believe that the primary source of these problems is conservatives, who are the ones most in need of help. While white conservatives may express a defensive response to triggers, many white liberals, both men and women, perpetuate the same mythology of white superiority and nonwhite inferiority. They just do it more passive aggressively.

In recent years, there has been a trend among religious groups, churches, and even entire denominations of "repudiating" the Doctrine of Discovery. On November 3, 2016, "a group of 524 clergy, spiritual leaders of 22 faith traditions called from all parts of the country, gathered in North Dakota for a day of solidarity and repentance on the Standing Rock Sioux Indian Reservation." The very protest of the water protectors already drew a line between conservative and liberal Christians as it was a clash between the rights of Native tribes verses the rights of corporations and the protection of the environment against the expansion of national economic development. So it was primarily liberal, left-leaning Christians who traveled to Standing Rock. As a "part of their pledge to fight the Dakota Access pipeline, several clergy repudiated the Doctrine of Discovery while gathered around the sacred fire at the Oceti Sakowin camp before representatives of the First Nations."[4]

Favorable reports emerged from this event proclaiming it as a beautiful and healing moment. Tears were shed and hugs exchanged as words of repudiation were uttered. I (Mark) was not at the event but visited Standing Rock a few weeks later. During my visit, I talked with one of the organizers of the event who was white. He was very excited about what had happened, but I was a bit more skeptical. I asked if any of the clergy, churches, or denominations had returned land to the Native tribes along with their statements of repudiation. I was informed that did not happen. That was regrettable yet understandable since the scheduling of this event probably occurred quickly and organizing a return of land would require quite a bit of advance planning.

I then asked if any of the churches or denominations had committed to not defend themselves in court should they be sued by a tribe for their land. Because the Doctrine of Discovery has been used as a legal instrument by the United States Supreme Court, its repudiation must be seen not only as a spiritual act but also as a legal act, in legal terms, with legal implications.

The Doctrine of Discovery serves as legal precedent for the land rights of white Americans and for the denial of land rights for Native peoples. If Native tribes sought any legal remedies regarding the return of lands that were stolen from them, as the Oneida Indian Nation did in 2005, ultimately the legal argument against restoring Native lands would rely upon the Doctrine of Discovery. For any of the clergy, churches, or denominations that repudiated the doctrine, they would also need to repudiate their right to defend themselves in court if ownership of any land in their possession were to be legally challenged by a Native nation. The repudiation must be comprehensive and include legal rights as well as a spiritual statement of remorse. Otherwise, the entire event would merely be a photo-op, good for media optics, but with no real cost or change for those in the photo. I was informed that no such legal commitment had been made around the sacred fire at the Oceti Sakowin camp at Standing Rock.

The inability to comprehensively address the full impact of the Doctrine of Discovery reveals a form of trauma. Because of the lack of awareness of how the pervasive narrative of whiteness and white supremacy has traumatized white Christian America, the trauma continues untreated. The trauma of white America often goes undiagnosed because it is often seen in only individual terms. The hyper-individualism of American society results in a captivity to the Western societal value of individualism and prevents white American Christians from acknowledging their collective sin and therefore from addressing their collective trauma.

Another challenge is that white American Christians fail to see themselves as part of a collective, global body of Christ. In the US, the way the Methodists see themselves as related to the Catholics, the way the Baptists see themselves related to the Presbyterians, and the way the Reformed churches see themselves related to the Anabaptists is not through their membership in a global body of believers, but as citizens of a Christian nation. The absence of an awareness of the corporate nature of the body of Christ means that the only available corporate identity is Christendom, implicit and embedded with the dysfunctional American Christian imagination.

Since Christendom rejected Christ and prostituted itself to empire, when the American church is confronted with systemic, transgenerational, communal sins, there is no theological space to wrestle with such transgressions. Individual sins like lying, sexual assault, theft, and even murder can be addressed by the American church as it offers Christ simply as a personal Savior. However, the need to address corporate sins like stolen lands, broken treaties, genocide, slavery, sexism, systematic injustice, white supremacy, and Christendom itself is ignored or outright rejected.

When the American church is confronted with the impact of the Doctrine of Discovery and the idea that what they thought they own is actually stolen property, the church has no meaningful theological response. A few individuals may ask for personal forgiveness, a congregation might call a person of color to the front of their service and have someone publicly wash their feet, or a group of clergy might gather to stand and read repudiations of the Doctrine of Discovery; but no land will be returned, no reparations will be paid, and no systemic changes will be made. For white Christians and the American church, bringing the blood of Christ into transgenerational, corporate, and systemic sins like the Doctrine of Discovery would require not only a complete rejection of the heresy of Christian empire but possibly a returning of all the fruits that were gained through that heresy.

Repentance is not just sorrow and confession, it is the turning around of wrong behavior towards right and just action. Repentance from sinful corporate behavior therefore requires systemic change. For many, the cost of that repentance may be too high. The mythology of American Christian exceptionalism and the trauma of white America is too deeply pervasive and deeply embedded in our narratives and systems. Lament does not allow for the simple glossing over of unrighteousness, but instead calls for a movement towards justice that unearths the historical trauma and the narratives that cause that trauma.

Merely mouthing the words of lament or a ceremony of repentance is insufficient. If the American church were to confess the sin of stolen lands, broken treaties, slavery, genocide, mass incarceration, Jim

Crow laws, internment camps, nuclear weapons, the New Jim Crow, and all the social sins justified by the acceptance of the heresy of Christendom, the trauma of such a confession would compel a people unable to cope with trauma to immediately seek out a form of hope. They would scour the Scriptures for a promise from Creator that their confession would not be in vain and that their brokenness would be healed. Many Christians would probably find that hope in 2 Chronicles 7:14, which states: "If my people, who are called by my name, will humble themselves and pray and seek my face and turn from their wicked ways, then I will hear from heaven, and I will forgive their sin and will heal their land." The promise of healing at the end of this verse is embraced by Christians throughout our country who seek out the promise of hope in the midst of suffering.

The passage from 2 Chronicles 7 is from the second dedication of the temple, where God is reiterating the terms of his land covenant with the people of Israel. The promise of healing for the land is directed towards the nation of Israel and cannot be co-opted by future nation-states who see themselves as exceptional and chosen nations. As Americans, even American Christians, we are not God's chosen people and Turtle Island is not the promised land for European Americans. The United States of America is not, never has been, nor will it ever be a Christian nation.

Where is hope if not in a land covenant with the God of Abraham? We have been trained to read the Scriptures, especially the Old Testament, incorrectly. We have been taught to put ourselves in the place of Abraham, Isaac, and Jacob. We read the Old Testament as if the United States is the chosen people of Israel. But in the Old Testament narrative, Americans would be the citizens of the pagan nations. Hope for the United States does not emerge from being the promised and chosen people like the Jews, but instead, we take our hope from how God treats the other nations in the biblical narrative.

The hope for the United States comes from a God who was willing to negotiate with Abraham over the fate of Sodom and Gomorrah. The hope for the United States comes from a God who pulled Rahab out of the city before he destroyed Jericho. The hope for the United States comes from a God who said to Jonah, "Should I not be concerned" when he protested that God had sent him to prophesy to the pagan city of Nineveh. The hope for America does not come from a land covenant with God—it comes from the character of God. And the character of God is not accessed by our exceptionalism but through a humility that emerges from the spiritual practice of lament.

TRAUMA AND THE REJECTION OF LAMENT

Traumatized people often cling to a false sense of security. The trauma of white America emerged from embracing a dysfunctional power that oppressed others. Out of that trauma, white America continues to cling to a false security. Despite the power of the gospel that attests to a divergent narrative, white American Evangelicals and white liberal Christians continue to cling to worldly notions of power. Instead of the biblical narratives of confession, mercy, and justice, American Christians have embraced narratives of exceptionalism and triumphalism. These dysfunctional narratives embraced by a traumatized people are amplified by a hyper-individualism that serves as a blinder to the reality of corporate sin and corporate trauma.[5]

The necessary corrective for this trauma is offered in the healing power of lament. Lament calls for truth telling that reveals the underlying trauma and can lead to the promise of healing. Lament removes any pretense of exceptionalism and triumphalism that is used to cover up trauma. In the book of Lamentations, the self-perception of exceptionalism prevented the people of God from embracing the fullness of God's hope and restoration. God's people had experienced the devastation of conquest and exile and struggled with this unexpected reality. Lamentations points out the faulty reasoning of exception-alism that the traumatized remnant of Jerusalem was experiencing. As noted in *Prophetic Lament*: "The fall of Jerusalem is particularly disturbing to the residents who held a high view of their own worth as a city. Jerusalem was David's city. . . . Jerusalem was home to the temple of the Lord. It was the place of affirmation that Israel had a unique covenantal relationship with YHWH."[6] The residents of Jerusalem embraced this sense of exceptionalism and believed them-selves to be impervious to YHWH's judgment and punishment.

The concept of an exceptional people is rooted not in any inherent worth of the people, but in God's grace and provision. They are the chosen people because God chose them, not because they deserve to be chosen. "Jerusalem naively believed that their status as the keepers of the temple meant that no judgment would befall them. The temple of YHWH was their protection. Surely God would never judge his chosen people and his very own temple of worship."[7] But Jerusalem would succumb to the Babylonian siege and was laid waste. Their sense of exceptionalism and their belief in their inevitable triumph did not protect them.

The dysfunctional narrative of American exceptionalism has no basis in Scripture. Even when the Bible describes the unique charac-teristic of Israel's status, no parallel pronouncement or scenario exists between the ancient theocracy of Israel and the modern United States. There is no guarantee that white American Christianity will continue to flourish under the provision of Christendom. To cling to that sense of dysfunctional and abusive power is a severely traumatizing reality.

White American Christianity has been operating under the faulty assumption of American exceptionalism and triumphalism. White America has traumatized itself with these dysfunctional narratives. The proper response to this scenario is found in the book of

Lamentations, with an acknowledgment of this sinful reality and a lament that confesses and repents from this reality.

> Lamentations reveals the folly of Jerusalem's self-perceived exceptionalism. Their belief that they were the center of worship because they were exceptional in some inherent way was debunked when the temple was destroyed. Their sense of strength and the projection of their power was torn down as their once powerful city laid waste. Words of strength have been replaced with words of weakness. Lamentations points out to the remnant of Jerusalem the great folly of their self-perceived exceptionalism.[8]

Traumatized white American Christians can follow the example of the remnant of Jerusalem, who are powerless over their current circumstance and can no longer cling to their self-perceived sense of exceptionalism and their belief in their inevitable triumph. Accepting the truth of their trauma leads to the healing power of lament.

APOLOGIES OF A TRAUMATIZED PEOPLE

On December 19, 2009, President Obama signed House Resolution 3326, the 2010 Department of Defense Appropriation Act. On page forty-five of this sixty-seven-page bill, subsection 8113 is titled "Apology to Native People of the United States." What follows is a seven–bullet-point apology that mentions no specific tribe, no specific treaty, and no specific injustice. It basically says, "You had some nice land, our citizens didn't take it very politely; let's just call it all of our land and steward it together." The subsection ends with a disclaimer stating that nothing in this apology is legally binding. To date, this apology has not been announced, publicized, or read by the White House or by Congress.

> House Resolution 3326, 111th Congress, Department of Defense Appropriations Act, 2010. Apology to Native Peoples of the United States.
>
> Sub-Section 8113

Section A—acknowledgement and apology. The United States acting through Congress–

(1) recognizes the special legal and political relationship Indian tribes have with the United States and the solemn covenant with the land we share;

(2) commends and honors Native Peoples for the thousands of years that they have stewarded and protected this land;

(3) recognizes that there have been years of official depredations, ill-conceived policies, and the breaking of covenants by the Federal Government regarding Indian tribes;

(4) apologizes on behalf of the people of the United States to all Native Peoples for the many instances of violence, maltreatment, and neglect inflicted on Native Peoples by citizens of the United States;

(5) expresses its regret for the ramifications of former wrongs and its commitment to build on the positive relationships of the past and present to move toward a brighter future where all the people of this land live reconciled as brothers and sisters, and harmoniously steward and protect this land together;

(6) urges the President to acknowledge the wrongs of the United States against Indian tribes in the history of the United States in order to bring healing to this land; and

(7) commends the State governments that have begun reconciliation efforts with recognized Indian tribes located in their boundaries and encourages all State governments similarly to work toward reconciling relationships with Indian tribes within their boundaries.

Section B—Disclaimer- Nothing in this section—

(1) authorizes or supports any claim against the United States; or

(2) serves as a settlement of any claim against the United States.[9]

I [Mark] learned about this apology on December 19, 2011, and was appalled. How could our nation and our leaders bury something like this in a Department of Defense appropriations bill? On December 19, 2012, I hosted a gathering of approximately 150 friends, partners, and fellow citizens. We stood in front of the US Capitol and publicly read this apology. We read several pages of the sections before the apology (to highlight how inappropriate it was to place this apology in a defense appropriations bill). We also had the apology translated into the languages of Navajo and Ojibwe. This was to model for Congress and the White House that when you apologize, you not only do it publicly, but you also make every effort to have the apology be accessible and understandable to the offended parties. We then gave people in the audience an opportunity to react and respond to the apology. Because when you apologize, the offended party should speak.

This buried apology was initiated by Senator Sam Brownback of Kansas and signed by President Barack Obama. Throughout their political careers both men have gone far beyond their predecessors in reaching out to Native peoples. I invited Sam Brownback (who in 2012 was the Governor of Kansas) to attend the reading of the apology and sent a letter to the White House inviting President Obama to attend. Governor Brownback declined my invitation, and I received a letter from the White House stating that neither President Obama nor any of his staff would be in attendance.

Over the course of the year leading up to the scheduled reading, I also invited national religious leaders, academic leaders, political leaders, social justice leaders, and business leaders. In the months and weeks prior to the event, various justifications were offered why these leaders, liberal and conservative, Republican and Democrat, religious and secular, could not be there.

In the absence of any national public leadership, after the apology was read and the people had a chance to respond, I stepped forward, took the microphone, and encouraged our Native leaders, our communities, and our people to not accept this apology. I was not trying to be divisive, nor was I trying to shame politicians, the church, or even our nation. But this event was about the historic relationship between indigenous peoples and our colonizers throughout the world.

That morning, in front of the US Capitol, December 19, 2012, our audience was not just the 150 people from the grassroots effort standing on the Capitol lawn, nor even the people watching online. That morning our audience was the entire globe. Our audience was history.

The United States of America is a leader in this world; its words are scrutinized, and its example followed. If the indigenous tribes of North America were to accept this apology in the vague, politicized, disrespectful, and self-protecting way it was given, then we would be condoning our government's actions and making a model of their methods. We would be communicating to indigenous peoples everywhere that we are still subservient to our colonizers, that we are not their equals, and that we should just be grateful for whatever scraps they bother to throw our way. We would be accepting the dysfunctional expressions of a traumatized people unable to seriously deal with the trauma they inflicted upon others and themselves.

In 2009, despite the fact that our nation had elected its first black president, we were in no way ready to apologize to Native peoples. Even today, ten years later, most Americans are unaware about the Doctrine of Discovery, which is still the basis for their land titles. Most Americans are ignorant about the unabashed white supremacy and genocidal policies of the man they consider to be their greatest president. Most Americans could not name the Native nation that was ethnically cleansed from the lands that their city, their community, even their very houses are built on. Because of the trauma of a white America still in the initial phase of shock and denial, the United States is incapable of offering a sincere, informed apology. Which is why even a white senator with deep moral convictions had to water down this apology, and why a black president, who in his first term in office was learning quickly to speak the language of "American exceptionalism" was unwilling to publicly acknowledge this apology. Another approach is needed that does not emerge from a dysfunctional response to trauma.

About the same time Senator Brownback was watering down his proposed Congressional Apology in an effort to gain its support in the white majority Congress, which was stuck in a state of denial, I had developed and was successfully using a metaphor to initiate dialogue between white Americans and indigenous peoples regarding this dehumanizing history. This metaphor did not emerge from the experience of trauma but rather framed the dialogue in a way that was both honest and constructive. I offer that metaphor here: It feels like our indigenous peoples are an old grandmother who lives in a very large house. It is a beautiful place with plenty of rooms and comfortable furniture. But years ago, some people came into her house and locked her upstairs in the bedroom. Today her home is full of people. They are sitting on her furniture. They are eating her food. They are having a party in her house. They have since come upstairs and unlocked the door to her bedroom, but now it is much later, and she is tired, old, weak, and sick; so she can't or doesn't want to come out.

But what is the most hurtful and what causes her the most pain is that virtually no one from this party ever comes upstairs to find the grandmother in the bedroom. No one sits down next to her on the bed, takes her hand, and simply says, "Thank you. Thank you for letting us be in your house."

On the surface, this metaphor seems to suggest an easy answer. "Is that it? All we need to do is say thank you?" But that's the beauty of this metaphor. Because that's not it at all. Saying thank you requires a fundamental shift in thinking. Saying thank you reverses the roles. Saying thank you decenters the white, landowning Christian male and the colonizers from Europe who falsely claimed to have "discovered" lands that were already inhabited. Saying thank you acknowledges that the indigenous peoples of Turtle Island are the hosts of this land. Saying thank you is not the end, but merely a step into the beginning.

CONCLUSION

Truth and Conciliation

To'aheed'lini baa shi'chiin. My paternal grandmother, May Casamero, was the daughter of Morgan Casamero. After surviving the Long Walk and the death camp at Bosque Redondo, he and his family returned to a tiny portion of our traditional lands and lived in a hogan situated in a canyon south of some beautiful red rocks that stretch for miles and can be found scattered throughout *Dinétah*. *Dinétah* is the home of our *Tó'aheedlíinii bá shíshchíín* people. It is bordered by four sacred mountains. To the east is *Tsisnaasjini'*—Dawn or White Shell Mountain (our colonizers call it Mount Blanca, located near Alamosa, Colorado). To the south is *Tsoodzil*—Blue Bead or Turquoise Mountain (our colonizers call it Mount Taylor, located near Grants, New Mexico). To the west is *Doko'oosliid*—Abalone Shell Mountain (our colonizers named it San Francisco Peaks, near Flagstaff, Arizona). And to the north is *Dibé Nitsaa* (Big Mountain Sheep)—Obsidian Mountain (our colonizers named it Mount Hesperus, part of the La Plata mountains).

My great-grandfather was born in the mid-1800s before the railroad was built, before *Hwéeldi*. I don't know much about his life except for the lessons my grandmother repeated to my father. One of those lessons was, "Treat your horses well." Horses were the major form of transportation for our people. They were used in herding sheep, hauling water, visiting family, and escaping danger. My first job, as a young teenager, was working for a rancher in New Mexico, taking care of his horses. I learned how to saddle them, exercise them, and even occasionally helped round up livestock with them. I imagine my *nalii* grew up in a similar way, but with even more of the traditions of our people. Greeting the morning sun with his prayers, growing corn, and herding sheep on horseback.

The high desert of the Southwest has a beauty that is unique unto itself and cannot be found anywhere else in the country. The horizon stretches for miles, and the sky seems to extend to eternity. In the mornings the sun rises behind the red rocks running from the northwest to the southeast. The placement of these rocks means that in the evening the setting sun not only lights up the vast sky, but it also shines brilliantly on the red rocks, lighting them up and making the colors on the ground nearly as brilliant as the colors in the sky.

It is an amazing view and can cause an observer to question which way to look. Do you turn to the west and watch the beauty of the sunset and the incredible colors of the sky, or do you look to the east and behold the brilliance of the red rocks, shining majestically like a precious metal? The red rocks are probably one reason Spanish explorers like Cortez, Juan de Onate, and others believed this area was laden with gold. It is most likely one of the reasons our colonizers, the European Americans, made the motto for the state of New Mexico "the Land of Enchantment."

The Indian Removal Act of 1830 allowed the United States government to remove tribes from their lands in the east to more empty lands farther to the west. The language of "choice" is actually used in the legislation: "Such tribes or nations of Indians as may choose to exchange the lands where they now reside."[1] Choice was hardly the experience of the thousands of Navajo and Apache people whose crops were burned, livestock killed, and homes destroyed by Abraham Lincoln's armies as he sought to ethnically cleanse the lands of what is now Arizona and New Mexico to make way for Manifest Destiny and the transcontinental railway. Choice was not what my great-grandfather felt when he was one of the ten thousand *Diné* people rounded up and forcibly marched from our traditional lands to Bosque Redondo. Fortunately, my great-grandfather was not one of the 2,300 people who died at this death camp, but that also meant he lived through five horrifying years of imprisonment, malnutrition, and the constant threat of execution until the treaty of Bosque Redondo was signed in 1868.

My great-grandfather and his family were fortunate to return from Bosque Redondo. Initially they lived in a hogan situated in some canyons south of the red rocks, but it was not long before they were forced to move once again. The US government claimed much of the land south of their newly constructed railway, and our family was forced to move. We eventually ended up settling near Marino Lake, an area about thirty miles north of the red rocks. This is where my grandmother was born and where many of my relatives, *To'aheed'lini*, reside today.

In 1881 the railroad was being built through the territory of New Mexico. Gallup, New Mexico, was founded "as headquarters along the construction right-of-way of the southern transcontinental route."[2] In 1896 the Christian Reformed Church purchased some land just east of Gallup. There they built a compound that served as a base of operations for their mission to the Indians of the Southwest. Their mission compound was located just south of where the red rocks end. On this mission compound the missionaries built a church. And in 1903 they opened an Indian boarding school. The approach of the mission reflected the social imagination of its time, which sought to kill the Indian in order to save the man.

By the late 1800s the United States of America had fully embraced the Doctrine of Discovery and its role as the next carrier of the mantle of Christendom. John Winthrop's narrative of claiming the promised land (akin to the Israel of the Old Testament) and the building of a city on a hill had become deeply ingrained in the national consciousness and imagination. Americans across the continent truly believed this nation was blessed by God and had a manifest destiny to rule the continent from sea to shining sea. Like most Christian denominations, the Christian Reformed Church was no different. They arrived with a doctrine that allowed them to discover new lands. They constructed a mythology which allowed them to claim it. And they co-opted a theology of promised lands that allowed them to ethnically cleanse it.

However, there was a problem. Those damn Indians were not going as quickly or as quietly as most Christian Americans had hoped. By the end of the nineteenth century, the explicit manifestation of the institution of slavery had changed with the Emancipation Proclamation and the passing of the Thirteenth Amendment. The evil structure of slavery had been brought down, but the narrative of white supremacy continued and found expression in Jim Crow, which would eventually be replaced by the New Jim Crow. The evil systems were being dismantled, but the narrative continued to perpetuate new systems. And that was the dynamic around the Indian problem.

The evil social structure of explicit genocide and intentional extermination of Native people was being challenged. One of the reasons my Navajo elders were able to negotiate a treaty with the US Army was because images and stories of the horrid conditions and inhumane treatment of our people were becoming public. The army and its leadership had a public relations problem. So the explicit slaughter of Native bodies was stopped, but the narrative of white supremacy continued on and created new systems of oppression. The army addressed their public relations problem by agreeing to send our people back to a portion of *Dinétah*, the land in the general vicinity of our four sacred mountains. We did not get all of our land back, but some of it was returned in the treaty we signed with the US government in 1868.

One of the sections of land that we did not get back was the land to the east of Gallup. I was one of the last babies born at the old mission hospital run by the Christian Reformed Church east of Gallup. In 1971 this hospital was moved off the mission compound and into the limits of the nearby town. My mother, Evelyn Natelborg, worked at the hospital on the mission compound as a nurse. Her parents, John and Mae Natelborg, were lifelong members of the Christian Reformed Church. She originally came to the denomination's Indian mission, Rehoboth, on her way to Africa. But during her stay she met my father, Theodore Charles. They fell in love and were soon married. She never left.

My father, Ted Charles, also lived on the same mission compound. He had recently completed his service in the US Marine Corps and was working at the CRC mission. His mother, May Casimero, was *Diné*, from the *To'aheed'lini* clan (where the waters flow together). She was a boarding school survivor born in a nearby community called Mariana Lake. My other *nali*, John Charles, was also *Diné*, from the *To'adchini* clan (Bitter Water). He too was a boarding school survivor who was raised more than an hour north of Gallup, in another area of our reservation called Blanco Canyon. My grandmother was one of the founding members of the Christian Reformed Church in Crownpoint, New Mexico. My grandfather was a former US government employee who later worked as a translator for the CRC missionaries serving at the CRC Indian mission in New Mexico.

My father's parents lived on campus at the CRC Indian mission near us. When I was in the first grade, our family moved from the mission compound to a neighborhood on the west side of Gallup to a new housing development on the very edge of town. There was a lot of open, undeveloped land to the west, and the border of the Navajo Reservation was located only a few miles to the north. As a result, there was a lot of free space. My grandparents moved to that neighborhood with us and purchased a house right next door to ours. We did not live in hogans, but our front doors did face the east, just like the front door of nearly every house and hogan on the reservation.

Not long after we moved there, my grandfather, who had never owned land before, decided to plant corn in our backyard. Corn is sacred to our people and is one of the few crops that has any chance of growing in this climate. Gallup is located in the high desert of the Southwest, where the ground is dry, rocky, and hard, and there is very little rain and almost no irrigation. This makes growing anything difficult and requires that the ground be dug up and tilled quite deep. Every day my grandfather was out in the yard with a shovel and a pick, breaking up the ground, removing rocks, and planting his corn just as his parents, grandparents, and great-grandparents did before him.

As my grandparents grew older, I began sleeping in an extra bedroom in their house so that I could help them, if necessary, in the middle of the night. My grandparents purchased some land several miles outside the city limits of Gallup. This land was nothing special. It was located up in the hills about four miles south of the highway. "The land," as my *nali* called it, was like most of the plots around there, off the grid and undeveloped. There were no houses, sheds, plumbing, running water, or electricity. It was just land, filled with trees, shrubs, rocks, and dirt. The road leading to it from the interstate wasn't even paved. Over the years, down the hill, closer to the road, a few houses and trailers began popping up. Up the hill, there was almost no development. Frequently, usually on the weekends, my grandparents would take us up to the land. I'm not sure why. There was not much to do there, but my brother, sister, and I would ride our bikes, climb the trees, and hike among the ravines while our parents, grandparents, and other friends and relatives would sit under the trees and talk.

Later, after I had left for college, and my grandparents were older and needed more constant care, they sold the land and bought two more plots farther up, near the top of the hill. There, our family built a two-story hogan, large enough for my parents and siblings to live in, as well as room for my grandparents to have their own apartment downstairs. They moved there after I had left for college, so I never lived in that hogan. But I loved returning home for a few weeks at a time to enjoy the peace and quiet of the land. One of my favorite spots was behind our hogan, to the south. Because we lived at the top of the hill, and the interstate was to the north, all of the land to the south was undeveloped. There were no roads, no houses, no buildings, no lights. Nothing. Just forest for miles and miles and miles. But when you began walking south, fewer than two hundred yards behind our hogan, the trees suddenly broke and you found yourself standing on the edge of beautiful canyon. It was amazing. I was attending college in the crowded and busy city of Los Angeles, so I relished the opportunity to come home, visit my parents, walk out to that canyon, sit down on the rocks, and behold, in complete silence, the magnificent beauty.

In our hogan there is a large window facing north. The view is breathtaking, looking down the hill, over the trees, and with an amazing view of the beautiful red rocks off in the distance. When the sun sets in the west, the red rocks light up magnificently. My grandmother loved sitting in her chair, looking out that window. I knew she had grown up about forty miles to the northeast in an area not unlike this. And I assumed she loved looking out of the windows because of the memories that the beauty of this land brought back. But several years later, my father explained to me why she loved this land so much. While they were building the hogan, he would bring my grandparents up there to see the progress on their new home. My grandmother at that point was in a wheelchair, and he would have to push her chair through the dirt to get up to the house. On one trip, she became reflective as he was helping her out of the car. "You know," she said to my dad, "my father, Morgan Casamero, your *cheii*, used to live in that canyon, the one just over this hill."

At the publishing of this book it will have been ten years since the apology to Native peoples was buried in the defense appropriations bill and seven years since a group of 150 people from the grassroots effort gathered to publicly read it in front of the US Capitol. But not much has changed. President Obama left office without ever publicizing it. President Trump has embraced the narrative of white American exceptionalism in his campaign rhetoric, environmental policies, blatant racism and sexism, his nationalism, his border wall, and his unabashed love for Andrew Jackson. To this day, most Americans do not know about this apology nor about the Doctrine of Discovery. Our nation still has no clue how to deal with its past. But for myself, my family, close friends, and the 150 people gathered in front of the US Capitol that cold December morning, December 19 is no longer just a normal day. It is an annual reminder. A reminder to not get stuck in anger or resentment. A reminder to press on. A reminder that there is much work to be done.

George Erasmus, an aboriginal leader from the Dene people in Canada, says, "Where common memory is lacking, where people do not share in the same past, there can be no real community. Where community is to be formed, common memory must be created."[3] The United States of America has a white majority that remembers a history of discovery, opportunity, expansion, and exceptionalism.

Meanwhile our communities of color have the lived experiences of stolen lands, broken treaties, slavery, Jim Crow laws, Indian removal, ethnic cleansing, lynchings, boarding schools, segregation, internment camps, mass incarceration, and families separated at our borders. Our country does not have a common memory.

The United States of America needs a national dialogue on race, gender, and class. A conversation on par with the Truth and Reconciliation Commissions that took place in South Africa, Rwanda, and Canada. It must be an inclusive dialogue, not one that takes place in specific silos. And the church must be involved. But because the American church has so broadly accepted the heresy of Christian empire and because the Western church wrote the Doctrine of Discovery, the church is currently incapable of leading this dialogue. It needs to participate, but it cannot lead.

Suppose there are two families living next door to each other. One family regularly attends church while the other does not. David, the husband of the churchgoing family, is committing adultery with Eliza, the wife from the family next door. As a result, the second couple is experiencing problems in their marriage. Eliza's husband, John, is unaware of the adulterous relationship and seeks help from a men's ministry at a church in the community. The church leadership greets John with open arms and informs him that they have a thriving ministry for men, especially those struggling in their marriages. In fact, this ministry is led by a church elder who just happens to live right next door!

When the two men meet, David realizes that John, who is seeking help, is Eliza's husband. But David has nothing to offer John. He cannot counsel him, he cannot comfort him, he cannot befriend him, he cannot even pray for him. The only role that David has in healing John's marriage is to get out of Eliza's bed.

Because the problems our nation are facing are systemic and corporate, because our problems are rooted in the Doctrine of Discovery and the heresy of Christian empire, and because the American church still broadly accepts the national identity of Christendom, the church in America literally has nothing to offer. Its only solution to our national problems is to "make the nation Christian again." But that is precisely what caused our problems in the first place.

In the Old Testament book of Hosea, God commands the prophet, "Go, marry a promiscuous woman and have children with her, for like an adulterous wife this land is guilty of unfaithfulness to the LORD" (Hosea 1:2-3). So, Hosea married Gomer. After giving birth to several children, Gomer returned to her promiscuous life on the streets, even working as a prostitute. Later the Lord commanded Hosea, "Go show your love to your wife again, though she is loved by another man and is an adulteress" (Hosea 3:1). Hosea went back to the streets, paid for the services of his wife, and brought her home.

Jesus is the prophet.

The Western/American church is Gomer.

Our adultery is with the empire.

And our only path to healing is through lament and learning how to accept some very unsettling truths.

Acknowledgments

How do you write acknowledgments for a book that details the heresies of your church, the dehumanizing and ethnic cleansing policies of your nation, and the genocide of your people? Acknowledgments for such a book may seem like an oxymoron, but the life experiences that went into researching and writing this book have been a journey. And for everyone who has been a part of that journey, I am extremely grateful. Here are a few:

Ahéhee', Rachel. When we were married twenty-one years ago, neither of us knew the adventure that lay before us: a journey that took us from southern California to Gallup, New Mexico; Denver, Colorado; eleven years on the Navajo Nation (including three years in a *hogan* with no running water or electricity); and most recently to Washington, DC. We have raised three incredible children together. I am exceedingly grateful not only for your friendship, your partnership, and your incredible attention to detail, but also I am humbled by your faith and love for Christ.

Ahéhee' Shimá dóó shizhéé, Theodore and Evie Charles. Thank you, mom and dad, for raising me not to be half Navajo and half white, but for giving me the tools to learn how to be whole—both *Dine'* and American of Dutch heritage.

I am grateful to the teachers and staff at *Tséhootsooí Diné Bi'Ólta'*, the Navajo immersion school in Window Rock, Arizona. Thank you for keeping our *Diné* language and culture alive and for your investment in our children. *Ahéhee'*.

I am grateful and indebted to my mentors Jim Northrup and Susie Silversmith. Not only did they both survive the horrors of boarding school, but they also retained their language and culture and went on, as a part of their healing, to share their stories publicly. Their courage and resilience is humbling. And their voices are awe-inspiring. *Ahéhee'*.

I am grateful for nearly five decades of siblings, friends, neighbors, relatives, colleagues, and organizations who journeyed with me and helped shape me: David, Denise, Mildred, Linda. Eric, Brenda, and Curtis. Leroy Barber. Louise, Roy, and Stanley. Marilyn, Jasbert, Tim, and Matt. Linda and Laverna. Ruth. Ben and Eunice Stoner, Johnny B. Dennison. Tim and Joy Stoner. Richard Twiss, Terry LeBlanc, Gavriel Gefen, Raymond Minniecon, and my Aboriginal aunties in Australia (WCGIP). Richard Silversmith (Christian Indian Center). Mike Hogeterp and the rest of our Doctrine of Discovery Task Force (CRCNA). John Witvliet and my colleagues at the Calvin Institute of Christian Worship. Doug Schaupp and Alex Van Riesen (IVCF at UCLA). Megan and Willie Krischke, Mike Kelly, Donnie and Renee Begay (Would Jesus Eat Frybread). *Ahéhee'*.

I am also humbled by the many voices of Native authors and academics who have been working to expose the Doctrine of Discovery for decades. This is not the first book on the Doctrine of Discovery, nor will it be the last. I am especially grateful for the work of Steve Newcomb. *Pagans in the Promised Land* is a must read and was one of my first exposures to the Doctrine of Discovery. *Ahéhee'* Steve.

I am grateful for the work of Maria Yellowhorse Braveheart. Her work on historical trauma is invaluable. *Ahéhee'* Maria.

I am deeply grateful for my friend and coauthor, Soong-Chan Rah, without whom this book could not have been written.

I am grateful to the Canadian nonprofit Native Land Digital. Their ongoing work to map and educate regarding the traditional lands, treaties, and languages of Native nations and peoples is exemplary. Their website (native-land.ca) allows anyone to enter an address, city, or zip code to learn what Native nation or indigenous tribe originally inhabited those lands, what treaties where written there, and what language groups are from there. While this resource is not the final authority, it is a great place to begin your research.

I am grateful for the online Native-run publications of *Indianz, Indian Country Today,* the *Navajo Times,* and *Native News Online.* This book was prefaced by nearly a decade of my blog articles, op-eds, and other literary musings, many of which were published by these organizations. *Ahéhee'.* Thank you for your commitment to lifting up the voices and stories of our Native peoples.

Ahéhee' my relatives. Walk in beauty.

Mark Charles

I am so grateful for the partnership and friendship with Mark Charles in coauthoring this book. At the beginning of this process I could not have imagined that we would have such a strong and productive symbiotic relationship in the writing process. But more than simply producing a book, this process has resulted in the deepening of our friendship, for which I am grateful. Special thanks to IVP for their patience and perseverance in seeing this project to the end. Particular thanks to our heroic champion and editor, Al Hsu.

I am unable to list all of the academic mentors who have shaped my formation as a scholar and as a writer. Through my journey in various academic institutions, Columbia (Randall Balmer, Penny Nixon), Gordon-Conwell (Eldin Villafañe, Doug and Judy Hall, Stephen Mott), Harvard (Harvey Cox, Cornel West), Duke (Willie Jennings, Kate Bowler, Grant Wacker, J. Kameron Carter, Ellen Davis, Emmanuel Katongole, Valerie Cooper), North Park (Michael Emerson, Dan Hodge, Michelle Clifton-Soderstrom), I have been blessed with teachers and colleagues who continue to shape and challenge my intellectual development. I am thankful for scholars who have contributed to my current endeavors: the late Richard Twiss, the late Wendy Peterson, Terry LeBlanc, Randy Woodley, Andrea Smith, Ray Aldred, Dan Hawk, JR Lilly, and Steve Newcomb. My gratitude to my students who wrestled with the concepts found in this book, through classroom discussion and papers. Thanks to my TAs, Peter Shin and Will Eastham. Special thanks to my students at Stateville Correctional Center who have taught me the true meaning of mobilizing for justice.

My ministry colleagues and spiritual mentors over the years have blessed me with a profound sense that writing is a calling that lifts up previously silenced voices. Thanks to many colleagues who have my utmost admiration in their faithful ministry endeavors (Ray and Gloria Hammond, Larry Kim, Liz Verhage, Bil Mooney-McCoy, Gary VanderPol, Vince Bantu, Peter Cha, Danny Martinez, Greg Yee). Over the course of this book project, dear friends stepped into the gap to provide spiritual support that I would not have survived without. Thank you Five Guys for your ongoing prayers and standing in the gap for me. Additional thanks to Jon Ido Warden, Charles Miyamoto, Neil Taylor, and Dave Kersten.

My deepest joy is in acknowledging the great gift of my children. Annah and Elijah continue to be my inspiration, source of great joy, and my impetus to keep moving forward.

Soong-Chan Rah

A Partial List of the Native Nations and Indigenous Tribes of Turtle Island (Located in the United States)

This is a list of nearly seven hundred Native nations, tribes, and people groups from the lands known today as the United States of America. I implore you to read (not skim or skip) but *read* every single one of these names. This is just a partial list of the indigenous hosts of Turtle Island. The basis of this list came from the National Congress of American Indians and was combined with another list from the Nation Conference of State Legislatures of American Indian Tribes that the United States federal government and states acknowledge. There are many other "unrecognized" tribes, as well as tribes that have been exterminated. There are also numerous tribes and nations located in the lands to the north and south (Canada and Mexico).

My debt and gratitude to the indigenous hosts of Turtle Island is unending. Everywhere I travel to speak, I do my best to acknowledge the Native nation or tribe whose land I am on, and I thank them for their stewardship of these lands. These are the people who lived here. These are the lands where they hunted, they fished, and they farmed. They gave birth to their children on these lands, and they buried their dead on these lands. Acknowledging the story and stewardship of the indigenous hosts of Turtle Island is not only respectful, but appropriate. Turtle Island has a history that greatly exceeds what is written in most US history books. Each of these nations and tribes not only have a past in these lands, but they also have an ongoing story moving forward. These nearly seven hundred names represent people and nations who survived, and they deserve not only to be acknowledged, but also honored.

Absentee-Shawnee Tribe of Indians of Oklahoma
Addai Caddo Tribe
Agdaagux Tribe of King Cove
Agua Caliente Band of Cahuilla Indians
Ak-Chin Indian Community
Akiachak Native Community (IRA)
Akiak Native Community (IRA)
Alabama-Coushatta Tribe of Texas
Alabama-Quassarte Tribal Town
Alatna Village
Aleut Community of St. Paul Island
Algaaciq Native Village
Allakaket Village
Alturas Rancheria
Angoon Community Association
Aniak Traditional Council
Anvik Traditional Council
Apache Tribe of Oklahoma
Arctic Village
Aroostook Band of Micmacs
Asaʼcarsarmiut Tribe
Atmautluak Traditional Council
Atqasuk Village
Augustine Band of Cahuilla Indians
Bad River Band of the Lake Superior Tribe
Barona Band of Mission Indians

Battle Mountain Band (Te-Moak Tribe of Western Shoshone Indians of Nevada)
Bay Mills Indian Community of Michigan
Bear River Band of Rohnerville Rancheria
Beaver Creek Indians
Beaver Village Council
Benton Paiute–U-tu Utu Gwaitu Paiute Tribe
Berry Creek Rancheria of Maidu Indians of California
Big Lagoon Rancheria
Big Pine Paiute Tribe of the Owens Valley
Big Sandy Rancheria
Big Valley Rancheria
Biloxi-Chitimacha Confederation of Muskogee
Birch Creek Tribal Council
Bishop Paiute Tribe
Blackfeet Nation
Blue Lake Rancheria
Bois Forte Band of Chippewa
Bridgeport Paiute Indian Colony
Buena Vista Rancheria of Me-Wuk Indians
Burns Paiute Tribe
Cabazon Band of Mission Indians

Cachil Dehe Band of Wintun Indians of
the Colusa Indian Rancheria
Caddo Indian Tribe of Oklahoma
Cahto Tribe of the Laytonville Rancheria
Cahuilla Band of Mission Indians of the
Cahuilla Reservation
California Valley Miwok Tribe
Campo Band of Mission Indians
Carson Colony (Washoe Tribes of
Nevada and California)
Capitan Grande Band of Diegueño
Mission Indians of California: Barona
Group of Capitan Grande Band of
Mission Indians of the Barona
Reservation; Viejas (Baron Long)
Group of Capitan Grande Band of
Mission Indians of the Viejas
Reservation
Catawba Indian Nation
Cayuga Nation of Indians
Cedarville Rancheria
Central Council Tlingit and Haida
Indian Tribes of Alaska
Chalkyitsik Village
Cheesh-Na Tribal Council
Chemehuevi Tribe
Cher-Ae Heights Indian Community of
the Trinidad Rancheria
Cher-O-Creek Intra Tribal Indians
Cheroenhaka (Nottoway)
Cherokee Nation
Cherokee Tribe of Northeast Alabama
Cherokees of Southeast Alabama
Chevak Native Village
Cheyenne Arapaho Tribes of Oklahoma
Cheyenne River Sioux Tribe
Chickahominy Indian Tribe
Chickaloon Native Village
Chickasaw Nation
Chicken Ranch Rancheria of Me-Wuk
Indians of California
Chignik Bay Tribal Council
Chignik Lake Village Council
Chilkat Indian Village (Klukwan) (IRA)
Chilkoot Indian Association (IRA)
Chinik Eskimo Community (aka
Golovin)

Chinook Indian Tribe
Chippewa Cree Tribe of the Rocky Boy's
Reservation
Chitimacha Indian Tribe of Louisiana
Chitina Traditional Indian Village
Council
Choctaw Nation of Oklahoma
Choctaw-Apache Community of Ebarb
Chuloonawick Native Village
Circle Native Community (IRA)
Citizen Potawatomi Nation
Clifton Choctaw
Cloverdale Rancheria
Cocopah Tribe of Arizona
Coeur d'Alene Tribe
Coharie Intra-Tribal Council, Inc.
Cold Springs Rancheria
Colorado River Indian Tribe
Comanche Nation
Confederated Salish and Kootenai Tribes
of the Flathead Nation
Confederated Tribes and Bands of the
Yakama Nation
Confederated Tribes of Chehalis
Reservation
Confederated Tribes of Colville
Reservation
Confederated Tribes of Coos, Lower
Umpqua and Siuslaw Indians
Confederated Tribes of Grand Ronde
Community of Oregon
Confederated Tribes of Siletz Reservation
Confederated Tribes of the Goshute
Reservation
Confederated Tribes of the Umatilla
Indian Reservation
Confederated Tribes of Warm Springs
Reservation of Oregon
Connecticut
Coquille Tribe
Cortina Band of Wintun Indians
Coushatta Indian Tribe of Louisiana
Cow Creek Band of Umpqua Tribe of
Indians
Cowlitz Indian Tribe
Coyote Valley Band of Pomo Indians
Craig Community Association (IRA)

Crow Creek Sioux Tribe

Crow Nation

Curyung Tribal Council

Delaware Nation

Delaware Tribe of Indians

Douglas Indian Association (IRA)

Dresslerville Colony (Washoe Tribes of Nevada and California)

Dry Creek Rancheria Band of Pomo Indians

Duckwater Shoshone Tribe of the Duckwater Reservation

Eastern Band of Cherokee Indians

Eastern Pequot Tribal Nation

Eastern Shawnee Tribe of Oklahoma

Echota Cherokee Tribe of Alabama

Edisto Natchez Kusso Tribe of South Carolina

Edzeno' Native Village Council

Egegik Village

Eklutna Native Village

Ekwok Village

Elem Indian Colony

Elk Valley Rancheria

Elnu Abenaki Tribe

Elko Band Council (Te-Moak Tribe of Western Shoshone Indians of Nevada)

Ely Shoshone Tribe of Nevada

Emmonak Village

Enterprise Rancheria Estom Yumeka Maidu Tribe

Evansville Village (aka Bettles Field)

Ewiiaapaayp Band of Kumeyaay Indians

Federated Indians of Graton Rancheria

Flandreau Santee Sioux Tribe

Fond du Lac Reservation Business Committee

Forest County Potawatomi Community

Fort Belknap Tribe

Fort Bidwell Paiute Indian Reservation

Fort Independence Indian Reservation

Fort McDermitt Paiute and Shoshone Tribes

Fort McDowell Yavapai Nation

Fort Mojave Indian Tribe of Arizona, California and Nevada

Fort Peck Tribes of Assiniboine and Sioux Tribes

Fort Sill Apache Tribe of Oklahoma

Four Winds Tribe, Louisiana Cherokee

Galena Village aka Louden Village

Georgia Tribe of Eastern Cherokee

Gila River Indian Community

Grand Caillou/Dulac Band

Grand Portage Reservation Tribal Council

Grand Traverse Band of Ottawa and Chippewa Indians

Greenville Rancheria

Grindstone Indian Rancheria

Guidiville Indian Rancheria

Gulkana Village

Gwichyaa Zhee Gwich'in Tribal Government–Native Village of Fort Yukon (IRA)

Habematolel Pomo of Upper Lake

Haliwa-Saponi Indian Tribe

Hannahville Indian Community of Michigan

Havasupai Tribe

Ho-Chunk Nation

Hoh Indian Tribe

Holy Cross Village

Hoonah Indian Association (IRA)

Hoopa Valley Tribe

Hopi Tribe

Hopland Band of Pomo Indians

Houlton Band of Maliseet Indians

Hualapai Tribe

Hughes Village–Hodotl'eekkaakk'e Tribe

Huslia Village

Hydaburg Cooperative Association (IRA)

Igiugig Village

Iipay Nation of Santa Ysabel Band

Inaja-Cosmit Band of Mission Indians

Inupiat Community of the Arctic Slope (IRA)

Ione Band of Miwok Indians

Iowa Tribe of Kansas and Nebraska

Iowa Tribe of Oklahoma

Iqurmiut Traditonal Council

Isle de Jean Charles Band

Ivanoff Bay Village
Jackson Rancheria
Jamestown S'Klallam Tribe
Jamul Indian Village
Jena Band of Choctaw Indians
Jicarilla Apache Nation
Juaneno Band of Mission Indians
Kaguyak Village
Kaibab Band of Paiute Indians
Kaktovik Village aka Barter Island
Kalispel Tribe
Kaltag Tribal Council
Karuk Tribe of California
Kaw Nation
Kenaitze Indian Tribe (IRA)
Ketchikan Indian Community
Kewa Pueblo
Keweenaw Bay Indian Community of
    Michigan
Kialegee Tribal Town
Kickapoo Traditional Tribe of Texas
Kickapoo Tribe in Kansas
Kickapoo Tribe of Oklahoma
King Island Native Community (IRA)
King Salmon Tribe
Kiowa Tribe of Oklahoma
Klamath Tribes
Klawock Cooperative Association
Knik Tribe
Koasek Abenaki Tribe
Koi Nation of Northern California
Kokhanok Village
Kootenai Tribe of Idaho
Koyukuk Native Village
La Jolla Band of Luiseno Indians
La Posta Band of Mission Indians
Lac Courte Oreilles Band of Lake
    Superior Chippewa Indians
Lac du Flambeau Band of Lake Superior
    Chippewa Indians
Lac Vieux Desert Band of Lake Superior
    Chippewa
Las Vegas Paiute Tribe
Leech Lake Band of Ojibwe
Lenape Indian Tribe of Delaware
Levelock Village Council
Lime Village

Lipan Apache Tribe of Texas
Little River Band of Ottawa Indians
Little Shell Tribe of Chippewa Indians of
    Montana
Little Traverse Bay Bands of Odawa Indians
Lone Pine Paiute Shoshone Reservation
Los Coyotes Band of Cahuilla and
    Cupeno Indians
Louisiana Choctaw Tribe
Lovelock Paiute Tribe
Lower Brule Sioux Tribe
Lower Elwha Klallam Tribe
Lower Lake Rancheria
Lower Muskogee Creek Tribe
Lower Sioux Indian Community
Lumbee Tribe of North Carolina
Lummi Nation
Lytton Rancheria of California
Ma-Chis Lower Creek Indian Tribe of
    Alabama
Makah Indian Tribe
Manchester Point Arena Band of Pomo
    Indians
Manley Hot Springs Village
Manokotak Village
Manzanita Band of Kumeyaay Nation
Mashantucket Pequot Tribe
Mashpee Wampanoag Tribe
Massachusetts
Match-E-Be-Nash-She-Wish Band of
    Pottawatomi Indians
Mattaponi
McGrath Native Village
Mechoopda Indian Tribe of Chico
    Rancheria
Meherrin Nation
Mendas Cha-Ag Tribe of Healy Lake
Menominee Indian Tribe of Wisconsin
Mentasta Lake Traditional Council
Mesa Grande Band of Mission Indians
Mescalero Apache Tribe
Metlakatla Indian Community, Annette
    Island Reserve
Miami Tribe of Oklahoma
Miccosukee Indian Tribe of Florida
Middletown Rancheria
Mille Lacs Band of Ojibwe

Minnesota Chippewa Tribe
Mississippi Band of Choctaw Indians
Mississquoi Abenaki Tribe
Moapa Band of Paiutes
Modoc Tribe of Oklahoma
Mohegan Indian Tribe
Monacan Indian Nation
Mooretown Rancheria
Morongo Band of Mission Indians
Mowa Band of Choctaw Indians
Muckleshoot Indian Tribe
Muscogee (Creek) Nation
Naknek Native Village
Nansemond Tribe
Nanticoke Indian Association, Inc.
Nanticoke-Lenni Lenape Tribal Nation
Narragansett Indian Tribe
Native Village of Afognak
Native Village of Akhiok
Native Village of Akutan
Native Village of Aleknagik
Native Village of Ambler
Native Village of Atka
Native Village of Barrow Inupiat
    Traditional Government
Native Village of Belkofski
Native Village of Bill Moore's Slough
Native Village of Brevig Mission
Native Village of Buckland (IRA)
Native Village of Cantwell
Native Village of Chenega aka Chanega
Native Village of Chignik Lagoon
    Council
Native Village of Chignik Lagoon
Native Village of Chitina
Native Village of Chuathbaluk (Russian
    Mission, Kuskokwim)
Native Village of Council
Native Village of Crooked Creek
Native Village of Deering
Native Village of Diomede (IRA) (aka
    Inalik)
Native Village of Eagle
Native Village of Eek
Native Village of Eklutna
Native Village of Ekuk
Native Village of Ekwok

Native Village of Elim (IRA)
Native Village of Eyak (Cordova)
Native Village of False Pass
Native Village of Gakona
Native Village of Gambell
Native Village of Georgetown
Native Village of Goodnews Bay
Native Village of Hamilton
Native Village of Hooper Bay
Native Village of Kanatak (IRA)
Native Village of Karluk (IRA)
Native Village of Kasigluk
Native Village of Kiana
Native Village of Kipnuk
Native Village of Kivalina (IRA)
Native Village of Kluti-Kaah (aka Copper
    Center)
Native Village of Kobuk
Native Village of Kongiganak
Native Village of Kotzebue (IRA)
Native Village of Koyuk (IRA)
Native Village of Kwigillingok (IRA)
Native Village of Kwinhagak (IRA)
Native Village of Larsen Bay
Native Village of Marshall (aka Fortuna
    Ledge)
Native Village of Mary's Igloo
Native Village of Mekoryuk (IRA)
Native Village of Minto
Native Village of Nanwalek (aka English
    Bay)
Native Village of Napaimute
Native Village of Napakiak (IRA)
Native Village of Napaskiak
Native Village of Nelson Lagoon
Native Village of Nightmute
Native Village of Nikolski (IRA)
Native Village of Noatak (IRA)
Native Village of Noorvik (IRA)
Native Village of Nuiqsut (aka Nooiksut)
Native Village of Nunapitchuk (IRA)
Native Village of Ouzinkie
Native Village of Paimiut
Native Village of Perryville
Native Village of Pitka's Point
Native Village of Point Hope (IRA)
Native Village of Point Lay

Native Village of Port Heiden
Native Village of Port Lions
Native Village of Saint. Michael (IRA)
Native Village of Savoonga (IRA)
Native Village of Selawik
Native Village of Shaktoolik (IRA)
Native Village of Sheldon Point - Nunam
    Iqua Tribal Council
Native Village of Shishmaref (IRA)
Native Village of Shungnak (IRA)
Native Village of South Naknek
Native Village of Stevens (IRA)
Native Village of Tanacross
Native Village of Tanana (IRA)
Native Village of Tatitlek (IRA)
Native Village of Tazlina
Native Village of Tetlin (IRA)
Native Village of Tyonek (IRA)
Native Village of Unalakleet (IRA)
Native Village of Wales (IRA)
Native Village of White Mountain
    (IRA)
Navajo Nation
Nenana Traditional Council
New Koliganek Village Council
New Jersey
New Stuyahok Village
Newhalen Village
Newtok Traditional Council
Nez Perce Tribe
Nikolai Village
Ninilchik Traditional Council
Nipmuc Nation
Nisqually Indian Tribe
Nome Eskimo Community
Nondalton Village
Nooksack Indian Tribe
Northern Arapaho Tribe
Northern Cheyenne Tribe
Northfork Rancheria
Northway Village
Northwestern Band of the Shoshone
    Nation
Nottawaseppi Huron Band of
    Potawatomi
Nottoway Indian Tribe of Virginia
Nulato Village

Nulhegan Band of the Coosuk Abenaki
    Nation
Nunakauyarmiut Tribe
Occaneechi Band of teh Saponi Nation
Oglala Sioux Tribe
Ohkay Owingeh
Omaha Tribe of Nebraska
Oneida Indian Nation
Oneida Tribe of Indians of Wisconsin
Onondaga Indian Nation
Organized Village of Grayling (IRA) (aka
    Holikachuk)
Organized Village of Kake (IRA)
Organized Village of Kasaan (IRA)
Organized Village of Kwethluk (IRA)
Organized Village of Saxman (IRA)
Orutsararmiut Traditional Native
    Council
Osage Nation
Oscarville Traditional Village
Otoe-Missouria Tribe of Indians
Ottawa Tribe of Oklahoma
Paiute Indian Tribe of Utah
Paiute-Shoshone Tribe of the Fallon
    Reservation and Colony
Pala Band of Mission Indians
Pamunkey Indian Tribe
Pascua Yaqui Tribe of Arizona
Paskenta Band of Nomlaki Indians
Passamaquoddy Tribe–Indian Township
    Reservation
Passamaquoddy Tribe–Pleasant Point
    Reservation
Pattawomeck
Pauloff Harbor Village
Pauma/Yuima Band of Mission
    Indians
Pawnee Nation of Oklahoma
Pechanga Band of Mission Indians
Pedro Bay Village
Pee Dee Indian Tribe
Pee Dee Indian Nation of Upper South
    Carolina
Pee Dee Indian Tribe of South Carolina
Penobscot Indian Nation
Peoria Tribe of Oklahoma
Petersburg Indian Association (IRA)

Picayune Rancheria of Chukchansi
Indians
Pilot Point Tribal Council
Pilot Station Traditional Village
Pinoleville Pomo Nation
Piqua Shawnee Tribe
Piscataway Conoy Tribe
Piscataway Indian Nation
Pit River Tribe
Platinum Traditional Village Council
Poarch Band of Creek Indians
Pointe-Au-Chien Indian Tribe
Pokagon Band of Potawatomi Indians
Ponca Tribe of Nebraska
Ponca Tribe of Oklahoma
Port Gamble S'Klallam Tribe
Port Graham Village Council
Portage Creek Village (aka Ohgenakale)
Potter Valley Rancheria
Prairie Band Potawatomi Nation
Prairie Island Indian Community
Pribilof Islands Aleut Communities of St.
Paul and St. George Islands
Pueblo of Acoma
Pueblo of Cochiti
Pueblo of Isleta
Pueblo of Jemez
Pueblo of Laguna
Pueblo of Nambe
Pueblo of Picuris
Pueblo of Pojoaque
Pueblo of San Felipe
Pueblo of San Ildefonso
Pueblo of Sandia
Pueblo of Santa Ana
Pueblo of Santa Clara
Pueblo of Santo Domingo
Pueblo of Taos
Pueblo of Tesuque
Pueblo of Ysleta Del Sur
Pueblo of Zia
Pueblo of Zuni
Puyallup Tribe of Indians
Pyramid Lake Paiute Tribe
Qagan Tayagungin Tribe of Sand Point
Village
Qawalangin Tribe of Unalaska

Quapaw Tribe of Oklahoma
Quartz Valley Reservation
Quechan Tribe of the Fort Yuma Indian
Reservation
Quileute Tribe
Quinault Indian Nation
Ramapough Lenape Nation
Ramona Band of Cahuilla
Rampart Village
Rappahannock Tribe
Red Cliff Band of Lake Superior
Chippewa Indians
Red Lake Band of Chippewa Indians
Redding Rancheria
Redwood Valley Little River Band of
Pomo Indians
Reno-Sparks Indian Colony
Resighini Rancheria
Rincon Band of Mission Indians
Robinson Rancheria
Rosebud Sioux Tribe
Round Valley Reservation
Ruby Tribal Council
Sac and Fox Tribe of the Mississippi in
Iowa
Sac and Fox Nation of Missouri in
Kansas and Nebraska
Sac and Fox Nation of Oklahoma
Saginaw Chippewa Indian Tribe
Salt River Pima-Maricopa Indian
Community
Samish Indian Tribe
San Carlos Apache Tribe
San Juan Southern Paiute Tribe
San Manuel Band of Mission Indians
San Pasqual Band of Diegueno Indians
Santa Rosa Band of Cahuilla Indians
Santa Rosa Rancheria Tachi Yokut Tribe
Santa Rosa Indian Community of the
Santa Rosa Rancheria
Santa Ynez Band Of Chumash Tribe
Santee Indian Organization
Santee Sioux Tribe
Sappony
Sauk-Suiattle Indian Tribe
Sault Ste. Marie Tribe of Chippewa
Indians

Scammon Bay Traditional Council
Schaghticoke Tribal Nation
Scotts Valley Band of Pomo Indians
Seldovia Village Tribe (IRA)
Seminole Indian Tribe of Florida
Seminole Nation of Oklahoma
Seneca Nation of Indians
Seneca-Cayuga Tribe of Oklahoma
Shageluk Native Village (IRA)
Shakopee Mdewakanton Sioux
  Community
Shawnee Tribe
Sheep Ranch Rancheria of Me-Wuk
  Indians
Sherwood Valley Rancheria
Shingle Springs Rancheria
Shinnecock Indian Nation
Shoalwater Bay Indian Tribe
Shoshone Tribe of Wind River Indian
  Reservation
Shoshone-Bannock Tribes of the Fort
  Hall Reservation
Shoshone-Paiute Tribes of the Duck
  Valley Indian Reservation
Sisseton-Wahpeton Oyate of the Lake
  Traverse Reservation
Sitka Tribe of Alaska (IRA)
Skagway Traditional Village
Skokomish Indian Tribe
Skull Valley Band of Goshutes Indians
Smith River Rancheria
Snoqualmie IndianTribe
Soboba Band of Luiseno Indians
Sokaogon Band of the Lake Superior
  Chippewa Indians
South Fork Band Council (Te-Moak
  Tribe of Western Shoshone Indians of
  Nevada)
Southeastern Mvskoke Nation, Inc.,
  formerly Star Clan of Muscogee
  Creeks
Southern Ute Indian Tribe
Spirit Lake Tribe
Spokane Tribe
Squaxin Island Tribe
St. Croix Chippewa Indians
St. George Traditional Council

St. Regis Mohawk Tribe
Standing Rock Sioux Tribe
Stebbins Community Association (IRA)
Stewart Community Council (Washoe
  Tribe of Nevada and California)
Stewarts Point Rancheria
Stillaguamish Tribe
Stockbridge-Munsee Community
Summit Lake Paiute Tribe of Nevada
Sun'aq Tribe of Kodiak
Suquamish Indian Tribe
Susanville Indian Rancheria
Swinomish Indian Tribe
Sycuan Band of the Kumeyaay Nation
Table Mountain Rancheria
Takotna Village
Tangirnaq Native Village aka Woody
  Island Tribal Council
Tejon Indian Tribe
Telida Native Village Council
Teller Traditional Council
Te-Moak of Western Shoshone Tribes of
  Nevada
The Eastern Chickahominy
The Golden Hill Paugussett
The Powhatan Renape Nation
The Waccamaw Indian People
Thlopthlocco Tribal Town
Three Affiliated Tribes of Mandan,
  Hidatsa and Arikara Nation
Timbisha Shoshone Tribe
Tohono O'odham Nation
Tolowa Dee-ni' Nation
Tonawanda Band of Seneca
Tonkawa Tribe of Oklahoma
Tonto Apache Tribe
Torres-Martinez Desert Cahuilla Indians
Traditional Village of Togiak
Tulalip Tribes
Tule River Indian Reservation
Tuluksak Native Community (IRA)
Tunica-Biloxi Tribe of Louisiana
Tuntutuliak Traditional Council
Tununak Council (IRA)
Tuolumne Me-Wuk Tribe
Turtle Mountain Band of Chippewa
  Indians

Tuscarora Nation
Twenty-Nine Palms Band of Mission
  Indians
Twin Hills Village Council
Ugashik Traditional Village Council
Umkumiut Native Village
Unga Tribal Council
United Auburn Indian Community
United Cherokee Ani-Yun-Wiya Nation
United Houma Nation
United Keetoowah Band of Cherokee
  Indians
Unkechaug Indian Nation
Upper Lake Band of Pomo Indians
Upper Mattaponi Tribe
Upper Sioux Community
Upper Skagit Indian Tribe
Ute Indian Tribe–Uintah and Ouray
Ute Mountain Ute Tribe
Venetie Village Council
Viejas Band of Kumeyaay Indians
Village of Alakanuk
Village of Anaktuvuk Pass
Village of Chefornak
Village of Clarks Point
Village of Dot Lake
Village of Iliamna
Village of Kalskag
Village of Kotlik
Village of Lower Kalskag
Village of Ohogamiut
Village of Old Harbor
Village of Red Devil

Village of Salamatoff
Village of Sleetmute
Village of Solomon
Village of Stony River
Village of Wainwright
Waccamaw Siouan Tribe
Walker River Paiute Tribe
Wampanoag Tribe of Gay Head
  (Aquinnah)
Washoe Tribes of Nevada and California
Wassamasaw Tribe of Varnertown
  Indians
Wells Indian Colony Band Council
White Earth Reservation Business
  Committee
White Mountain Apache Tribe
Wichita and Affiliated Tribes
Wilton Rancheria
Winnebago Tribe of Nebraska
Winnemucca Indian Colony Council
Wiyot Tribe
Woodfords Community Council
Wrangell Cooperative Association (IRA)
Wyandotte Nation
Yakutat Tlingit Tribe
Yankton Sioux Tribe
Yavapai-Apache Nation
Yavapai-Prescott Indian Tribe
Yerington Paiute Tribe
Yocha Dene Wintun Nation
Yomba Shoshone Tribe
Yupiit of Andreafski
Yurok Tribe

Notes

INTRODUCTION

[1]This section was adapted from Mark Charles, "Lessons from a Donkey," September 28, 2011, https://worship.calvin.edu/resources/resource-library/lessons-from -a-donkey.

1 THE DOCTRINE OF DISCOVERY AND WHY IT MATTERS

[1]Robert J. Miller, Jacinta Ruru, Larissa Behrendt, and Tracey Lindberg, *Discovering Indigenous Lands* (New York: Oxford University Press, 2010), 1.

[2]Latin translation: *Bullariym Patronatus Portugalliae Regum*. See the following for the English translation: "Dum Diversas," Doctrine of Discovery, Indigenous Values, July 23, 2018, www.doctrineofdiscovery.org/dum-diversas/.

[3]"The Bull Romanus Pontifex," Doctrine of Discovery, Indigenous Values, July 23, 2018, https://doctrineofdiscovery.org/the-bull-romanus-pontifex-nicholas-v/.

[4]"The Bull Romanus Pontifex."

[5]"The Bull Romanus Pontifex."

[6]"The Bull Romanus Pontifex."

[7]Willie James Jennings, *The Christian Imagination* (New Haven, CT: Yale University Press, 2010), 16.

[8]Jennings, *Christian Imagination,* 18.

[9]Jennings, 19.

[10]Jennings, 22.

[11]"Inter Caetera," Doctrine of Discovery, Indigenous Values, July 23, 2018, https:// doctrineofdiscovery.org/inter-caetera.

[12]"Inter Caetera."

[13]"Inter Caetera."

[14]Seth Adema, editor, *The Christian Doctrine of Discovery: A North American History* (Doctrine of Discovery Task Force of the Christian Reformed Church of North America: November 2013), 10.

[15]"Inter Caetera."

[16]Edward M. Sullivan, "The Faith of Columbus the Evangelizer," National Christopher Columbus Association, https://christophercolumbus.org/2006/10/11/the -faith-of-columbus-the-evangelizer, accessed May 28, 2019.

[17]Christopher Columbus, *Libro de las profecías*, trans. and ed. Delno C. West and August Kling (Gainesville: University of Florida Press, 1991), 101.

[18]Turtle Island is the indigenous name for the land we now identify as the United States.

[19]Stephen T. Newcomb, *Pagans in the Promised Land: Decoding the Doctrine of Christian Discovery* (Golden, CO: Fulcrum, 2008), 94.

[20]Seth Adema, editor, *Christian Doctrine of Discovery*, 2.

2 THE POWER OF NARRATIVES AND THE IMAGINATION

[1]Peter Berger and Thomas Luckmann, *The Social Construction of Reality* (New York: Random House, 1966).

[2]Reinhold Niebuhr in *Moral Man in Immoral Society* posits the challenge that an externalized institution does not have the moral capacity of individual humans. Niebuhr acknowledges the reality of externalized systems but also sees the ethical limitations of that system. See Reinhold Niebuhr, *Moral Man and Immoral Society: A Study in Ethics* (New York: Charles Scribner's Sons, 1995).

[3]See also Soong-Chan Rah, *Many Colors: Cultural Intelligence for a Changing Church* (Chicago: Moody Publications, 2010).

[4]C. Wright Mills, *The Sociological Imagination* (New York: Oxford University Press, 1959), 6-7.

[5]William Cavanaugh, *Torture and Eucharist* (Malden, MA: Blackwell Publishing, 1998), 57.

[6]Willie James Jennings, *The Christian Imagination* (New Haven: Yale University Press, 2010), 6.

[7]Walter Brueggemann, *The Prophetic Imagination* (Minneapolis: Fortress Press, 2001), 3.

[8]Jennings, *Christian Imagination*, 6.

[9]Franklin Graham, cited from Facebook account, June 4, 2017, www.facebook .com/FranklinGraham/posts/since-911-i-have-been-warning-america-about -the-dangers-of-the-teachings-of-isla/1528265163896326/. See also, Carol E. Lee, "Rev. Franklin Graham: Islam 'Evil,'" Politico Now Blog, October 3, 2010, www

.politico.com/blogs/politico-now/2010/10/rev-franklin-graham-islam
-evil-029683.

[10]See Mae Cannon, Lisa Sharon Harper, Troy Jackson, and Soong-Chan Rah, *Forgive Us: Confessions of Compromised Faith* (Grand Rapids: Zondervan, 2014).

[11]George Lakoff, *Women, Fire, and Dangerous Things* (Chicago: The University of Chicago Press), xi.

[12]"Here's Donald Trump's Presidential Announcement Speech," *Time*, June 16, 2015, http://time.com/3923128/donald-trump-announcement-speech.

[13]Louis Nelson, "Trump Told Howard Stern It's OK to Call Ivanka a 'Piece of A--,'" Politico, October 8, 2016, www.politico.com/story/2016/10/trump-ivanka-piece-of-ass-howard-stern-229376.

[14]"Presidential Candidate Donald Trump at the Family Leadership Summit," C-SPAN, July 18, 2015, www.c-span.org/video/?327045-5/presidential-candidate-donald-trump-family-leadership-summit.

[15]David Brody, "Exclusive: Donald Trump Says If Evangelicals Show Up and Vote 'We're Going to Win the Election,'" CBN News, October 27, 2016, www1.cbn.com/thebrodyfile/archive/2016/10/27/brody-file-exclusive-donald-trump-says-if-evangelicals-show-up-and-vote-we-rsquo-re-going-to-win-the-election.

[16]Lakoff, *Women, Fire and Dangerous Things*, xvii.

[17]Walter Wink, *The Powers That Be: Theology for a New Millennium* (New York: Galilee, 1989), 1.

[18]See Soong-Chan Rah, *The Next Evangelicalism: Freeing the Church from Western Cultural Captivity* (Downers Grove, IL: InterVarsity Press, 2009).

[19]Wink, *Powers That Be*, 3.

[20]Wink, *Powers That Be*, 5.

[21]Wink, *Powers That Be*, 7.

[22]Walter Brueggemann in the foreword to James E. Atwood's *America and Its Guns: A Theological Expose* (Eugene, OR: Wipf and Stock, 2012), xi-xii.

[23]Wink, *Powers That Be*, 35-36.

[24]See Stephen C. Mott, *Biblical Ethics and Social Change* (New York: Oxford University Press, 1982).

4 THE RISE AND DEFENSE OF CHRISTENDOM

Eusebius, *Life of Constantine*, trans. Averil Cameron and Stuart G. Hall (Oxford: Clarendon Press, 1999), 81.

[1]Eusebius Pamphilus, *The Ecclesiastical History of Eusebius Pamphilus*, trans. C.F. Cruse (London: George Bell & Sons, 1908), 417.

[2]Eusebius, *Ecclesiastical History*, 320.

[3]Eusebius, *Ecclesiastical History*, 321.

[4]Eusebius, *Ecclesiastical History*, 374.

[5]Eusebius, *Life of Constantine*, 81.

[6]Eusebius, *Life of Constantine*, 81.

[7]Raymond Van Dam, *Remembering Constantine at the Milvian Bridge* (Cambridge, UK: Cambridge University Press, 2011), 8.

[8]Van Dam, *Remembering Constantine*, 8.

[9]Van Dam, *Remembering Constantine*, 14.

[10]Van Dam, *Remembering Constantine*, 14.

[11]John Langan, "The Elements of St. Augustine's Just War Theory," *The Journal of Religious Ethics* 12, no. 1 (Spring 1984): 24.

[12]Justo Gonzalez, *The Story of Christianity: The Early Church to the Dawn of the Reformation*, vol. 1 (New York: Harper Collins, 1984), 214.

[13]Saint Augustine of Hippo, "The Political Writings of Saint Augustine; Treatise on the Correction of the Donatists," ed. Henry Paolucci (Washington DC, 1962), 212.

[14]Richard Shelly Hartigan, "Saint Augustine on War and Killing: The Problem of the Innocent" in *Journal of the History of Ideas* 27, no. 2 (April-June 1966): 196.

[15]Augustine, "The Political Writings of Saint Augustine," 214.

[16]Langan, "Elements of St. Augustine's Just War," 25.

[17]Nico Vorster, "Just War and Virtue: Revisiting Augustine and Thomas Aquinas," *South African Journal of Philosophy* 34, no. 1 (2015): 60.

[18]St. Thomas Aquinas, *The "Summa Theologica" of St. Thomas Aquinas*, trans. Fathers of the English Dominican Province (London: R. & T. Washbourne, LTD, 1920), 154.

[19]Vorster, "Just War and Virtue," 61.

[20]The ideas in this paragraph come from Seth Adema, editor, *The Christian Doctrine of Discovery: A North American History* (Doctrine of Discovery Task Force of the Christian Reformed Church of North America, November 2013), 7.

[21]Eusebius, *Ecclesiastical History*, 3.

[22]Eusebius, *Ecclesiastical History*, 419.

[23]Eusebius, *Ecclesiastical History*, 418.

[24]Eusebius, *Ecclesiastical History*, 417.

5 A DYSFUNCTIONAL THEOLOGY BROUGHT TO THE "NEW" WORLD

[1]US Constitution, art. I, sec. 2., cl. 2.

[2]"The Complete Transcript of Netanyahu's Address to Congress," *The Washington Post*, March 3, 2015, www.washingtonpost.com/news/post-politics/wp/2015/03/03/full-text-netanyahus-address-to-congress/?utm_term=.3e685fc2056e.

[3]John Winthrop, "A Model of Christian Charity," accessed May 26, 2018, http://templetonhonorscollege.com/wp-content/uploads/2014/06/5.-A-Model-of-Christian-Charity-by-Governor-John-Winthrop.pdf.

[4]Winthrop, "A Model of Christian Charity."

[5]Kelly Brown Douglas, *Stand Your Ground* (Maryknoll, New York: Orbis Books, 2015), 5.

[6]Douglas, *Stand Your Ground,* 6.

[7]Hugh A. MacDougall, *Racial Myth in English History: Trojans, Teutons, and Anglo-Saxons* (London: University Press of New England, 1982), 2.

[8]Douglas, *Stand Your Ground,* 8.

[9]Douglas, *Stand Your Ground,* 8-9.

[10]John Wilsey, *American Exceptionalism and Civil Religion* (Downers Grove, IL: IVP Academic, 2015), 29.

[11]Steven T. Newcomb, *Pagans in the Promised Land: Decoding the Doctrine of Christian Discovery* (Golden, CO: Fulcrum, 2008), 37.

[12]Donald Trump, "2018 Naval Academy Commencement Address," *The Atlantic,* May 25, 2018, www.theatlantic.com/politics/archive/2018/05/read-president-trumps-us-naval-academy-commencement-address/561206/.

[13]Wilsey, *American Exceptionalism and Civil Religion,* 31.

[14]Roger Cohen, "Palin's American Exception," *The New York Times,* September 25, 2008, www.nytimes.com/2008/09/25/opinion/25Cohen.html.

[15]Greg Jaffe, "Obama's New Patriotism," *The Washington Post,* June 3, 2015, www.washingtonpost.com/sf/national/2015/06/03/obama-and-american-exceptionalism/?utm_term=.b9984fdf2c53.

[16]"Hillary Clinton Acceptance Speech," C-SPAN, July 28, 2016, www.c-span.org/video/?412848-101/hillary-clinton-acceptance-speech.

[17]"Full Transcript: Second 2016 Presidential Debate," *Politico,* October 10, 2016, www.politico.com/story/2016/10/2016-presidential-debate-transcript-229519.

[18]Will Drabold, "Read Cory Booker's Speech at the Democratic Convention," *Time,* July 26, 2016, http://time.com/4421756/democratic-convention-cory-booker-transcript-speech.

6 EXCEPTIONALISM AND THE FOUNDING DOCUMENTS OF THE UNITED STATES

[1]US Declaration of Independence (1776).

[2]Mark Charles, "The Doctrine of Discovery, War, and the Myth of America," *Leaven* 24:3, article 9, 2016, 150, http://digitalcommons.pepperdine.edu/leaven/vol24/iss3/9.

[3]Anthony Hoekema, *Created in God's Image* (Grand Rapids, MI: Eerdmans Publishing, 1986), 19.

[4]Richard Twiss, *Rescuing the Gospel from the Cowboys* (Downers Grove, IL: InterVarsity Press, 2015), 15.

[5]Willie James Jennings, *The Christian Imagination* (New Haven: Yale University Press, 2010), 58-59.

[6]See Steven Newcomb, *Pagans in the Promised Land: Decoding the Doctrine of Christian Discovery* (Golden, CO: Fulcrum, 2008).

[7]Cf. Sangkeun Kim, *Strange Names of God: The Missionary Translation of the Divine Name and the Chinese Responses to Matteo Ricci's* Shangti *in Late Ming China, 1583–1644* (Berlin: Peter Lang, 2005).

[8]US Constitution, art. I, sec. 2., cl. 3.

[9]US Census Bureau, National Health Statistics Reports, "Income, Poverty and Health Insurance Coverage in the United States: 2017," September 12, 2018, www.census.gov/newsroom/press-releases/2018/income-poverty.html.

[10]Stephen J. Rose and Heidi I. Hartmann, "Still a Man's Labor Market: The Slowly Narrowing Gender Wage Gap," Institute for Women's Policy Research, https://iwpr.org/publications/still-mans-labor-market.

[11]Peter Wagner and Joshua Aiken, "Racial Disparities in United States Prisons and Jails," Prison Policy Initiative, December 2016, www.prisonpolicy.org/graphs/disparities2010/US_racial_disparities_2010.html.

[12]See also Michelle Alexander, *The New Jim Crow: Mass Incarceration in the Age of Colorblindness* (New York: The New Press, 2010) and Dominique Gilliard, *Rethinking Incarceration: Advocating for Justice that Restores* (Downers Grove, IL: InterVarsity Press, 2018).

[13]Roe v. Wade, 410 S. Ct. 113. See also Roe v. Wade (website), www.phschool.com/curriculum_support/interactive_constitution/scc/scc35.htm.

[14]Curtiss Paul DeYoung, Michael O. Emerson, George Yancey, and Karen Chai Kim in *United by Faith* (New York: Oxford University Press USA, 2004), citing Lester B. Scherer, *Slavery and the Churches in Early America 1619–1819* (Grand Rapids: Eerdmans, 1983), 64.

[15]Ibram X. Kendi, *Stamped from the Beginning* (New York: Nation Books, 2016), 6.

[16]Albert Barnes, *The Church and Slavery* (Philadelphia: Parry & McMillan, 1857), 12-13.

[17]Charles F. Irons, *The Origins of Proslavery Christianity* (Chapel Hill: University of North Carolina Press, 2008), 1.

[18]James G. Birney, *The American Churches, The Bulwarks of American Slavery* (Newburyport, MA: Charles Whipple, 1842). Republished by Arno Press, 1969, 9-10.

7 Dysfunctional Theology and the Spread of Settler Colonialism

[1]"Understanding Implicit Bias," *The Ohio State University Kirwan Institute for the Study of Race and Ethnicity*, Kirwan Institute, May 27, 2019, http://kirwaninstitute.osu.edu/research/understanding-implicit-bias.

[2]John Wilsey, *American Exceptionalism and Civil Religion* (Downers Grove, IL: IVP Academic, 2015), 17.

[3]Wilsey, *American Exceptionalism and Civil Religion,* 17.

[4]Ace Collins, *Stories Behind the Hymns that Inspire America* (Grand Rapids: Zondervan, 2003), 9. See also, Melinda M. Ponder, "Majestic Lyrics" in *The Chicago Tribune*, July 4, 1993, www.chicagotribune.com/news/ct-xpm-1993-07-04 -9307040168-story.html.

[5]Katherine Lee Bates, "America the Beautiful," accessed May 27, 2019, https:// hymnary.org/text/o_beautiful_for_spacious_skies.

[6]Kenneth W. Osbeck, *Amazing Grace* (Grand Rapids: Kregel, 1990), 164.

[7]"Transcript of Dred Scot v. Sanford (sic)," Our Documents, accessed May 27, 2019, www.ourdocuments.gov/doc.php?flash=false&doc=29&page=transcript.

[8]"Cherokee Nation v. Georgia, 30 U.S. 1 (1831)," Justia: US Supreme Court (website), accessed May 27, 2019, https://supreme.justia.com/cases/federal/us/30/1/.

[9]"Cherokee Nation v. Georgia."

[10]The case 21 US 8 Wheat. 543 (1823) is referred to by various names: *Johnson*; *Johnson v. M'Intosh*, *M'Intosh*, etc. When citing a source, we will retain the author's specific way of citing the case. When we cite the case, we will use the short reference: *M'Intosh*.

[11]Robert J. Miller, Jacinta Ruru, Larissa Behrendt, and Tracey Lindberg, *Discovering Indigenous Lands* (New York: Oxford University Press, 2010), 9.

[12]Eric Kades, "History and Interpretation of the Great Case of Johnson v. M'Intosh," *Faculty Publications* 50 (2001), 67, 69, http://scholarship.law.wm.edu/facpubs/50.

[13]Stuart Banner, *How the Indians Lost Their Land: Law and Power on the Frontier* (Cambridge: Harvard University Press, 2005), 33.

[14]Kades, "History and Interpretation," 81-82.

[15]The estimated cost of the land purchased by the Illinois Land Company was $24,000 and $31,000 for the Wabash Land Company. Kades, 82, 85.

[16]Kades, "History and Interpretation," 84, 86.

[17]Kades, "History and Interpretation," 90.

[18]Robert J. Miller, Jacinta Ruru, Larissa Behrendt, and Tracey Lindberg, *Discovering Indigenous Lands: The Doctrine of Discovery in the English Colonies* (New York: Oxford University Press, 2010), 69.

[19]Miller, et.al., 76.

[20]Kades, "History and Interpretation," 94.

[21]Stephen T. Newcomb, *Pagans in the Promised Land: Decoding the Doctrine of Christian Discovery* (Golden, CO: Fulcrum, 2008), xvi.

[22]Lindsay G. Robertson, *Conquest by Law* (New York: Oxford University Press, 2005), 75-76.

[23]Newcomb, *Pagans in the Promised Land,* 94.

[24]Newcomb, xxi.

[25]Robertson, *Conquest by Law,* 57.

[26]Robertson, *Conquest by Law,* 118.

[27]Robertson, *Conquest by Law*, 125.

[28]Robertson, *Conquest by Law*, 126.

[29]"A Brief History of the Trail of Tears," Cherokee Nation (website), accessed May 27, 2019, www.cherokee.org/about-the-nation.

[30]Quotation from "The Loss of Turtle Island" drawn from script adapted for use in the CRCNA. The CRCNA acknowledges with deep thanks the work of MCC USA to develop this content and Kairos Canada's ongoing work on the Blanket Exercise—the inspiration for the US version, "The Loss of Turtle Island."

[31]Andrew K. Frank, "Trail of Tears (term)," *The Encyclopedia of Oklahoma History and Culture*, www.okhistory.org/publications/enc/entry.php?entry=TR003.

[32]Ken Drexler, "Indian Removal Act: Primary Documents in American History," Library of Congress Research Guides (website), January 30, 2019, www.loc.gov/rr /program/bib/ourdocs/Indian.html. See also Theda Perdue and Michael D. Green, *The Cherokee Nation and the Trail of Tears* (New York: Viking Penguin, 2007).

[33]William Shorey Coodey, "Letter dated August 13, 1840," in Vicki Rozema, editor, *Voices from the Trail of Tears* (Winston-Salem, NC: John F. Blair, 2003), 134.

[34]Daniel Sabine Butrick, "Excerpts for Journal," in Vicki Rozema, editor, *Voices from the Trail of Tears* (Winston-Salem, NC: John F. Blair, 2003), 147-148.

[35]Frank, "Trail of Tears."

[36]Benjamin Madley, *An American Genocide: The United States and the California Indian Catastrophe, 1846–1873* (Yale University Press, 2016), Introduction.

[37]Chris Clarke, "Untold History: The Survival of California's Indians," KCET: Tending the Wild, September 26, 2016, www.kcet.org/shows/tending-the-wild /untold-history-the-survival-of-californias-indians.

[38]"New Perspectives on the West," PBS, accessed May 27, 2019, www.pbs.org/weta /thewest/events/1850_1860.htm.

[39]"Native American Adversity in California," Pechanga Band of Luiseño Indians, accessed May 27, 2019, www.pechanga-nsn.gov/index.php/history/facts-or-myths /pechanga-history-fact-or-myth/native-american-adversity-in-california.

[40]Peter Burnett, "The State of the State Address," The Governors' Gallery, accessed May 27, 2019, http://governors.library.ca.gov/addresses/s_01-Burnett2.html.

[41]"Massacre at Wounded Knee," *Eyewitness to History*, accessed May 27, 2019, www .eyewitnesstohistory.com/knee.htm.

[42]"Medal of Honor Recipients: Indian Wars Period," US Army Center of Military History August 13, 2013, https://history.army.mil/moh/indianwars.html.

8 Genocide, the Impact of a Dysfunctional Theology

[1]Emil Brunner, *Man in Revolt* (Philadelphia: The Westminster Press, 1939), 140.

[2]Calvin Luther Martin, *In the Spirit of the Earth: Rethinking History and Time* (Baltimore: Johns Hopkins University Press, 1992), 18.

[3]Willie James Jennings, *The Christian Imagination* (New Haven: Yale University Press, 2010), 40, 58, 59.

[4]Richard H. Pratt, "The Advantages of Mingling Indians with Whites," in *Proceedings of the National Conference of Charities and Corrections*, ed. Isabel C. Barrows (Boston: Press of Geo. H.Ellis, 1892), 46.

[5]Pratt, "The Advantages of Mingling Indians with Whites," 50-51.

[6]Pratt, "The Advantages of Mingling Indians with Whites," 51.

[7]Jennings, *The Christian Imagination*, 35-36.

[8]Pratt, "The Advantages of Mingling Indians with Whites," 57.

[9]Dietrich Bonhoeffer, *Creation and Fall* (New York: Touchstone, 1959), 57.

[10]Bonhoeffer, *Creation and Fall*, 51-58.

[11]Pratt, "The Advantages of Mingling Indians with Whites," 51, 52, 56.

[12]Lindsay G. Robertson, *Conquest by Law* (New York: Oxford University Press, 2005), 57.

[13]8 Wheat. at 21 U.S. 587.

[14]City of Oneida v. Oneida Indian Nation: [Federal Common Law].

[15]City of Sherrill v. Oneida Indian Nation of N.Y., 544 U.S. 197 (2005).

[16]County of Oneida v. Oneida Indian Nation of N.Y., 470 U.S. 226, 234 (1985).

[17]City of Sherrill v. Oneida Indian Nation of N.Y., 544 U.S. 197 (2005).

[18]City of Sherrill v. Oneida Indian Nation of N.Y., 544 U.S. 197 (2005).

[19]Johnson & Graham's Lessee v. McIntosh, 21 U.S. 543 (1823).

[20]City of Sherrill v. Oneida Indian Nation of N.Y., 544 U.S. 197 (2005).

[21]City of Sherrill v. Oneida Indian Nation of N.Y., 544 U.S. 197 (2005).

[22]City of Sherrill v. Oneida Indian Nation of N.Y., 544 U.S. 197 (2005).

9 ABRAHAM LINCOLN AND THE NARRATIVE OF WHITE MESSIAHSHIP

[1]Alison Smale, "Former SS Member, on Trial in Germany, Says He Was 'Morally Complicit' at Auschwitz," *The New York Times*, April 21, 2015, www.nytimes.com /2015/04/22/world/europe/oskar-groning-auschwitz-birkenau-guard-trial.html.

[2]"'Auschwitz bookkeeper' gets four years' jail," The Local DE, July 15, 2005, www .thelocal.de/20150715/auschwitz-bookkeeper-faces-judgement-day.

[3]*The Fog of War: Eleven Lessons from the Life of Robert S. McNamara*, directed by Errol Morris, Sony Pictures Classics, 2003.

[4]"US Army Service, Campaign Medals and Foreign Awards Information: Legion of Merit," US Veteran Medals, accessed May 28, 2018, https://veteranmedals .army.mil/awardg&d.nsf/374fbd6468877ab385256b6600590a90/43110baf632e7eed 85256b660062b7fc.

[5]William A. Buckingham, Jr., *Operation Ranch Hand: The Air Force and Herbicides in Southeast Asia 1961-1971* (Office of Air Force History, United States Air Force, 1982), iii.

[6] *The Fog of War.*

[7] *The Fog of War.*

[8] "About African American History Month," African American History Month: Library of Congress, accessed May 28, 2019, https://africanamericanhistory month.gov/about/.

[9] Abraham Lincoln, "The Gettysburg Address," accessed May 27, 2019, http://rmc .library.cornell.edu/gettysburg/good_cause/transcript.htm.

[10] Paul Ryan, "This is the Party of Lincoln," YouTube, March 1, 2016, www.youtube .com/watch?v=vTChA8lfMuA.

[11] Edwin E. Sparks, *The Lincoln-Douglas Debates* (Dansville, N.Y.: F.A. Owen Publishing Company, 1918), 30.

[12] Sparks, *The Lincoln-Douglas Debates*, 76-77.

[13] Abraham Lincoln, *The Writings of Abraham Lincoln* (New York and London: G.P. Putnam's Sons, 1906), 243.

[14] Edward McPherson, *The Political History of the United States of America, During the Great Rebellion, from November 6, 1860, to July 4, 1864* (Washington, DC: Philip and Solomons, 1865), 50.

[15] Daniel W. Crofts, *Lincoln and the Politics of Slavery: The Other Thirteenth Amendment and the Struggle to Save the Union* (Chapel Hill: University of North Carolina Press, 2016), 8.

[16] United States Congress, *The Statutes at Large, Treaties and Proclamations of the United States of America from December 5, 1859 to March 3, 1863* (Boston: Little Brown and Company, 1863), 251. www.loc.gov/law/help/statutes-at-large/36th -congress/c36.pdf.

[17] Abraham Lincoln, "First Inaugural Address," Lincoln Home (website), March 4, 1861, www.nps.gov/liho/learn/historyculture/firstinaugural.htm.

[18] Lincoln, "First Inaugural Address."

[19] Crofts, *Lincoln and the Politics*, 287.

[20] Abraham Lincoln, "Abraham Lincoln papers: Series 2. General Correspondence. 1858 to 1864: Abraham Lincoln to Horace Greeley, Friday, August 22, 1862 (Clipping from Aug. 23, 1862 Daily National Intelligencer, Washington, DC)" Library of Congress (website), www.loc.gov/item/mal4233400/.

[21] Abraham Lincoln, "Transcription of the Proclamation," National Archives (website), last reviewed May 5, 2017, www.archives.gov/exhibits/featured -documents/emancipation-proclamation/transcript.html.

[22] US Constitution, Amendment 14.

10 ABRAHAM LINCOLN AND NATIVE GENOCIDE

[1] "Public Acts of the Thirty-Seventh Congress of the United States," Library of Congress (1863), 489, www.loc.gov/law/help/statutes-at-large/37th-congress /c37.pdf.

[2]"Public Acts," 1862.

[3]"Pacific Railway Act (1862)," Our Documents, May 27, 2019, www.ourdocuments .gov/doc.php?flash=false&doc=32.

[4]Duane Schultz, *Over the Earth I Come: The Great Sioux Uprising of 1862* (New York: St. Martin's Press, 1992), 44.

[5]Colette Routel, "Minnesota Bounties on Dakota Men during the U.S.-Dakota War," *William Mitchell Law Review* 40, no. 1 (2013): article 2, http://open.mitchell hamline.edu/wmlr/vol40/iss1/2.

[6]Carol Chomsky, "The United States-Dakota War Trials: A Study in Military Injustice," *Stanford Law Review* 43 (1990): 13, https://scholarship.law.umn.edu /faculty_articles/226.

[7]Abraham Lincoln, *The Writings of Abraham Lincoln* (Including the Full Text of the Lincoln-Douglas Debates Together with the Essay on Lincoln), edited by Arthur Brooks Lapsley, vol. 6 (New York: G.P. Putnam's Sons, 1906), 216.

[8]Dee Brown, *Bury My Heart at Wounded Knee* (New York: Henry Holt & Company, 1970), 60.

[9]Brown, *Bury My Heart*, 60.

[10]Lincoln, *Writings of Abraham Lincoln,* 216.

[11]"That all treaties heretofore made and entered into by the Sisseton, Wahpaton, Medawakanton, and Wahpakoota bands of Sioux or Dakota Indians, or any of them, with the United States, are hereby declared to be abrogated and annulled, so far as said treaties or any of them purport to impose any future obligation on the United States, and all lands and rights of occupancy within the State of Minnesota, and all annuities and claims heretofore accorded to said Indians, or any of them, to be forfeited to the United States." From Charles Kappler, ed., *Indian Affairs, Laws and Treaties,* vol. 2 (Washington, DC: US Government Printing Office, 1903), 594.

[12]"The President is authorized and hereby directed to assign to and set apart for the Sisseton, Wahpaton, Medawakanto, and Wahpakoota bands of the Sioux Indians a tract of un-occupied land outside of the limits of any state." From An Act for the Removal of the Sisseton, Wahpaton, Medawakanton, and Wahpakoota Bands of Sioux or Dakota Indians, and for the Disposition of Their Lands in Minnesota and Dakota, March 3, 1863, Thirty-Seventh Congress, session 3, chap 119, www.loc .gov/law/help/statutes-at-large/37th-congress/session-3/c37s3ch119.pdf.

[13]William E. Lass, "The Removal from Minnesota of the Sioux and Winnebago Indians," *Minnesota History* (December 1963): 363, http://collections.mnhs.org /MNHistoryMagazine/articles/38/v38i08p353-364.pdf.

[14]Lass, "Removal from Minnesota," 363.

[15]General Orders No. 41 stated it is "imperatively necessary that extraordinary measures should be adopted for the more complete protection of our frontier and the extirpation of the savage fiends who commit these outrages. It is therefore ordered

that a corps of volunteer scouts be organized . . . to scour the Big Woods from Sauk Centre to the Northern boundary line of Sibley county." *Report of the Adjutant General of the State of Minnesota,* "The Military Law. An Act to provide for the Organization, Equipment and Discipline of the Military Forces of the State of Minnesota," (Saint Paul, MN: Press Print Co., 1863) 132, https://babel.hathitrust .org/cgi/pt?id=njp.32101071984569;view=1up;seq=256.

[16]General Orders No. 60 by order of the commander-in-chief, Oscar Malmros, Adjutant General.

[17]Lincoln, *Writings of Abraham Lincoln*, 433.

[18]Raymond Friday Locke, *The Book of the Navajo* (Los Angeles: Mankind Publishing, 1992), 356.

[19]Locke, *Book of the Navajo*, 358.

[20]United States, Executive Office of the President [Abraham Lincoln]: New Mexico. Bosque Redondo Reserve. 15. Jan. 1864. Indian Affairs. Laws and Treaties. Vol. 1 (LAWS). 870–Part III. Executive Orders Related to Reserves.

[21]Brown, *Bury My Heart*, 33.

[22]Brown, *Bury My Heart*, 33.

[23]Brown, *Bury My Heart*, 33.

[24]Jerome Greene, *Washita: the U.S. Army and the Southern Cheyennes, 1867–1869* (Norman, OK: University of Oklahoma Press, 2014), 27.

[25]"Sand Creek Massacre," HistoryNet, May 27, 2019, www.historynet.com /sand-creek-massacre.

[26]Colorado Senate Joint Resolution 14-030.

[27]Lincoln, *Writings of Abraham Lincoln,* 257-258.

[28]Lincoln, *Writings of Abraham Lincoln*, 21.

[29]Lincoln, *Writings of Abraham Lincoln*, 219.

[30]Lincoln, *Writings of Abraham Lincoln*, 417.

11 THE COMPLEX TRAUMA OF THE AMERICAN STORY

[1]"Post-traumatic stress disorder (PTSD)," Mayo Clinic (website), May 28, 2019, www .mayoclinic.org/diseases-conditions/post-traumatic-stress-disorder /symptoms-causes/syc-20355967.

[2]Tribal Law and Policy Institute, "Tribal Legal Code Resource: Juvenile Justice," June 2015, www.tribal-institute.org/download/codes/JJGuide6-29-15.pdf.

[3]See Maria Yellow Horse Brave Heart, "Wakiksuyapi: Carrying the Historical Trauma of the Lakota" in *Tulane Studies in Social Welfare* (2000): 245-266, and Maria Yellow Horse Brave Heart, "The Return to the Sacred Path," *Smith College Studies in Social Work* 68, no. 3 (1998): 287-305.

[4]"Transgenerational Trauma," Wikipedia, last edited May 6, 2019, https:// en.wikipedia.org/wiki/Transgenerational_trauma.

[5]Judith Herman, *Trauma and Recovery: The Aftermath of Violence—From Domestic Abuse to Political Terror* (New York: Basic Books, 2015), 119.

[6]John J. Sigall and Morton Weinfeld, *Trauma and Rebirth: Intergenerational Effects of the Holocaust* (New York/London: Praeger, 1989). See also, Pierre Fossion, et. al., "Family Approach with Grandchildren of Holocaust Survivors," *American Journal of Psychotherapy* 57, no. 4 (2002), 519-527, https://psychotherapy.psychiatryonline .org/doi/pdf/10.1176/appi.psychotherapy.2003.57.4.519.

[7]Robin DiAngelo, "White Fragility," *International Journal of Critical Pedagogy* 3, no. 3 (2011): 54-70. See also DiAngelo, *White Fragility* (Boston: Beacon Press, 2018).

[8]Rachel McNair, *Perpetration-Induced Traumatic Stress: The Psychological Consequences of Killing* (New York/London: Praeger, 2002), back cover.

[9]McNair, *Perpetration-Induced Traumatic Stress*, 7.

[10]"Trauma," American Psychological Association (website), accessed May 27, 2019, www.apa.org/topics/trauma.

12 THE CHRISTIAN WORLDVIEW AND THE
FAILURE OF RE-CONCILIATION

[1]Christian Reformed Church of North America (CRCNA), Acts of Synod 2016 (Grand Rapids: Christian Reformed Church of North America, 2016), 922.

[2]"Truth and Reconciliation Commission of Canada," Government of Canada (website), modified February 19, 2019, www.rcaanc-cirnac.gc.ca/eng/1450124405592 /1529106060525.

[3]CRCNA, Acts of Synod 2016, 922.

[4]Connie Larkman, "More than 500 Clergy Gather for Prayer, Solidarity and Repentance at Standing Rock," *United Church of Christ News*, November 7, 2016, www.ucc.org /news_more_than_500_clergy_gather_for_prayer_solidarity_and_repentance_at _standing_rock_11072016.

[5]See Michael Emerson and Christian Smith, *Divided by Faith: Evangelical Religion and the Problem of Race in America* (Oxford: Oxford University Press, 2001); see also Soong-Chan Rah, *The Next Evangelicalism: Freeing the Church from Western Cultural Captivity* (Downers Grove, IL: InterVarsity Press, 2009).

[6]Soong-Chan Rah, *Prophetic Lament: A Call for Justice in Troubled Times* (Downers Grove, IL: InterVarsity Press, 2015), 91-97.

[7]Rah, *Prophetic Lament*, 91-97.

[8]Rah, *Prophetic Lament*, 91-97.

[9]Department of Defense Appropriations Act of 2009, Pub. L. No. 111–118, § 8113, 123 STAT. 3453 (2009).

CONCLUSION

[1]"A Century of Lawmaking for a New Nation: U.S. Congressional Documents and Debates, 1774–1875," Library of Congress, May 27, 2019, http://memory.loc.gov /cgi-bin/ampage?collId=llsl&fileName=004/llsl004.db&recNum=459.

[2]"Brief History of Gallup," Greater Gallup Economic Development Corporation, accessed May 27, 2019, www.gallupedc.com/live-here.

[3]Erasmus made this statement in a press release on March 2, 2008. See "From Truth to Reconciliation," Aboriginal Healing Foundation Press Release, accessed May 27, 2019, http://media.knet.ca/node/3522. He is quoting from H. Richard Niebuhr, *The Meaning of Revelation* (New York: The Macmillan Company, 1941), 115.

Name and Subject Index

Christendom, 10, 21, 29, 31, 33, 52-68, 77, 160-62, 182-89, 200

Christianity, 8, 20, 28, 52, 53, 57-59, 64, 73, 189

church, 2-5, 16-18, 20, 22, 26, 28, 39-40, 49-51, 53, 55, 57-68, 72-73, 75, 128, 161

church, American, 4, 8-11, 29, 33, 39, 80-81, 86-87, 95-97, 101-2, 130, 169, 179-86, 192, 199-201, 205-6

Columbus, Christopher, 13-14, 19-22, 73, 137-39

Diné (Navajo), 1, 2, 4, 87, 128, 129, 153-55, 158, 160, 162, 169, 171, 181, 192, 197-99, 201-2

Doctrine of Discovery (discovery doctrine), 10, 13-17, 19-22, 24, 26, 28, 33, 37-38, 64, 66, 70-77, 80-85, 88, 95-97, 100-109, 112-18, 124-28, 137-39, 153, 159, 161-62, 179-86, 193, 200, 204-5

exceptionalism, 8-10, 35-38, 57, 59, 66, 70, 74, 77-81, 82-87, 91, 101-2, 115, 121, 133, 145, 160-61, 182-90, 194, 204

genocide, 10, 43, 63, 72-73, 100, 109, 113, 119-23, 153-63, 170, 181, 186, 200

imagination (social, theological), 3, 10-11, 14-15, 18-23, 24-30, 33-38, 47, 56, 59, 64, 72-74, 78, 80, 83-90, 94-97, 100-104, 107-8, 119, 121-23, 133, 140, 148, 153, 158, 182, 185, 200

Johnson v. M'Intosh (*M'Intosh* verdict), 104-10, 112, 124-28

lament, 5, 8-9, 11, 183, 188-90

Lincoln, Abraham, vii, 10, 139-47, 148, 150-62, 169, 171, 181, 199

narratives, 3, 4, 10-11, 21-29, 33-40, 42, 51, 55-56, 63, 70-78, 80, 82, 94-97, 100-102, 115, 118, 132-47, 160-61, 179, 182, 185-89, 200-201, 204

"other," 15-22, 24, 45, 63-64, 75, 84-85, 88, 91, 97, 99, 117, 121-22, 145, 188, 193

papal bull(s), 15-22, 72, 101

promised land, 41, 48, 53, 70-76, 102, 107, 130-31, 138, 187, 200

Puritans, 71-76

Supreme Court decisions, 1, 32, 91, 103-5, 107-9, 116, 124-28, 179, 184-85

theology (dysfunctional), 8-9, 17, 22, 28, 33, 69-81, 84-90, 95, 98-116, 122, 182-83, 200

trauma, 11, 164-77, 178-95

triumphalism, 8-9, 145, 160-61, 188-89

Trump, Donald, 31-32, 56, 77-79, 139, 140, 179, 204

white supremacy, 10-11, 20-23, 24, 29, 33, 37-38, 75, 77, 80-97, 100, 108, 116, 121-24, 128, 145-47, 153, 159, 185-86, 193, 200-201